A Dictionary of Legal Quotations

A
DICTIONARY
OF
LEGAL
QUOTATIONS

Compiled and edited by Simon James and Chantal Stebbings

Macmillan Publishing Company
NEW YORK

Macmillan Publishing Company.
866 Third Avenue, New York, NY 10022

Library of Congress Catalog Card Number: 87-12255

Printed and bound in Great Britain

printing number
1 2 3 4 5 6 7 8 9 10

Library of Congress Cataloging-in-Publication Data

A Dictionary of legal quotations.

  Includes indexes.
    1. Law — Quotations — Dictionaries. I. James, Simon R.
II. Stebbings, Chantal.
K58.D53 1987   340.02   87-12255
ISBN 0-02-916002-2

Contents

List of Topics

LIST OF TOPICS

Preface

The quotations that follow are arranged by topic, a list of which appears on page vii. The allocation of quotations between topics is sometimes rather arbitrary because, of course, many quotations refer to two or more subjects. However, there is a key-word index which should enable the reader to find particular quotations without too much difficulty.

The key-word index gives a two-figure reference for each quotation in which the key word plays an important part. The first figure refers to the number of the topic and the second to the quotation itself. Part of the quotation is also given to indicate the context. For example, an entry under 'Convenience' reads: 'C. and justice 83.1'. This refers to the first quotation appearing under the 83rd topic, which is Justice. The numbers and titles of the topics appear at the top of the pages, and within each topic the quotations are arranged alphabetically by author or source.

There is also an index of authors on page 178. While the years of birth and death have been given wherever possible for deceased authors, no attempt has been made to provide the dates of birth for living persons. Some inconsistency also arises where authors have changed their names or titles or both. Although there is an argument for using the same name throughout, this does lead to anomalies. For example 'Lord Brougham' would seem to sit unhappily over a reference to the House of Commons and he therefore appears over such references under his previous name. Similarly, with authors of books it generally seemed better to use the name under which they published, and also judges in cases are given the titles they had at the time.

Finally, we should like to express our gratitude for the patient and expert assistance of the staff of a number of libraries, in particular the staff of the British Library of Political and Economic Science and the staff of the University of Exeter Library.

Simon James
Chantal Stebbings

University of Exeter

A Brief Guide to Legal Citations

The reports of cases decided by the courts referred to in the *Dictionary*, and indeed in all law reports, fall into two groups. The first group, which covers the period from the early sixteenth century to 1865, consists of the 'private' reports. The second group dates from 1865 and consists of 'authorised' law reports.

The 'private' group are reports of cases compiled by private individuals, often for their own use, and subsequently published. Such cases can be recognised by their date and the way they are cited. They are generally cited by reference to the name of the reporter in an accepted abbreviation. So, for example, '*R.* v. *Wilkes* (1770), 4 Burr. 2527' refers to the case of the Crown against Wilkes, reported by Burrows in the fourth volume of his reports at page 2527. The date here is not necessary to locate the report, and accordingly it is in round brackets and is followed by a comma to indicate that it is not an essential element in the citation.

Many, but not all, law libraries have copies of all the private reports. All should, however, keep the English Reports, a series of 176 volumes in which most of the private reports are reprinted. Instructions for locating a case in the English Reports are generally found with that series in law libraries.

The year 1865 marks the beginning of modern law reporting, for it saw the issue of a series of authorised law reports, authorised in the sense that they are examined before publication by the judges who decided the cases. They are known simply as the Law Reports. A case is cited here by reference to its date and the court in which it was heard. Thus, for example, the report of the case cited as '*Le Lievre* v. *Gould*, [1893] 1 Q.B. 491' is to be found in the first volume of the reports of cases for 1893 in the Queen's Bench Division of the High Court at page 491. Here the date is necessary for locating the case, and accordingly the year is placed in square brackets with the comma before it to indicate that it is an essential part of the citation. A separate series covers cases that reach the House of Lords.

Some private reports exist today that are authorised in the same way as the Law Reports, and notable examples include the All England Law Reports. These reports are to be found in law libraries as well.

Finally, the above is intended only as a very brief and general guide to legal citations. A list of abbreviations used in the *Dictionary* is to be found below, and Donald Raistrick's *Index to legal citations and abbreviations* (1981) provides the full instructions needed to find any report.

List of Abbreviations

A.C.	Law Reports, Appeal Cases 1891–	Car. & P.	Carrington & Payne's Nisi Prius Reports 1823–41
A.G.	Attorney-General		
All E.R.	All England Law Reports 1936–	Ch.	Law Reports, Chancery 1891–
App. Cas.	Law Reports, Appeal Cases 1875–90	Ch.D.	Law Reports, Chancery Division 1875–90
B.	Baron	Cl. & Fin.	Clark & Finnelly's House of Lords Cases 1831–46
B. & A.	Barnewell & Alderson's King's Bench Reports 1817–22		
		Cox C.C.	Cox's Criminal Cases 1843–1945
B. & G.	Brownlow & Goldesborough's Common Pleas Reports 1569–1624	D.P.P.	Director of Public Prosecutions
		Dick.	Dicken's Chancery Reports 1599–1798
Bing.	Bingham's Common Pleas Report 1822–34	Doug.	Douglas' King's Bench Reports 1778–85
Black. W.	Sir William Blackstone's King's Bench Reports 1746–80	El. & Bl.	Ellis & Blackburn's Queen's Bench Reports 1851–8
Bos. & Pul.	Bosanquet & Puller's Common Pleas Reports 1796–1804	Eq.	Law Reports, Equity Cases 1865–75
Bulstr.	Bulstrode's King's Bench Reports 1609–25	Gould.	Gouldsborough's King's Bench Reports 1586–1601
Burr.	Burrow's King's Bench Reports tempore Lord Mansfield 1757–71	H.L.	Law Reports, House of Lords, English & Irish Appeals 1866–75
C.B.	(1) Common Bench Reports by Manning, Granger & Scott 1845–56 (2) Chief Baron	Hag. Con.	Haggard's Consistorial Reports 1789–1821
		Hag. Ecc.	Haggard's Ecclesiastical Reports 1827–33
C.J.	Chief Justice	Hob.	Hobart's Common Pleas Reports 1613–25
C. Rob.	Christopher Robinson's Admiralty Reports 1799–1808	I.C.R.	Industrial Court Reports
		J.	Justice

LIST OF ABBREVIATIONS

J.P.	Justice of the Peace	Q.B.	Law Reports, Queen's Bench Division 1891– 1901, 1952–
K.B.	Law Reports King's Bench Division 1891–		
L.C.	Lord Chancellor	Q.B.D.	Law Reports, Queen's Bench Division 1875– 90
L.J.	Lord Justice		
L.J. Eq.	Law Journal Reports, Chancery, New Series 1831–1946	Rep.	Coke's King's Bench Reports 1572–1616
L.J. Mag. Cas. N.S.	Law Journal Reports, Magistrates' Cases, New Series, 1831–96	Sc. & Div.	Law Reports, Scotch and Divorce Appeals 1866–75
Ld. Ray.	Lord Raymond's King's Bench Reports 1694– 1732	Show. K.B.	Shower's King's Bench Reports ed. Butt 1678– 95
Ll. L. Rep.	Lloyd's List Law Reports 1919–50	Sir T. Ray.	Sir T. Raymond's King's Bench & Common Pleas Reports 1660–84
Lofft	Lofft's King's Bench Reports 1772–74	Sty.	Style's King's Bench Reports 1646–55
M.L.R.	Modern Law Review	Swans.	Swanston's Chancery Reports 1818–19
M.R.	Master of the Rolls		
Mac. & G.	Macnaghten and Gordon's Chancery Reports 1848–51	T.L.R.	Times Law Reports 1884–1952
Mod.	Modern Reports 1669– 1755	T.R.	Durnford & East's Term Reports 1785–1800
P.	Law Reports, Probate Division 1891–1971	Taunt.	Taunton's Common Pleas Reports 1808–19
P.D.	Law Reports, Probate, Divorce and Admiralty Division 1875–90	Tax. Cas.	Reports of Tax Cases 1875–
Pea. (2)	Peake's Additional Cases 1795–1812	U.S.	United States Supreme Court Reports 1790–
Peere Wms.	Peere Williams' Chancery & King's Bench Cases 1695– 1735	V.C.	Vice-Chancellor
		Ves. Jr.	Vesey Junior's Chancery Reports 1789–1817
		Ves. Sen.	Vesey Senior's Chancery Reports 1747–1756
Pr. Ch.	Precedents in Chancery (Finch) 1689–1722	W.L.R.	Weekly Law Reports 1953–

The Quotations

1. ACCOMPLICE

1. Accomplice, *n.* One associated with another in a crime, having guilty knowledge and complicity, as an attorney who defends a criminal, knowing him guilty. This view of the attorney's position in the matter has not hitherto commanded the assent of attorneys, no one having offered them a fee for assenting.

   Ambrose Bierce (1842–1914?), *The devil's dictionary*, 1911

2. I am your accessory.

   William Shakespeare (1564–1616), *All's well that ends well*, 1602–4, II.i

2. ACCOUNTANTS

1. Accountants are the witch doctors of the modern world.

   Harman J. (1894–1970), *Miles* v. *Clarke*, [1953] 1 W.L.R. 537 at 539

3. ACCUSE

1. Accuse, *v.t.* To affirm another's guilt or unworth; most commonly as a justification of ourselves for having wronged him.

   Ambrose Bierce (1842–1914?), *The devil's dictionary*, 1911

2. He that first cries out stop thief, is often he that has stolen the treasure.

   William Congreve (1670–1729), *Love for love*, 1695, III.iv

3. How useful and necessary it is for republics to have laws which allow the masses a way to express their displeasure against a citizen. Because if this is not provided, the masses will resort to illegal methods which will produce much worse effects.

   Niccolo Machiavelli (1469–1527), *Discourses*, bk I, ch. VII

4. Do not cast away an honest man for a villain's accusation.

   William Shakespeare (1564–1616), *Henry VI, Pt II*, 1590–1, I.iii

5. Yet I am richer than my base accusers
   That never knew what truth meant.

   William Shakespeare (1564–1616), *Henry VIII*, 1612–13, II.i

6. Accuse some innocent and forswear myself.

   William Shakespeare (1564–1616), *Titus Andronicus*, 1593–4, V.i

7. *J'accuse.* — I accuse.

   Émile Zola (1840–1902), Letter, 13 January 1898

4. ADULTERY

1. Villains are usually the worst casuists, and rush into greater crimes to avoid less. Henry the eighth committed murder, to avoid the imputation of adultery; and in our times, those who commit the latter crime attempt to wash off the stain of seducing the wife, by signifying their readiness to *shoot* the *husband*!

   C.C. Colton (1780–1832), *Lacon*, 1820, vol. I, CXXXI

2. The husband who commits adultery within a few weeks of marriage, or who commits adultery promiscuously with more than one woman or with his wife's sister, or with a servant in the house, may probably be labelled as exceptionally depraved.

   Denning L.J., *Bowman* v. *Bowman*, [1949] 2 All E.R. 127 at 128–9

3. Adultery is the application of democracy to love.

   H.L. Mencken (1880–1956), *Sententiae*

4. He that hath known pleasure unlawfully, will hardly be restrained from unlawful pleasure.

   Francis Quarles (1592–1644), *Enchyridion*, 1641, third century, XI

5. Adulterers by an enforced obedience of planetary influence.

   William Shakespeare (1564–1616), *King Lear*, 1605–6, I.ii

6. She's an adulteress ...
   A bed-swerver, even as bad as those
   That vulgars give the boldest titles.

   William Shakespeare (1564–1616), *A winter's tale*, 1610–11, II.i

7. I may say that I have met reasonably well-educated and well-informed business men of forty and upwards who honestly thought and said: 'Adultery is having sexual connexion with a woman who is not your wife, who is not over fifty years of age; and it is not adultery if she is over fifty'. It was, at first, not easy to convince them that the woman's age was irrelevant. Other instances of ignorance on the part of petitioners of the real meaning of the word 'adultery' which have come to the notice of the King's Proctor are: 'I did not think it was adultery during the daytime'; 'I thought it meant getting a girl into trouble'; and 'I thought it meant drinking with men in public houses'.

   Wallington J. (1876–1962), *Barnacle* v. *Barnacle*, [1948] P. 257 at 261

5. ADVOCACY

1. Then shifting his side (as a lawyer knows how,)

He pleaded again on behalf
of the Eyes:
But what were his arguments few
people know,
For the court did not think
they were equally wise.

William Cowper (1731–1800),
Report of an adjudged case

2. Th' most ardent advocate o' anything is th' feller who can't lose.

Frank McKinney Hubbard (1868-
-1930), *New sayings by Abe Martin*, 1917

3. My lawsuit has nothing to do with
assault, battery or poisoning. It is
about three goats my neighbour
stole. The judge wants this proved
but you, with big words and
extravagant gestures, talk about
the Battle of Cannae, the Mithri-
datic war and the perjuries of
Carthaginians, the Syllae, the Marii
and the Mucii. Now, Postumus,
say something about my three
goats.

Martial (*c.*AD40–*c.*104), *Epigrams*, bk VI, epig. XIX

4. The first rule of advocacy. Never
ask your witness a question unless
you're quite sure of the answer.

John Mortimer, *The trials of
Rumpole*, 1979, 'Rumpole and the
showfolk'

5. The advocates of a criminal are
seldom artists enough to turn the
beautiful terribleness of the deed
to the advantage of the doer.

Friedrich Nietzsche (1844–1900),
Beyond good and evil, ch. 4

6. [Cicero] was indeed the man who

most effectually showed the
Romans what charms eloquence
can add to truth, and that justice is
invincible when properly supported.

Plutarch (46–120), *Lives: Cicero*

6. AGENCY

1. Let every eye negotiate for itself,
And trust no agent.

William Shakespeare (1564–
1616), *Much ado about nothing*,
1598–9, II.i

7. ALIBI

1. Never mind the character, and
stick to the alleybi. Nothing like a
alleybi, Sammy, nothing.

Charles Dickens (1812–70), *The
Pickwick papers*, 1837, ch.
XXXIII

2. If your governor don't prove a
alleybi, he'll be what the Italians
call reg'larly flummoxed.

Charles Dickens (1812–70), ibid.

3. Oh Sammy, Sammy vy worn't
there a alleybi.

Charles Dickens (1812–70), ibid.,
ch. XXXIV

8. ALIMONY

1. Alimony — The ransom that the
happy pay to the devil.

H.L. Mencken (1880–1956),
Sententiae

3

2. The wages of sin is alimony.

   Carolyn Wells (1862–1942), Attributed

9. APPEALS

1. Appeal, *v.t.* In law, to put the dice into the box for another throw.

   Ambrose Bierce (1842–1914?), *The devil's dictionary*, 1911

2. The Court of Appeal is the focal point of the jurisdiction in English Law.

   Lord Hailsham, House of Lords, 5 February 1985

3. Being a Lord Justice of Appeal would be fascinating, but I don't think I'm a good enough lawyer.

   Sir Michael Havers, *Observer*, 'Sayings of the week', 9 December 1984

4. One effect of running causes fast through the courts below is that they go by scores to appeal.

   Sir Walter Scott (1771–1832), *Journal*, 9 June 1826

10. ARREST

1. Arrest, *v.t.* Formally to detain one accused of unusualness.

   Ambrose Bierce (1842–1914?), *The devil's dictionary*, 1911

2. 'It is my duty to warn you that it will be used against you' cried the inspector, with the magnificent fair play of the British criminal law.

   Sir Arthur Conan Doyle (1859–1930), *The return of Sherlock Holmes*, 1904, 'The adventure of the dancing men'

11. ARSON

1. Arson: To be careless in the use of fire.

   Frank McKinney Hubbard (1868–1930), *The Roycroft dictionary*, 1923

2. It takes only the hand of a Liliputian to light a fire but would require the diuretic powers of Gulliver to extinguish it.

   Sir Walter Scott (1771–1832), *Journal*, 25 November 1825

3. First, go and set London Bridge on fire; and, if you can, burn down the Tower too.

   William Shakespeare (1564–1616), *Henry VI, Pt II*, 1590–1, IV.vi

4. Arson, after all, is an artificial crime. Some crimes are crimes in themselves, would be crimes without any law ... but the burning of things is in itself neither good nor bad. A large number of houses deserve to be burnt.

   H.G. Wells (1866–1946), *History of Mr. Polly*, ch. X, 1

12. AUDITORS

1. It is the duty of the auditor to see that the authority to charge is not made a pretext for extravagance or favouritism.

   Lush J. (1807–81), *R.* v. *Cumberlege* (1877), 2 Q.B.D. 366 at 370

13. BANKING

1. Bankers have no right to establish a customary law among themselves, at the expence of other men.

   Foster J. (1689–1763), *Hankey* v. *Trotman* (1746), 1 Black. W. 1 at 2

2. A 'sound' banker, alas! is not one who foresees danger and avoids it, but one who, when he is ruined, is ruined in a conventional and orthodox way along with his fellows, so that no one can really blame him.

   John Maynard Keynes (1883–1946), 'The consequences to the banks of the collapse of money values', in *Essays in persuasion*, 1933, pt II

14. BANKRUPTCY

1. How often have I been able to trace bankruptcies and insolvencies to some lawsuit about ten or fifteen pounds, the costs of which have mounted up to large sums.

   Henry Peter Brougham (1778–1868), House of Commons, 7 February 1828

2. Bankrupt of life, yet prodigal of ease.

   John Dryden (1631–1700), *Absalom and Achitophel*

3. Beggars can never be bankrupts.

   Thomas Fuller (1654–1734), *Gnomologia*, 1732, no. 963

4. A cynic has observed that if you go 'bust' for £700 you are probably a fool, if you go 'bust' for £7,000 you are probably in the dock, and if you go 'bust' for £7 million you are probably rescued by the Bank of England.

   Lord Meston, House of Lords, 15 January 1985

5. I am ashamed to owe debts I cannot pay but I am not ashamed of being classed with those to whose rank I belong. The disgrace is in being an actual bankrupt not in being made a legal one.

   Sir Walter Scott (1771–1832), *Journal*, 16 February 1826

6. Poor bankrupt.

   William Shakespeare (1564–1616), *Romeo and Juliet*, 1595–6, II.ii

7. Bankrupts, hold fast,
   Rather than render back, out with
   your knives
   And cut your trusters' throats.

   William Shakespeare (1564–1616), *Timon of Athens*, 1607–8, IV.i

8. Blessed bankrupt.

   William Shakespeare (1564–1616), *Venus and Adonis*, 1592

15. BIGAMY

1. Bigamy is having one husband too many. Monogamy is the same.

   Anonymous, quoted in Erica Jong, *Fear of flying.*

2. Marriage is bound to be a failure if

a woman can only have one husband at a time.

Anonymous

3. Bigamy, *n.* A mistake in taste for which the wisdom of the future will adjudge a punishment called trigamy.

Ambrose Bierce (1842–1914?), *The devil's dictionary*, 1911

4. Bigamy is not a vice of wealth, the rich can find other less illegal outlets for their emotions.

Lord Buckmaster (1861–1934), *Observer*, 'Sayings of the week', 15 October 1922

5. One wife is too much for most husbands to hear
But two at a time there's no mortal can bear.

John Gay (1685–1732), *The beggar's opera*, 1728, III.xi

6. There was an old party of Lyme,
Who married three wives at one time.
When asked, 'Why the third?'
He replied, 'One's absurd,
And bigamy, sir, is a crime!'

William Cosmo Monkhouse (1840–1901), attributed

7. Will Bigamy. This gentleman, knowing that marriage fees were a considerable perquisite to the clergy, found out a way of improving them *cent. per. cent* for the *good of the Church.* His invention was to marry a second wife while the first was alive, convincing her of the lawfulness of it by such arguments.

Jonathan Swift (1667–1745), *The examiner*, no. 22, 4 January 1710

16. BILL OF RIGHTS

1. A bill of rights is what the people are entitled to against every government on earth, general or particular; and what no just government should refuse, or rest on inference.

Thomas Jefferson (1743–1826), Letter to James Madison, 20 December 1787

2. The Bill of Rights, contained in the first ten amendments to the Constitution, is every American's guarantee of freedom.

Harry S. Truman (1884–1972), *Years of trial and hope 1945–1953*, ch. XIX

3. A Bill of Rights against the encroachment of an elective legislature, that is, against our *own* encroachments on *ourselves*, is a curiosity in government.

Noah Webster (1758–1843), *A collection of essays*, no. III, 1788, p. 45

17. BLACKMAIL

1. After all, there couldn't be any blackmail if there wasn't something black to go on.

A.P. Herbert (1890–1971), *More uncommon law*, 1982 '*Rex* v. *Rungle*, Codd's Last Case'

18. BRIBERY

1. A bribe in hand betrays mischief at heart.

Aesop (fl. c. 550 BC), 'The thief and the dog', *Fables*

2. There is no one act, in which tyranny, malice, cruelty, and oppression can be charged, that does not at the same time carry evident marks of pecuniary corruption.

   Edmund Burke (1729–97), *Impeachment of Warren Hastings*, 17 February 1788

3. Bribes throw dust into cunning men's eyes.

   Thomas Fuller (1654–1734), *Gnomologia*, 1732, no. 1,018

4. Bribes will enter without knocking.

   Thomas Fuller (1654–1734), Ibid., no. 1,019

5. Gold delights to penetrate through the midst of guards, and to break through stone walls.

   Horace (65–8 BC), *Odes*, trans. C. Smart, bk III, ode XVI

6. The chief justice was rich, quiet and infamous.
   [Chief Justice Impey, India]

   Lord Macaulay (1800–59), *Warren Hastings*, October 1841

7. Alas! the small discredit of a bribe
   Scarce hurts the lawyer, but undoes the scribe.

   Alexander Pope (1688–1744), *Epilogue to the satires*, 1731, dialogue II, 1. 46

8. An open hand makes a blind eye.

   Francis Quarles (1592–1644), *Enchyridion*, 1641, Third Century, LXV

9. Honesty stands at the gate and knocks, and bribery enters in.

   Barnabe Rich (1540?–1617), Attributed

10. In the corrupted currents of this world,
    Offence's gilded hand may shove by justice,
    And oft 'tis seen the wicked prize itself.

    William Shakespeare (1564–1616), *Hamlet*, 1599–1600, III.iii

19. BURGLARY
See also 145. Theft

1. An eminent foreigner, smarting from painful experience, said to me … that burglary was the only well-organised institution which England possessed.

   James Anthony Froude (1818–94), *Short studies on great subjects*, 1894, 'Reciprocal duties of state and subject'

2. We inflict atrocious injuries on the burglars we catch in order to make the rest take effectual precautions against detection.

   George Bernard Shaw (1856–1950), *Major Barbara*, 1905, Preface

20. CERTAINTY

1. There's no certainty in the law.

   Lord Denning, *Observer*, 'Sayings of the week', 30 September 1979

2. They [the Law Lords] think the

great aim is certainty in the law. My aim is justice.

Lord Denning, *Sunday Times*, 1 August 1982, p. 25

3. It is better the law should be certain, than that every Judge should speculate upon improvements in it.

    Lord Eldon L.C. (1751–1838), *Sheddon* v. *Goodrich* (1803), 8 Ves. Jr. 481 at 497

4. Certainty is the mother of repose, and therefore the law aims at certainty.

    Lord Hardwicke L.C. (1690–1764), *Walton* v. *Tryon* (1753), Dick. 244 at 245

5. The law is not the same at morning and at night.

    George Herbert (1593–1633), *Jacula prudentum*, 1651

6. The instability of our laws is really an immense evil.

    Thomas Jefferson (1743–1826), Letter to James Madison, 20 December 1787, postscript

7. The more certain justice is, the less severe it need be.

    Sir Robert Mark, Quoted in *US news and world report*, 10 May 1976, p. 41

8. One of the essential elements of the law is some measure of uniformity. One of the important elements of law is predictability.

    Megaw L.J., *The Mihalis Angelos*, [1971] 1 Q.B. 164 at 205

9. If absolute certainty was the pre-condition for decision, the judicial process would be paralyzed.

    Louis Nizer, *The jury returns*, 1966, 'Fruehauf'

10. When people have to have recourse to the courts of justice, it should be because of the nature of the constitution rather than the contradiction or uncertainty of the law.

    Charles de Secondat, Baron de Montesquieu (1689–1755), *The spirit of the laws*, 1748, bk VI, 1

21. CHARACTER

1. Mankind is made up of inconsistencies, and no man acts invariably up to his predominant character. The wisest man sometimes acts weakly, and the weakest sometimes wisely.

    Lord Chesterfield (1694–1773), Letter to his son, 26 April 1748

2. Everyone had a 'good character' once.

    John Mortimer, *Rumpole of the Bailey*, 1978, 'Rumpole and the alternative society'

3. An accused man should have the benefit of the presumption of integrity which arises from the virtue of a lifetime.

    Lord O'Hagan (1812–85), *Symington* v. *Symington* (1875), 2 Sc. & Div. 415 at 425

4. The highest of characters is his who is as ready to pardon the moral errors of mankind as if he were every day guilty of them himself; and as cautious of committing

a fault as if he never forgave one.

Pliny the Younger (AD 61–112), *Letters*, VIII

5. There is in many, if not in all men a constant inward struggle between the principles of good and evil; and because a man has grossly fallen, and, at the time of his fall added the guilt of hypocrisy to another sort of immorality, it is not necessary, therefore, to believe that his whole life has been false, or that all the good which he ever professed was insincere or unreal.

Lord Selborne (1812–95), *Symington* v. *Symington* (1875), 2 Sc. & Div. 415 at 428

22. CHARITY

1. Charity shall cover the multitude of sins.

Bible, Authorized Version, 1 Peter, 4: 8

2. The care of the aged poor and the like is a charity ... whether the persons who devote their lives to it are actuated by the love of God, a desire for their own salvation, or mere pique, or disgust with the world.

Farwell J. (1845–1915), *Re Delany*, [1902] 2 Ch. 642 at 647–8

23. CHILDREN

1. Children cannot be happy because they are not old enough to be capable of noble acts.

Aristotle (384–322 BC), *Ethics*, bk I, ch. IX

2. Train up a child in the way he should go:
   And when he is old, he will not depart from it.

Bible, Authorized Version, Proverbs, 22:6

3. There are many things in life more worth while than money. One of these things is to be brought up in this our England, which is still 'the envy of less happier lands.' I do not believe that it is for the benefit of children to be uprooted from England and transported to another country simply to avoid tax ... Children are like trees: they grow stronger with firm roots.

Lord Denning M.R., *Re Weston's Settlements*, [1969] 1 Ch. 223 at 245–6

4. It is highly undesirable that any child should learn that a court has publicly declared his or her birth was a mistake or a disaster.

Mr Justice Jupp, *Observer*, 'Sayings of the week', 20 February 1983

24. CIVIL DISOBEDIENCE

1. If [the injustice] is of such a nature that it requires you to be the agent of injustice to another, then, I say, break the law.

Henry D. Thoreau (1817–62), *Civil disobedience*, 1849

2. Under a government which imprisons unjustly, the true place for a just man is also prison.

Henry D. Thoreau (1817–62), *Resistance to civil government*, 1849

9

3. I do not want to break the laws of this land, but if they pass laws which are quite unjust, then I will break that law.

   Desmond Tutu, *Observer*, 'Sayings of the week', 4 August 1985

25. CIVIL LAW

1. The civil code is at bottom only the penal code under another aspect: it is not possible to understand the one without understanding the other.

   Jeremy Bentham (1748–1832), *Principles of the civil code*, Introduction

2. In civil jurisprudence it too often happens that there is so much law that there is no room for justice.

   C.C. Colton (1780–1832), *Lacon*, 1820, vol. II, XXIV

3. The folly of being counsel for yourself is so notorious in civil cases, that it has grown into a proverb.

   Sydney Smith (1771–1845), *Counsel for prisoners*

4. *Nurses*: The Civil Law has found it otherwise.
   Compasse: The Civil Law! Why then the Uncivil Law shall make it mine agen.

   John Webster (*c.* 1580–*c.*1625), *A cure for a cuckold*, III.2

26. CLASS

1. Written laws are like spiders' webs and, like them, only entangle and hold the poor and weak, while the rich and powerful easily break through.

   Anacharsis (fl. 600 BC), Quoted in Plutarch, *Lives: Solon*

2. The law doth punish man or woman
   That steals the goose from off the common,
   But lets the greater felon loose,
   That steals the common from the goose.

   Anonymous, 18th century

3. Our dangerous class is not at the bottom, it is near the top of society. Riches without law are more dangerous than is poverty without law.

   Henry Ward Beecher (1813–87), *Proverbs from Plymouth pulpit*, 1887

4. I sow corn: partridges eat it, and if I attempt to defend it against the partridges, I am fined or sent to jail: all this, for fear a great man, who is above sowing corn, should be in want of partridges.

   Jeremy Bentham (1748–1832), *Truth v. Ashhurst; or, law as it is*, 1823

5. Ask of politicians the end for which laws were originally designed; and they will answer, that the laws were designed as a protection for the poor and the weak, against the oppression of the rich and powerful. But surely no pretence can be so ridiculous; a man might as well tell me he has taken off my load, because he has changed the burden.

   Edmund Burke (1729–97), *A vindication of natural society*

6. The tendency of our laws is very much to bring the agricultural community again to two classes — namely, the proprietor and the peasant ... the middle class is the best security, as it is the best consequence, of civilisation.

   Benjamin Disraeli (1804–81), House of Commons, 11 February 1851

7. The law in its majestic egalitarianism, forbids the rich as well as the poor to sleep under bridges, to beg in the streets, and to steal bread.

   Anatole France (1884–1924), *Le lys rouge*, 1894, ch. 7

8. Laws grind the poor, and rich men rule the law.

   Oliver Goldsmith (1728–74), *The traveller*, 1764, 1. 385

9. The poor and ignorant will continue to lie and steal as long as the rich and educated show them how.

   Elbert Hubbard (1856–1915), *Notebook*, p. 146

10. What are laws but expressions of the opinions of some class which has power over the rest of the community. By what was the world ever governed but by the opinion of some person or persons? By what else can it ever be governed?

    Lord Macaulay (1800–1859), *Southey's colloquies on society*, January 1830

11. Law, morality, religion, are to him [the proletarian] so many bourgeois prejudices, behind which lurk in ambush just as many bourgeois interests.

    Karl Marx (1818–83) and **Friedrich Engels** (1820–95), *The communist manifesto*, 1848, I

12. Here's a fish hangs in the net like a poor man's right in the law; 'twill hardly come out.

    William Shakespeare (1564–1616), *Pericles*, 1608–9, II.i

27. COMMERCE

1. It is the privilege of a trader in a free country, in all matters not contrary to law, to regulate his own mode of carrying it on according to his own discretion and choice.

   Alderson B. (1787–1857), *Hilton* v. *Eckersley* (1855), 6 El. & Bl. 47 at 74

2. The great source of the flourishing state of this kingdom is its trade, and commerce, and paper currency, guarded by proper regulations and restrictions, is the life of commerce.

   Ashhurst J. (1725–1807), *Jordaine* v. *Lashbrooke* (1798), 7 T.R. 601 at 605

3. Prudent business men in their dealings incur risk.

   Bacon V.C. (1798–1895), *Re Godfrey* (1883), 23 Ch.D. 483 at 493

4. We are suffering from the intolerable competition of a foreign rival, who is placed ... in a condition so infinitely superior to ours for the production of light, that he *inundates* our *national market* at a marvellously reduced price ... This rival ... is no other than the sun ...

We pray that you will be pleased to make a law ordering that all windows, skylights, inside and outside shutters, curtains, fan-lights, bull's-eyes, carriage-blinds, in short that all openings, holes, chinks, and crevices should be closed, by which the light of the sun can penetrate into houses, to the injury of the flourishing trade with which we have endowed our country. [The candlemakers].

Frédéric Bastiat (1801–50), *Sophismes economiques,* trans. G.R. Porter, ch. VII, pp. 79–80

5. Organised business is a thing of law; and law is always hard and unrelenting toward the weak.

Henry Ward Beecher (1813–87), *Proverbs from Plymouth pulpit,* 1887

6. Regulating the prices of goods in general would be an endless task, and no legislator has ever been weak enough to think of attempting it.

Jeremy Bentham (1748–1832), *Defence of usuary,* Letter V

7. Most businesses require liberal dealings.

Bowen L.J. (1835–94), *Hutton* v. *West Cork Railway Co.* (1883), 23 Ch.D. 654 at 672

8. It is when merchants dispute about their own rules that they invoke the law.

Brett J. (1815–99), *Robinson* v. *Mollett* (1875), 7 H.L. 802, at 817

9. How extraordinary and contrary to reason is this ordinance for man to legislate about buying and selling or fix a definite price; for it is quite sure that the fertility or barrenness of the earth and all living things, yes, of everything that multiplies, rests in the power of God alone.

Canon of Bridlington (1307–77?), quoted by Alan and Veronica Palmer, *Quotations in history*

10. Commercial law ... lies within a narrow compass, and is far purer and freer from defects than any other part of the system.

Henry Peter Brougham (1778–1868), House of Commons, 7 February 1828

11. It has been uniformly laid down in this Court, as far back as we can remember, that good faith is the basis of all mercantile transactions.

Buller J. (1746–1800), *Salomons* v. *Nissen* (1788), 2 T.R. 674 at 681

12. Merchants know perfectly well what they mean when they express themselves, not in the language of lawyers, but in the language of courteous mercantile communication.

Lord Cairns (1819–85), *Shepherd* v. *Harrison* (1871), 5 H.L. 116 at 133

13. The great object of the law is to encourage commerce.

Chambre J. (1739–1823), *Beale* v. *Thompson* (1803), 3 Bos. & Pul. 405 at 421

14. The English trader is generally too much occupied with his business to devote much time to the invention

of new or fancy words, and he is not always gifted with that degree of fancy which is capable of coining new words. Besides the English public is not so ready, apparently, to buy articles passing under an entirely new name, which may give rise to a suspicion of adulteration.

Chitty J. (1828–99), *Re Trade-Mark 'Alpine'* (1885), 29 Ch.D. 877 at 880

15. It must be remembered that all trade is and must be in a sense selfish; trade not being infinite, nay, the trade of a particular place or district being possibly very limited, what one man gains another loses. In the hand to hand war of commerce, as in the conflicts of public life, whether at the bar, in Parliament, in medicine, in engineering (I give examples only), men fight on without much thought of others, except a desire to excel or to defeat them.

Lord Coleridge C.J. (1820–94), *Mogul Steamship Co. Ltd.* v. *McGregor, Gow & Co.* (1888), 21 Q.B.D. 544 at 553

16. In trade, in commerce, even in a profession, what is one man's gain is another's loss.

Lord Coleridge C.J. (1820–94), *Connor* v. *Kent* (1891), 61 L.J. Mag. Cas. N.S. 9 at 18

17. Trade is in nature free, finds its own channel, and best directeth its own course: and all laws to give it rules and directions, and to limit and circumscribe it, may serve the particular ends of private men, but are seldom advantageous to the public.

Charles D'avenant (1656–1714), *An essay on the East India trade*

18. It is not a presumption of law that a hire-purchase finance company cannot be innocent.

Diplock L.J. (1907–85), *Snook* v. *London and West Riding Investments, Ltd.*, [1967] 2 Q.B. 786 at 801

19. I cannot consent that the laws regulating the industry of a great nation should be made the shuttlecock of party strife.

Benjamin Disraeli (1804–81), Speech, House of Commons, 11 February, 1851

20. In the days when the nation depended on agriculture for its wealth it made the Lord Chancellor sit on a woolsack to remind him where the wealth came from. I would like to suggest we remove that now and make him sit on a crate of machine tools.

Duke of Edinburgh, *Observer*, 'Sayings of the week', 3 August 1986

21. The usual trade and commerce is cheating all round by consent.

Thomas Fuller (1654–1734), *Gnomologia*, 1732

22. Commerce never really flourishes so much, as when it is delivered from the guardianship of legislators and ministers.

William Godwin (1756–1836), *Enquiry concerning political justice*, 1798, vol. II, bk VI, ch. I

27. COMMERCE

23. The buyer needs a hundred eyes, the seller not one.

    George Herbert (1593–1633), *Jacula prudentum*, 1651

24. I should regret to find that the law was powerless to enforce the most elementary principles of commercial morality.

    Lord Herschell (1837–99), *Reddaway* v. *Banham*, [1896] A.C. 199 at 209

25. Laws for the regulation of trade should be most carefully scanned. That which hampers, limits, cripples and retards must be done away with.

    Elbert Hubbard (1856–1915), *Notebook*, p. 16

26. Let the buyer beware. (*Caveat emptor.*)

    Legal maxim

27. A proceeding may be perfectly legal and may yet be opposed to sound commercial principles.

    Lindley L.J. (1828–1921), *Verner* v. *General and Commercial Investment Trust*, [1894] 2 Ch. 239 at 264

28. A trader is trusted upon his character, and visible commerce: that credit enables him to acquire wealth. If by secret liens, a few might swallow up all, it would greatly damp that credit.

    Lord Mansfield (1705–1793), *Worseley* v. *Demattos* (1758), 1 Burr. 467 at 483

29. Convenience is the basis of mercantile law.

    Lord Mansfield (1705–93), *Medcalf* v. *Hall* (1782), 3 Doug. 113 at 115

30. The word Commission sounds sweet in a merchant's ear.

    Sir William Scott (1745–1836), *The Gratitudine* (1801), 3 C. Rob. 240 at 277

31. This is the kind of order which makes the administration of justice stink in the nostrils of commercial men.

    A.L. Smith L.J. (1836–1901), *Graham* v. *Sutton, Carden & Co.*, [1897] 1 Ch. 761 at 765

32. By means of glasses, hotbeds and hotwalls, very good grapes can be raised in Scotland, and very good wine too can be made of them at about thirty times the expense for which at least equally good can be brought from foreign countries. Would it be a reasonable law to prohibit the importation of all foreign wines, merely to encourage the making of claret and burgundy in Scotland.

    Adam Smith (1723–90), *Wealth of nations*, 1776, vol. I, bk IV, ch. II

33. Trade and commerce, if they were not made of India rubber, would never manage to bounce over the obstacles which legislators are continually putting in their way.

    Henry D. Thoreau (1817–62), *Resistance to civil government*, 1849

34. While competition cannot be created by statutory enactment, it can in large measure be revived by

changing the laws and forbidding the practices that killed it, and by enacting laws that will give it heart and occasion again. We can arrest and prevent monopoly.

Woodrow Wilson (1856–1924), Speech, 7 August 1912

28. COMMON LAW

1. The common law is the best and most common birth-right that the subject hath for the safeguard and defence, not only of his goods, lands and revenues, but of his wife and children, his body, fame and life also.

   Sir Edward Coke (1552–1634), *A commentary upon Littleton (The first part of the institutes of the Laws of England)*, 1628, 19th edn., 1832, 142a

2. After all, that is the beauty of the common law; it is a maze and not a motorway.

   Diplock L.J. (1907–1985), *Morris v. C.W. Martin & Sons Ltd*, [1966] 1 Q.B. 716 at 730

3. The common law is not a brooding omnipresence in the sky, but the articulate voice of some sovereign or quasi-sovereign that can be identified.

   Holmes J. (1841–1935), *Southern Pacific Co.* v. *Jensen* (1917), 244 U.S. 205 at 222

4. The common law, though not to be found in the written records of the realm, yet has been long well known. It is coeval with civilised society itself, and was formed from

time to time by the wisdom of man. Good sense did not come with the Conquest, or at any other one time, but grew and increased from time to time with the wisdom of mankind.

Lord Kenyon (1732–1802), *R.* v. *Rusby* (1800), Pea. (2) 189 at 192

5. The object of the common law is to solve difficulties and adjust relations in social and commercial life. It must meet, so far as it can, sets of fact abnormal as well as usual. It must grow with the development of the nation. It must face and deal with changing or novel circumstances. Unless it can do that it fails in its function and declines in its dignity and value. An expanding society demands an expanding common law.

   McCardie J. (1869–1933), *Prager v. Blatspiel, Stamp & Heacock Ltd.*, [1924] 1 K.B. 566 at 570

6. So venerable, so majestic, is this living temple of justice, this immemorial and yet freshly growing fabric of the Common Law.

   Sir Frederick Pollock (1845–1937), *Oxford lectures*, 1890, p. 111

7. The common law assumes that people intend the consequences of their acts and are deemed to know what they are likely to be. Man in society is assumed by the lawyer to be a rational creature.

   William Robson, *Man and the social sciences*, 1972, Introduction, p. xxiv

8. Lawyers hate Common Law (possibly because it makes much of

their specialist knowledge redundant).

Auberon Waugh, *Sunday Telegraph*, 1 June 1986

29. COMPANIES

1. The director is really a watch-dog, and the watch-dog has no right without the knowledge of his master to take a sop from a possible wolf.

   Bowen L.J. (1835–94), *Re The North Australian Territory Co. Ltd.* (1891), 61 L.J. Eq. 129 at 135

2. It appears to me that the atmosphere of the temple of Justice is polluted by the presence of such things as ... companies.

   James L.J. (1807–81), *Wilson* v. *Church* (1879), 13 Ch.D. 1 at 44

3. There is no ideal time for the consolidation of companies legislation. Company law is not static, and if consolidation were to wait until all the measures in the pipeline at that time were enacted it would be delayed almost indefinitely.

   Lord Lucas, House of Lords, 7 February 1985

30. COMPREHENSIBILITY

1. The lies and nonsense the law is stuffed with, forms so thick a mist, that a plain man, nay, even a man of sense and learning, who is not in the trade, can see neither through nor into it.

   Jeremy Bentham (1748–1832), *Truth* v. *Ashhurst; or law as it is*, 1823 (but written in 1792)

2. The matter of these law-books must be made up into sentences of moderate length, such as men use in common conversation, and such as the laws are written in France, with no more words than necessary: not like the present statutes, in which I have seen a single sentence take up thirteen such pages as would fill a reasonable volume, and not finished after all: and which are stuffed with repetitions and words that are of no use, that the lawyers who draw them may be the better paid for them. Just like their deeds, such as you may see in any attorney's office, each filling from one to a hundred skins of parchment, long enough to reach the breadth or the length of Westminster Hall; all of which stuff you must carry in your mind at once, if you would make head or tail of it; for it makes altogether but one sentence; so well do they understand the art of poisoning language in order to fleece their clients. All which deeds might be drawn, not only more intelligibly, but surer, in short sentences, and in a twentieth part of the room.

   Jeremy Bentham (1748–1832), ibid.

3. Scarce any man has the means of knowing a twentieth part of the laws he is bound by. Both sorts of law are kept most happily and carefully from the knowledge of the people: statute law by its shape and bulk; common law by its very essence.

   Jeremy Bentham (1748–1832), ibid.

4. A good parson once said, that where mystery begins, religion

ends. Cannot I say, as truly at least, of human laws, that where mystery begins justice ends? It is hard to see whether the doctors of law or divinity have made the greater advances in the lucrative business of mystery.

Edmund Burke (1729–97), *A vindication of natural society*

5. Sometimes Administration of Justice Bills are dismissed by the unwary as mere lawyers' law and therefore likely to be incomprehensible or, at any rate, of no real importance to anyone but lawyers themselves — so often and so wrongly deemed to be the sole beneficiaries of complex legislation.

Lord Elwyn-Jones, House of Lords, 14 January 1985

6. Law, grown a forest, where perplex
The mazes, and the brambles vex;
Where its twelve verdurers every day
Are changing still the public way:
Yet if we miss our path and err,
We grevious penalties incur;
And wanderers tire, and tear their skin
And then get out where they went in.

Matthew Green (1696–1737), *The spleen*, 1. 292

7. Laws are generally not understood by three sorts of persons *viz.* by those that make them, by those that execute them, and by those that suffer if they break them.

Lord Halifax (1633–95), *Political thoughts and reflections*

8. There is something monstrous in commands couched in invented and unfamiliar language; an alien master is the worst of all. The language of the law must not be foreign to the ears of those who are to obey it.

Learned Hand (1872–1961), Speech, Washington DC, 11 May 1929

9. A body of law is more rational and more civilized when every rule it contains is referred articulately and definitely to an end which it subserves and when the grounds for desiring that end are stated, or are ready to be stated, in words.

Mr. Justice Oliver Wendell Holmes (1841–1935), Address, 1897, Quoted in *Wigmore on evidence*, vol. I

10. What can be more strange than to see a people obliged to obey laws they never understood.

Michel de Montaigne (1533–92), *Essays*, bk I, 'Of custom'

11. My one code by its simplicity, has done more good in France than the mass of all the laws that preceeded me. Under my reign, crimes were rapidly decreasing; whilst among our neighbours, the English, they increased, on the contrary, in a frightful manner.

Napoleon I (1769–1821), *Table talk and opinions*, 1868, p. 73

12. It has been the custom in modern Europe to regulate, upon most occasions, the payments of the attorneys and clerks of courts according to the number of pages which they had occasion to write;

the court, however, requiring, that each page should contain so many lines, and each line so many words. In order to increase their payment, the attorneys and clerks have contrived to multiply words beyond all necessity, to the corruption of the law language of, I believe, every court of justice in Europe.

Adam Smith (1723–90), *The wealth of nations*, 1776, bk V, ch. 1, pt II, 'Of the expense of justice'

13. The society [of lawyers] hath a peculiar cant and jargon of their own, that no other mortal can understand, and wherein all their laws are written, which they take special care to multiply; whereby they have wholly confounded the very essence of truth and falsehood, of right and wrong.

Jonathan Swift (1667–1745), *Gulliver's travels*, 1726, pt IV, ch. V

14. The manufacture of a five-pronged implement for digging results in a fork even if the manufacturer, unfamiliar with the English language, insists that he intended to make and has made a spade.

Lord Templeman, *Street* v. *Mountford* [1985], 2 W.L.R. 877 at 884

15. Let all the laws be clear, uniform and precise: to interpret laws is almost always to corrupt them.

Voltaire (1694–1778), *Philosophical dictionary*

16. The maxim 'for the lower orders one's language cannot be too plain' (that is, *clear* and *perspicuous*, so as to require no learning nor

ingenuity to understand it).

Richard Whately (1787–1863), *Thoughts and apothegms* 1856, pt VI

31. CONFESSIONS

1. He confesseth himself guilty, who refuses to come to a trial.

Thomas Fuller (1654–1734), *Gnomologia*, 1732, no. 1,828

2. He that repents of his own act, either is, or was a fool by his own confession.

Thomas Fuller (1654–1734), ibid., no. 2,264

3. In confessing the greatest offences, a criminal gives himself credit for his candour. You and he seem to have come to an amicable understanding on his character at last.

William Hazlitt (1773–1830), *Characteristics*, 1823, CCLXII

4. Confession of a fault is half amends.

James Kelly, *Scottish Proverbs*, 1721, C, no. 56

5. Open confession is good for the soul.

James Kelly, ibid., O, no. 16

6. A confession made in court is of greater effect than any proof. (*Confessio facta in judicio omni probatione major est.*)

Legal maxim

7. There are a great number of

people ... who make the most extraordinary confessions, as they just feel that they want to get out of the police station and back home as fast as possible.

Lord Mishcon, House of Lords, 9 July 1984

8. He's half absolv'd who has confess'd.

Matthew Prior (1664–1721), *Alma*, 1719, canto II, 1. 22

9. His confession is taken, and it shall be read to his face.

William Shakespeare (1564–1616), *All's well that ends well*, 1602–4, IV. iii

10. I will confess what I know without constraint; if ye pinch me like a pasty I can say no more.

William Shakespeare (1564–1616), ibid.

11. I confess me much guilty.

William Shakespeare (1564–1616), *As you like it*, 1596–1600, I.ii

12. I confess nothing, nor I deny nothing.

William Shakespeare (1564–1616), *Much ado about nothing*, 1598–9, IV.i

13. If it be confessed, it is not redressed.

William Shakespeare (1564–1616), *The merry wives of Windsor*, 1597–1601, I.i

14. To deny all is to confess all.

Spanish proverb

32. CONGRESS

1. Congress, *n*. A body of men who meet to repeal laws.

Ambrose Bierce (1842–1914?), *The devil's dictionary*, 1911

2. In no country [America] perhaps in the world is the law so general a study. The profession itself is numerous and powerful; and in most provinces it takes the lead. The greater number of the deputies sent to the congress were lawyers.

Edmund Burke (1729–97), *Speech on conciliation with America*, 22 March 1775

3. All legislative powers herein granted shall be vested in a Congress of the United States, which shall consist of a Senate and House of Representatives.

Constitution of the United States, Art. I, 1789

4. How'd it do fer congress t' pass a law requirin' dealers in th' necessities o' life t' wait till ther wuz really a crisis before holdin' up th' consumer?

Frank McKinney Hubbard (1868–1930), *New sayings by Abe Martin*, 1917

5. If the present Congress errs in too much talking, how can it be otherwise, in a body to which the people send one hundred and fifty lawyers, whose trade it is to question everything, yield nothing and talk by the hour? That one hundred and fifty lawyers should

do business together, ought not to be expected.

Thomas Jefferson (1743–1826), *Autobiography*

6. Congress's internal organization and processes constitute a vast terrain of booby traps for the presidential program.

Louis W. Koenig, *The chief executive*, 3rd edn., 1975, ch. 7

33. CONSCIENCE

1. Law and conscience are one and the same.

Bacon J., *Watson* v. *Watson* (1647), Sty. 56

2. What do you get in place of a conscience? Don't answer. I know: a lawyer.

Kirk Douglas, Quoted in H. Haun, *The movie quote book*

3. A good conscience is never lawless in the worst regulated state, and will provide those laws for itself, which the neglect of legislators hath forgotten to supply.

Henry Fielding (1707–54), *Tom Jones* 1749, bk XVII, ch. II

4. He is one that will not plead that cause wherein his tongue must be confuted by his conscience.

Thomas Fuller (1608–61), *The holy state*, 1642, 'The good advocate'

5. A clear conscience laughs at false accusations.

Thomas Fuller (1654–1734), *Gnomologia*, 1732, no. 42

6. A guilty conscience never thinketh itself safe.

Thomas Fuller (1654–1734), Ibid., no. 208

7. A quiet conscience causes a quiet sleep.

Thomas Fuller (1654–1734), ibid., no. 374

8. A quiet conscience sleeps in thunder.

Thomas Fuller (1654–1734), ibid., no. 375

9. It is always term-time in the court of conscience.

Thomas Fuller (1654–1734), ibid., no. 2, 914

10. The pain which conscience give the man who has already done wrong, is soon got over. Conscience is a coward, and those faults it has not strength enough to prevent, it seldom has justice enough to accuse.

Oliver Goldsmith (1728–74), *The Vicar of Wakefield*, 1766, ch. XIII

11. Conscience ... The muzzle of the will.

Frank McKinney Hubbard (1868–1930), *The Roycroft dictionary*, 1923

12. If I had a guilty conscience I would not say anything, and would not blame others for an offence which I commit.

St Jerome (*c.* 342–420), *Letters*, CXVII

13. No guilty man is ever acquitted by

the verdict of his own conscience.

Juvenal (fl. AD 1st–2nd cent.), *Satires*, XIII

14. A guilty conscience self accuses.

James Kelly, *Scottish proverbs*, 1721, A, no. 48

15. A safe conscience makes a sound sleep.

James Kelly, ibid., no. 78

16. There is no witness so terrible, no accuser so dreaded, as the conscience that lives in all our hearts.

Polybius (*c.*208–*c.*126 BC), *Histories*, bk XVIII, 43

17. Our character often makes our conscience.

Joseph Roux (1834–1905), *Meditations of a parish priest*, trans. Hapgood, 1886, ch. IV, XXXII

18. Thus conscience does make cowards of us all.

William Shakespeare (1564–1616), *Hamlet*, 1599–1600, III.i

19. My conscience tells me you are innocent.

William Shakespeare (1564–1616), *Henry VI Pt II*, 1590–1, III.i

20. Wringing of the conscience.

William Shakespeare (1564–1616), *Henry VIII*, 1612–13, II.ii

21. The wild sea of my conscience.

William Shakespeare (1564–1616), ibid., IV

22. The witness of a good conscience.

William Shakespeare (1564–1616), *The merry wives of Windsor*, 1597–1601, IV.ii

23. The guilt of conscience take thou for thy labour.

William Shakespeare (1564–1616), *Richard II*, 1595–6, V.vi

24. The worm of conscience still begnaw thy soul!

William Shakespeare (1564–1616), *Richard III*, 1592–3, I.iii

25. When he opens his purse to give us our reward, the conscience flies out.

William Shakespeare (1564–1616), ibid., IV

26. My conscience hath a thousand several tongues,
And every tongue brings in a several tale,
And every tale condemns me for a villain.

William Shakespeare (1564–1616), ibid., V.iii

27. Conscience is but a word cowards use,
Devis'd at first to keep the strong in awe.
Our strong arms be our conscience, swords our law.

William Shakespeare (1564–1616), ibid.

28. I'll haunt thee like a wicked conscience still,
That mouldeth goblins swift as frenzy's thoughts.

William Shakespeare (1564–

1616), *Troilus and Cressida*, 1597–1602, V.x

29. I appeal to your conscience, sir.

William Shakespeare (1564–1616), *A winter's tale*, 1610–11, III.ii

30. Conscience makes egotists of us all.

Oscar Wilde (1856–1900), *The picture of Dorian Gray*, 1891, ch. VIII

34. CONSPIRACY

1. Conspiracies no sooner should be
                                form'd
Than executed.

   Joseph Addison (1672–1719), *Cato*, 1721, I.ii

2. O conspiracy,
Sham'st thou to show thy danger-
                        ous brow by night,
When evils are most free?

   William Shakespeare (1564–1616), *Julius Caesar*, 1599–1600, II.i

3. Take no care
Who chafes, who frets, or where
                        conspirers are

   William Shakespeare (1564–1616), *Macbeth*, 1606–7, IV.i

4. Open-eyed conspiracy
His time doth take.

   William Shakespeare (1564–1616), *The tempest*, 1611–12, I.ii

35. CONSTITUTION

1. The blessings of society depend entirely on the constitutions of government.

   John Adams (1735–1826), *Thoughts on government*, 1776

2. The nation's armour of defence against the passions of men is the Constitution. Take that away, and the nation goes down into the field of its conflicts like a warrior without armour.

   Henry Ward Beecher (1813–87), *Proverbs from Plymouth pulpit*, 1887

3. Those three great institutions, Parliament, the Press and the Judges, are safeguards of justice and liberty: and they embody the spirit of the constitution.

   Lord Denning, *The changing law*, 1953, p. 18

4. Our Constitution is in actual operation, everything appears to promise that it will last, but in this world nothing is certain but death and taxes.

   Benjamin Franklin (1706–90), Letter to Jean-Baptiste Leroy, 13 November 1789

5. Constitutions should consist only of general provisions; the reason is that they must necessarily be permanent, and they cannot calculate for the possible change of things.

   Alexander Hamilton (1757–1804), Speech, 28 June 1788

6. The United States, like Britain, has an unwritten constitution, though, unlike Britain, this is used along-

side the written one.

Simon Hoggart, *Observer*, 10 August 1986

7. No society can make a perpetual constitution, or even a perpetual law.

   Thomas Jefferson (1743–1826), Letter to James Madison, 6 September 1789

8. No constitution can work smoothly if politicians play too rough.

   Sir John Kerr, *Sydney Morning Herald*, 'Sayings of the week', 14 September 1985

9. Where in the same constitution there is a monarchy, an aristocracy and a democracy, each serves as a check upon the others.

   Niccolo Machiavelli (1469–1527), *Discourses*, I, ch. II

10. A constitution ... is to a government what the laws made afterwards by that government are to a Court of Judicature. The Court of Judicature does not make the laws, neither can it alter them; it only acts in conformity to the laws made: and the government is in like manner governed by the constitution.

    Thomas Paine (1737–1809), *Rights of man*, 1791

11. There is a higher law than the constitution.

    William Henry Seward (1801–72), Speech, US Senate, 11 March 1850

12. I evince my love of the Constitution, by making it the guardian

of all men's rights and the source of their freedom.

Sydney Smith (1771–1845), *The Peter Plymley letters*, 1807, V

36. CONTRACTS

1. A verbal contract isn't worth the paper it's written on.

   Samuel Goldwyn (1882–1974), attributed

2. A contract is a mutual promise.

   William Paley (1743–1805), *The principles of moral and political philosophy*, 1784, bk III, pt I, ch. VI

3. Men keep their agreements when it is an advantage to both parties not to break them.

   Solon (*c.*630–*c.*555 BC), quoted in Plutarch, *Lives: Solon*

4. [Contracts] must not be the sports of an idle hour, mere matters of pleasantry and badinage, never intended by the parties to have any serious effect whatever.

   Lord Stowell (1745–1836), *Dalrymple* v. *Dalrymple* (1811), 2 Hag. Con. 54 at 105

37. COPYRIGHT

1. The law in respect to literature ought to remain upon the same footing as that which regards the profits of mechanical inventions and chemical discoveries.

   William Wordsworth (1770–1850), Letter to Sergeant Talfourd, 18 April 1838

2. But the property here claimed is all ideal; a set of ideas which have no bounds or marks whatever, nothing that is capable of a visible possession, nothing that can sustain any one of the qualities or incidents of property. Their whole existence is in the mind alone; incapable of any other modes of acquisition or enjoyment, than by mental possession or apprehension; safe and invulnerable, from their own immateriality: no trespass can reach them: no tort affect them; no fraud or violence diminish or damage them. Yet these are the phantoms which the author would grasp and confine to himself.

Yates J. (1722–70), *Millar* v. *Taylor* (1769), 4 Burr. 2303 at 2361–2

38. CORPORATIONS

1. We have much to fear from great corporated, moneyed institutions. We are today more in danger from organised money than ever we were from slavery. And the battle for the future is going to be a battle with Mammon.

Henry Ward Beecher (1813–87), *Proverbs from Plymouth pulpit,* 1887

2. Corporation, *n.* An ingenious device for obtaining individual profit without individual responsibility.

Ambrose Bierce (1842–1914?), *The devil's dictionary,* 1911

3. [Corporations] cannot commit treason, nor be outlawed, nor excommunicate, for they have no souls.

Sir Edward Coke (1552–1634), *Case of Sutton's Hospital* (1612), 10 Rep. 23a at 32b

4. A corporation aggregate of many is invisible, immortal, and rests only in intendment and consideration of the law.

Sir Edward Coke (1552–1634), ibid.

5. The simple answer is that in these courts ... the privilege [against self-incrimination] is not available to a corporation. It has no body to be kicked or soul to be damned.

Lord Denning M.R., *British Steel Corporation* v. *Granada TV,* [1981] 1 All E.R. 417 at 439

6. There is the veil of corporate personality which protects the individual from any personal liability at all. That is the fundamental principle of our company law.

Lord Denning, House of Lords, 15 January 1985

7. To supervise wisely the great corporations is well; but to look backward to the days when business was polite pillage and regard our great business concerns as piratical institutions carrying letters of marque and reprisal is a grave error born in the minds of little men. When these little men legislate they set the brakes going uphill.

Elbert Hubbard (1856–1915), *Notebook,* p. 16

8. They [corporations] were invisible,

immortall, and ... had no soule; and therefore no subpoena lieth against them, because they have no conscience nor soule; a corporation, is a body aggregate, none can create soules but God, but the King creates them, and therefore they have no soules.

Manwood C.B. (1525–92), *Tipling* v. *Pexall* (1614), 2 Bulstr. 233

9. The biggest corporation, like the humblest private citizen, must be held to strict compliance with the will of the people.

Theodore Roosevelt (1858–1919), speech, 1902

10. It is truly enough said, that a corporation has no conscience; but a corporation of conscientious men is a corporation *with* a conscience.

Henry D. Thoreau (1817–62), *Resistance to civil government*, 1849

11. Did you ever expect a corporation to have a conscience, when it has no soul to be damned and no body to be kicked?

Lord Thurlow (1731–1806), attributed

39. CORRUPTION

1. Nepotism is only kin deep.

Anonymous

2. Corruption is a tree, whose branches are of an unmeasurable length, they spread everywhere, and the dew that drops from thence, hath infected some chairs and stools of authority.

Francis Beaumont (1584–1616) and **John Fletcher** (1579–1625), *The honest man's fortune*, III.i

3. Take all the robes of all the good judges that have ever lived on the face of the earth, and they would not be large enough to cover the iniquity of one corrupt judge.

Henry Ward Beecher (1813–87), *Proverbs from Plymouth pulpit*, 1887

4. And love is the keeping of her laws; and the giving heed unto her laws is the assurance of incorruption.

Bible, Authorized Version, The wisdom of solomon, 6: 18

5. Among a people generally corrupt, liberty cannot long exist.

Edmund Burke (1729–97), Letter to the Sheriffs of Bristol, 3 April 1777

6. Instances there have been many, wherein the punishment of minor offences, in inferior persons, has been made the means of screening crimes of a high order, and in men of high description.

Edmund Burke (1729–97), *Impeachment of Warren Hastings*, 15 February 1788

7. An arbitrary system indeed must always be a corrupt one ... There never was a man who thought he had no law but his own will, who did not soon find that he had no end but his own profit.

Edmund Burke (1729–97), ibid., 17 February 1788

8. Corruption is like a ball of snow, when once set a rolling it must increase.

   C.C. Colton (1780–1832), *Lacon*, 1820, vol. II, VI

9. 'Tis the most certain sign, the
   world's accurst,
   That the best things corrupted are
   the worst.

   Sir John Denham (1615–69), *The progress of learning*

10. Every actual state is corrupt. Good men must not obey the laws too well.

    Ralph Waldo Emerson (1803–82), *Essays, second series*, 1844, 'Politics'

11. Corruption, the most infallible symptom of constitutional liberty.

    Edward Gibbon (1737–94), *The decline and fall of the Roman Empire*, ch. XXI

12. A bad citizen cannot cause serious trouble in a republic unless it is already corrupt.

    Niccolo Machiavelli (1469–1527), *Discourses*, bk III, ch VIII

13. At length corruption, like a general
    flood,
    (So long by watchful ministers
    withstood)
    Shall deluge all; and avarice creep-
    ing on,
    Spread low like a low-born mist,
    and blot the sun;
    Statesman and patriot ply alike the
    stocks,
    Peeress and butler share alike the
    box,
    And judges job, and bishops bite
    the town,
    And mighty dukes pack cards for
    half a crown.
    See Britain sunk in lucre's sordid
    charms.

    Alexander Pope (1688–1744), *Moral essays*, III, 'Epistle to Bathurst', 1733, 1. 135

14. Whilst rank corruption, mining all
    within,
    Infects unseen.

    William Shakespeare (1564–1616), *Hamlet*, 1599–1600, III. iv

15. Corruption wins not more than honesty.

    William Shakespeare (1564–1616), *Henry VIII*, 1612–13, III. ii

16. Thieves for their robbery have
    authority
    When judges steal themselves.

    William Shakespeare (1564–1616), *Measure for measure*, 1604–5, II. i

17. When the state was most corrupt, legislation abounded.

    Tacitus (*c.*55–117), *Annals*, bk III, sec. 27

40. COSTS
See also 60. Fees

1. There is one panacea which heals every sore in litigation, and that is costs.

   Bowen L.J. (1835–94), *Cropper v. Smith* (1884), 26 Ch.D. 700 at 711

2. Agree, for the law is costly.

   Thomas Fuller (1654–1734), *Gnomologia*, 1732, no. 781

3. In a thousand pounds' worth of law, there is not a shilling's worth of pleasure.

   Thomas Fuller (1654–1734), ibid., no. 2,811

4. Sympathy pays no costs.

   A.P. Herbert (1890–1971), *More uncommon law*, 1982, *Fester* v. *The King*; *Fester* v. *Philpott, Rory and Company Ltd.*; *Fester* v. *Platt*

41. COURTS

1. Courts do not exist for the sake of discipline, but for the sake of deciding matters in controversy.

   Bowen L.J. (1835–94), *Cropper* v. *Smith* (1884), 26 Ch.D. 700 at 710.

2. Courts are made for the suitors, and not the suitors for the court.

   Edmund Burke (1729–97), *Report from the Committee of the House of Commons, appointed to inspect the Lords' Journals*, 30 April 1794

3. The relation of the rules of practice to the work of justice is intended to be that of handmaid rather than mistress.

   Collins M.R. (1842–1911), *Re Coles and Ravenshear*, [1907] 1 K.B. 1 at 4

4. One of the worst of all judicial fail-

ings is a desire to be humorous in court.

Mr Justice Comyn, *Sunday Telegraph*, 29 September 1985

5. So Tongue was the lawyer, and
   argued the cause
   With a great deal of skill, and a wig
   full of learning;
   While Chief-Baron Ear sat to
   balance the laws,
   So famed for his talent in nicely
   discerning.

   William Cowper (1741–1800), *Report of an adjudged case*

6. One of the most important tasks of the courts is to see that the powers of the executive are properly used, that is, used honestly and reasonably for the purposes authorised by Parliament and not for any ulterior motive.

   Lord Denning, *Freedom under the law*, 1949, p. 102

7. People who go voluntarily to law, or are taken forcibly there, for the first time, may be allowed to labour under some temporary irritation and anxiety.

   Charles Dickens (1812–70), *The Pickwick papers*, 1837, ch. XXXIII

8. In some countries the course of the courts is so tedious, and the expense so high, that the remedy, *Justice*, is worse than *injustice*, the disease.

   Benjamin Franklin (1706–90), *Poor Richard's almanac*, 1742

9. A friend in court is as good as a

penny in pocket.

Thomas Fuller (1654–1734), *Gnomologia*, no. 117

10. A mere scholar at court is an ass among apes.

Thomas Fuller (1654–1734), ibid., no. 322

11. At court, everyone for himself.

Thomas Fuller (1654–1734), ibid., no. 825

12. Hell and Chancery are always open.

Thomas Fuller (1654–1734), ibid., 1732, no. 2,486

13. It is at courts, as it is in ponds; some fish, some frogs.

Thomas Fuller (1654–1734), ibid., no. 2,912

14. When I wanted an honest man, I never thought to go to court for him.

Thomas Fuller (1654–1734), ibid., no. 5,560

15. A friend in court
Makes the process short.

Thomas Fuller (1654–1734), ibid., no. 6,311

16. The charge is prepared; the lawyers are met;
The judges all ranged (a terrible show!)

John Gay (1685–1732), *The beggar's opera*, 1728, II. xi, air LVII

17. It is evident that there is no process of a court by which the observance of the laws can, in the last resort, be enforced.

Alexander Hamilton (1757–1804), *The Federalist*, 1788, no. XV

18. Laws are a dead letter without courts to expound and define their true meaning and operation.

Alexander Hamilton (1757–1804), ibid., 1788, no. XXII

19. It is as important to keep out of court as it is to keep out of debt.

E.W. Howe (1853–1937), *Country town sayings*, 1911

20. Prosecutor: ... One who abets a crime after it has or has not been committed.

Frank McKinney Hubbard (1868–1930), *The Roycroft dictionary*, 1923

21. A friend in court is worth a penny in the purse.

James Kelly, *Scottish proverbs*, 1721, A, no. 66

22. Let the judges answer to the question of law, and the jurors to the matter of fact. (*Ad quaestionem juris respondeant judices ad quaestionem facti respondeant juratores.*)

Legal maxim

23. In the common pleas there is all law and no conscience, in the queen's bench both law and conscience, in the chancery all conscience and no law, and in the exchequer neither law nor conscience.

[On the four high Courts of Justice].

Sir Roger Manwood (1525–92), quoted in *The dictionary of national biography*

24. Prosecutors should not be scalp-hunters.

Justice Lionel Murphy, *Sydney Morning Herald*, 24 May 1986

25. Courts of justice do not pretend to furnish cures for all the miseries of human life. They redress or punish gross violations of duty, but they go no farther; they cannot make men virtuous; and, as the happiness of the world depends upon its virtue, there may be much unhappiness in it which human laws cannot undertake to remove.

Sir William Scott (1745–1836), *Evans* v. *Evans* (1790), 1 Hag. Con. 35 at 38

26. He must, then to the inns of court shortly: I was once of Clement's-inn; where I think they will talk of mad Shallow yet.

William Shakespeare (1564–1616), *Henry IV, Pt II*, 1597–8, III.ii

27. Our court shall be a little Academe,
Still and contemplative in living art.

William Shakespeare (1564–1616), *Love's labour's lost*, 1594–5, I.i

28. The court of Chancery [was] ... like a boa constrictor; it swallowed up the estates of English gentle-men in haste, and digested them at leisure.

Sydney Smith (1771–1845), W. Jerrold, *Bon-Mots of Sydney Smith and R. Brinsley Sheridan*, p. 110

29. A person who is ignorant of legal matters is always liable to make mistakes when he tries to photograph a court scene with his pen.

Mark Twain (1835–1910), *Puddn'head Wilson*, 1894, 'A whisper to the reader'

30. One should never allow lawyers to present one's case in court.

Auberon Waugh, *Private Eye*, no. 592, 24 August 1984

31. I have been to three or four courts martial in my time and in every case it struck me that the nearest the proceeding got to any kind of human truth was in the speech of mitigation by the prisoner's friend.

John Winton, *One of our warships*, 1975, ch. IV

32. Pray baul soundly for me at the Kings-Bench; bluster, splutter, question, cavil; but be sure your argument be intricate enough to confound the court.

William Wycherley (1640–1716), *The plain-dealer*, III.i

42. CRIME

1. He is the criminal that plans the crime:
On the contriver falls the penalty.

Vittorio Alfieri (1749–1803), *Antigone*, 1783, II.ii

2. Too many criminals these days are giving crime a bad name.

   Anonymous

3. Crime may be said to be injury voluntarily inflicted in defiance of the law.

   Aristotle (384–322 BC), *The rhetoric*, trans. Welldon, bk I, ch. X

4. The magnitude of a crime is proportionate to the magnitude of the injustice which prompts it. Hence the smallest crimes may be actually the greatest.

   Aristotle (384–322 BC), ibid., ch. XIV

5. Misdemeanor, *n.* An infraction of the law having less dignity than a felony and constituting no claim to admittance into the best criminal society.

   Ambrose Bierce (1842–1914?), *The devil's dictionary*, 1911

6. It is not the revolutionary man but the respectable man who would commit any crime — to save his respectability.

   G.K. Chesterton (1874–1936), *The secret of Father Brown*, 1927, 'The secret of Flambeau'

7. You may think a crime horrible because you could never commit it. I think it horrible because I could commit it.

   G.K. Chesterton (1874–1936), ibid.

8. Every crime depends on somebody not waking up too soon.

   G.K. Chesterton (1874–1936), ibid., 'The song of the flying fish'

9. But who can judge of crimes by punishment,
   Where parties rule, and law's subservient.
   Justice with change of int'rest learns to bow:
   And what was merit once, is murther now.

   Daniel Defoe (1660–1731), *A hymn to the pillory*, 1703

10. We must conceal crimes we cannot cure.

    Daniel Defoe (1660–1731), *The true-born Englishman*, 1701, pt II

11. If once a man indulges himself in murder, very soon he comes to think little of robbing; and from robbing he comes next to drinking and sabbath-breaking, and from that to incivility and procrastination. Once begin upon this downward path, you never know where you are to stop.

    Thomas De Quincey (1785–1859), *Supplementary paper on murder considered as one of the fine arts*

12. As often happens, a crime committed with outstanding audacity is more successful than others.

    Feodor Dostoevski (1821–81), *The brothers Karamazov*, 1879, bk VI, ch. II

13. Crime and its control amount to a regressive tax on the community.

    David Downes, *Law and order: theft of an issue*, 1983, ch. 1

14. The most commonplace crime is often the most mysterious, because it presents no new or special features from which deductions may be drawn.

    Sir Arthur Conan Doyle (1859–1930), *A study in scarlet*, 1887, pt 1, ch. 7, 'Light in the darkness'

15. But treason is not own'd when 'tis descried;
    Successful crimes alone are justified.

    John Dryden (1631–1700), *The medal*, 1682

16. There is no den in the wide world to hide a rogue. Commit a crime, and the earth is made of glass. Commit a crime, and it seems as if a coat of snow fell on the ground, such as reveals in the woods the track of every partridge and fox and squirrel and mole ... Some damning circumstance always transpires. The laws and substances of nature ... become penalties to the thief.

    Ralph Waldo Emerson (1803–82), *Essays, first series*, 1841 'Compensation'

17. Men never speak of crime as lightly as they think.

    Ralph Waldo Emerson (1803–82), *Essays, second series*, 1844, 'Experience'

18. No man at last believes that he can be lost, nor that the crime in him is as black as in the felon.

    Ralph Waldo Emerson (1803–82), ibid.

19. Crimes, like virtues, are their own rewards.

    George Farquhar (1678–1707), *The inconstant*, IV.ii

20. Crimes may be secret: but yet not secure.

    Thomas Fuller (1654–1734), *Gnomologia*, 1732, no. 1,205

21. Knowledge rendereth a crime inexcusable.

    Thomas Fuller (1654–1734), ibid., no. 3,140

22. The greater the man, the greater the crime.

    Thomas Fuller (1654–1734), ibid., no. 4,566

23. The number of malefactors, authorizes not the crime.

    Thomas Fuller (1654–1734), ibid., no. 4,687

24. It is not a crime to intend to commit a crime.

    Lord Gifford, House of Lords, 2 July 1984

25. If Canberra is about middle-aged men discovering sex, royal commissions into crime are about middle-aged men discovering crime.

    Richard Hall, *Sydney Morning Herald*, 'Sayings of the week', 28 June 1986

26. There is a heroism in crime as well as in virtue.

    William Hazlitt (1778–1830), *Characteristics*, 1823, CCCLIV

27. The hole calls the thief.

> **George Herbert** (1593–1633), *Jacula prudentum*, 1651

28. The source of every crime, is some defect of the understanding; or some error in reasoning; or some sudden force of the passions.

> **Thomas Hobbes** (1588–1679), *Leviathan*, 1651, pt II, ch. XXVII

29. Hear, the gods
Grow angry with your patience. 'Tis their care
And must be yours, that guilty
men escape not.
As crimes do grow, justice should
rouse itself.

> **Ben Jonson** (1573–1637), *Cataline*, III.v

30. Men commit the same crime, but often with very different results. One man ends up on a cross, and another wearing a crown.

> **Juvenal** (fl. AD 1st–2nd cent.), *Satires*, XIII

31. Those who are incapable of committing great crimes do not easily suspect them in others.

> **François, Duc de La Rochefoucauld** (1630–80), *Maxims*, 1678

32. Crime in every possible form, like business, has progressed to the stage where the little unorganised participant hasn't much chance of success.

> **Emanuel H. Lavine**, *The third degree*, 1930, ch. IV

33. Crime is never founded upon reason.

> **Livy** (59 BC–AD 17), *The history of Rome*, bk XXVIII, sec. XXVIII

34. Whatever offence is committed by many goes unpunished.

> **Lucan** (AD 39–65), *Pharsalia*, bk V

35. The common sense of mankind ... will always recognise a distinction between crimes which originate in an inordinate zeal for the commonwealth, and crimes which originate from selfish cupidity.

> **Lord Macaulay** (1800–59), *Warren Hastings*, October 1841

36. The surest and quickest way to reduce crime and achieve a more humane and enlightened penal system is to increase the likelihood that the guilty will be convicted.

> **Sir Robert Mark**, *Policing a perplexed society*, 1977, 'Liberty without responsibility'

37. The contagion of crime is like that of the plague.

> **Napoleon I** (1769–1821), *Table talk and opinions*, 1868, p. 100

38. Most felons never considered being caught, which was why prison rarely deterred.

> **G.F. Newman**, *Sir, you bastard*, 1970, ch. VIII

39. All, all look up with reverential
awe,
At crimes that 'scape, or triumph
o'er the law:
While truth, worth, wisdom, daily
they decry —

'Nothing is sacred now but villany.'

Alexander Pope (1688–1744), *Epilogue to the satires*, 1731, dialogue I, 1. 167

40. Crime like virtue has its degrees; and timid innocence was never known to blossom suddenly into extreme licence.

Jean Racine (1639–99), *Phèdre*, 1677, IV.ii

41. Most crime consists of breaking laws that even the most determined evangelist would have to admit are Caesar's not God's.

Robert Rice, *The business of crime*, 1956, 'The argument of this book'

42. Crime must be concealed by crime.

Seneca (4 BC–AD 65), *Hippolytus*

43. Successful crime goes by the name of virtue.

Seneca (4 BC–AD 65), *Hurcules furens*

44. He who does not prevent a crime when he can, encourages it.

Seneca (4 BC–AD 65), *Troades*

45. Our crimes would despair if they were not cherished by our virtues.

William Shakespeare (1564–1616), *All's well that ends well*, 1602–4, IV. iii

46. The offender's scourge is weigh'd, But never the offence.

William Shakespeare (1564–1616), *Hamlet*, 1599–1600, IV. iii

47. That argues but the shame of your offence:
A rotten case abides no handling.

William Shakespeare (1564–1616), *Henry IV Pt II*, IV. i

48. Tremble thou wretch,
That has within thee undivulged crimes,
Unwhipp'd of justice.

William Shakespeare (1564–1616), *King Lear*, 1605–6, III. ii

49. When rich villains have need of poor ones, poor ones may make what price they will.

William Shakespeare (1564–1616), *Much ado about nothing*, 1598–9, III. iii

50. The offender's sorrow lends but weak relief
To him that bears the strong offence's cross.

William Shakespeare (1564–1616), *Sonnets*, no. XXXIV

51. Crimes, like lands, are not inherited.

William Shakespeare (1564–1616), *Timon of Athens*, 1607–8, V. iv

52. Weigh but the crime.

William Shakespeare (1564–1616), *Timon of Athens*, 1607–8, III. v

53. For such petty crimes as these.

William Shakespeare (1564–1616), *Two gentlemen of Verona*, 1594–5, IV. i

54. Crime is only the retail department

of what, in wholesale, we call penal law.

George Bernard Shaw (1856–1950), *Maxims for revolutionists*, 1903

55. The worst of our crimes is poverty.

George Bernard Shaw (1856–1950), *Major Barbara*, 1905, Preface

56. A man is not in law bound to assume that the natural consequence of a lawful act which he does will be the commission of unlawful acts by others.

F.E. Smith (1872–1930), quoted in *The life of F.E. Smith by his son*, 1959, ch. 7

57. There is, indeed, one excuse for attempts to spread education by artificial means, namely, the anxiety to diminish crime, of which education is supposed to be a preventive.

Herbert Spencer (1820–1903), *Social statics*, 1870, pt III, ch. XXVI, sec. 9

58. Ignorance and crime are not cause and effect; they are coincident results of the same cause.

Herbert Spencer (1820–1903), ibid.

59. Had I a hundred tongues, a hundred mouths, and a voice of iron, I could not sum up all the types of crime nor all their punishments.

Virgil (70–19 BC), *The Aeneid*, bk VI

60. History is nothing more than the portrayal of crimes and misfortunes.

Voltaire (1694–1778), *L'Ingénu*, 1767, ch. 10

61. Nobody ever commits a crime without doing something stupid.

Oscar Wilde (1854–1900), *The picture of Dorian Gray*, 1891, ch. XIV

62. Mankind must have a knowledge of what is their duty, in order to observe it by abstaining from every violation of it: the breach of a duty must be wilful to make it criminal.

Yates J. (1722–70), *Millar* v. *Taylor* (1769), 4 Burr. 2303 at 2365

43. CRIMINAL JUSTICE

1. I do not think it right to unsettle the minds of those numerous and ignorant classes, on whom its [criminal law's] sanctions are principally intended to operate. It might produce no good effects if they were all at once to learn, that the Criminal Code in the mass, as it were, had been sentenced to undergo a revision.

Henry Peter Brougham (1778–1868), House of Commons, 7 February 1828

2. If the success of a system of criminal prosecution is to be measured by the proportion of criminals whom it convicts and punishes, the English system must be regarded as a failure.

Lord Devlin, quoted by Sir Robert Mark, in the *Observer*, 12 July 1981

3. If you make the criminal code sanguinary, juries will not convict. If the law is too mild, private vengeance comes in.

   Ralph Waldo Emerson (1803–82), *Essays, first series*, 1841, 'Compensation'

4. He whose father is judge goes safe to his trial.

   Thomas Fuller (1654–1734), *Gnomologia*, 1732, no. 2,400

5. Much better never to catch a rogue, than to let him go again.

   Thomas Fuller (1654–1734), ibid., no. 3,476

6. Whenever the offence inspires less horror than the punishment, the rigour of penal law is obliged to give way to the common feelings of mankind.

   Edward Gibbon (1737–94), *The decline and fall of the Roman Empire*, ch. XIV

7. It is abominable to convict a man behind his back.

   Holt, C.J. (1642–1710), *R. v. Dyer* (1703), 6 Mod. 41

8. Shall we indict one man for making a fool of another?

   Holt C.J. (1642–1710), *R. v. Jones* (1704), 2 Ld. Ray. 1013

9. The criminal justice system [in the US] would collapse if the courts had to try all, or even a substantial minority, of the indicted.

   Morton M. Hunt, *The mugging*, 1972, ch. 4, VI

10. It is safer for an evil person not to be prosecuted, than that he should be tried and acquitted.

    Livy (59 BC–AC 17), *The history of Rome*, bk XXXIV, sec. IV

11. The objective of criminal justice should be the establishment of the truth rather than the technical determination of guilt.

    Sir Robert Mark, speech, Toronto, August 1965

12. Let there be no doubt that a minority of criminal lawyers do very well from the proceeds of crime. A reputation for success, achieved by persistent lack of scruple in the defence of the most disreputable, soon attracts other clients who see little hope of acquittal in any other way. Experienced and respected metropolitan detectives can identify lawyers in criminal practice who are more harmful to society than the clients they represent.

    Sir Robert Mark, Dimbleby lecture, November 1973

13. The criminal-justice system can be likened to a vacuum cleaner. The police are the mouth and the suction power. The courts are the hose. And the prisons are the bag. We've increased the size of the mouth and the suction power but not the other things.

    Hans W. Mattick, quoted in *US News and World Report*, 10 May 1976, p. 40

14. The hungry judges soon the sentence sign

And wretches hang that jury-men
may dine.

Alexander Pope (1688–1744),
The rape of the lock, 1714, canto
III, 1. 21

15. The typical method of conviction is
by the accused's plea of guilty ...
Mostly, therefore, the system of
administering criminal justice in
the United States is a system of
justice *without* trial.

Jerome H. Skolnick, *Justice without trial*, 1966, ch. 1

44. CRIMINALS

1. No one is entirely useless. Even
the worst of us can serve as horrible examples.

Anonymous, *State Prison Newspaper*, Salt Lake City, quoted in
the *Observer*, 23 January 1949

2. Essentially, criminals are evil and
I'm not.

Ronald Biggs, (20 years after the
Great Train Robbery), *Sydney
Morning Herald*, 'Sayings of the
week', 3 August 1985

3. There is no such thing as a criminal
type among those whose crimes
are far-reaching or important. It
only exists in those whose offences
are the minor ones.

Francis Carlin, *Reminiscences of
an ex-detective*, 3rd edn., ch.
XVIII

4. The criminal is the creative artist;
the detective only the critic.

G.K. Chesterton (1874–1936),

The innocence of Father Brown,
1910, 'The blue cross'

5. Those criminals with small minds
are always quite conventional.
They become criminals out of
sheer conventionality.

G.K. Chesterton (1874–1936),
The secret of Father Brown, 1927,
'The secret of Flambeau'

6. Is it not known that the common
people throughout Russia call
crime a 'misfortune,' and the
criminal an 'unfortunate'?

Feodor Dostoevski (1821–81),
The house of the dead, 1861, pt I,
ch. V

7. When a felon's not engaged in his
employment...
Or maturing his felonious little
plans...
His capacity for innocent enjoyment...
Is just as great as any honest man's.

Sir W.S. Gilbert (1836–1911),
The pirates of Penzance, 1880, II

8. It is often hard to tell whether
English thriller writers copy the
wiles of the criminal, or whether
the English criminal learns his
plotting from his fiction reading.

Timothy Green, *The smugglers*,
1969, ch. 10

9. The criminal is not wholly a criminal — he is only a criminal at
times.

Elbert Hubbard (1856–1915),
Notebook, p. 35

10. Criminal: One who does by illegal

means what all the rest of us do legally.

Frank McKinney Hubbard (1868–1930), *The Roycroft dictionary*, 1923

11. Even the most hardened criminal a few years ago would help an old lady across the road and give her a few quid if she was skint.

Charles Kray, *Observer*, 'Sayings of the week', 9 February 1986

12. Most dangerous criminals are like elephants, difficult to define but easy to recognise.

Lord Justice Lawton, *Observer*, 'Sayings of the week', 30 August 1981

13. The criminal is often enough not equal to his deed: he extenuates and maligns it.

Friedrich Nietzsche (1844–1900), *Beyond good and evil*, ch. 4

14. It seems that criminals move in and out of the criminal-justice system as though it had a revolving door.

Patrick R. Oster and **Donald P. Doane**, '"Revolving door" justice', *US News and World Report*, 10 May 1976, p. 36

15. I only wish that we could have a code of practice for the criminals.

Baroness Phillips, House of Lords, 2 July 1984

16. Life is nothing but a competition to be the criminal rather than the victim.

Bertrand Russell (1872–1970), quoted in Alistair Cooke, *Six Men*, 1977

17. I am surprised, in visiting jails, to find so few respectable looking convicts.

Charles Dudley Warner (1829–1900), *Backlog studies*, 1873, 'Eighth study', p. 208

45. CROSS-EXAMINATION

1. I believe it's a sort of legal rule, a sort of legal tradition — for all investigating lawyers — to begin their attack from afar, with a trivial, or at least an irrelevant subject, so as to encourage, or rather, to distract the man they are cross-examining, to disarm his caution and then all at once to give him an unexpected knock-down blow with some final question.

Feodor Dostoevski (1821–81), *Crime and punishment*, 1866, pt IV, ch. V

2. In real life the witness's fortitude in the face of exposure [by cross-examination] is as remarkable as a human body's resistance to incredible torment.

Louis Nizer, *My life in court*, 1962, 'Prologue'

3. The cross-examiner must have speedy reactions in an emergency not unlike a driver of a car.

Louis Nizer, *The jury returns*, 1966, 'Fruehauf'

4. That kind of skill by which, in oral examination of witnesses, a cross-examiner succeeds in alarming, misleading, or bewildering an honest witness, may be characterized as the most, or one of the

most, base and depraved of all employments of intellectual power.

Richard Whately (1787–1863), *Thoughts and apothegms*, 1856, pt VI

46. CUSTOM

1. Prescription and custom are brothers, and ought to have the same age, and reason ought to be the father, and congruence the mother, and use the nurse, and time out of memory to fortify them both.

   Sir Edward Coke (1552–1634), *Rowles* v. *Mason* (1612), 2 B. & G. 192 at 198

2. Custom, that unwritten law,
   By which the people keep even kings in awe.

   Charles Davenant (1656–1714), *Circe*, II. iii

3. I very much doubt the propriety as a general principle, of legalizing customs. The moment you legalize a custom you fix its particular character; but the value of a custom is its flexibility, and that it adapts itself to all the circumstances of the moment and of the locality. All these qualities are lost the moment you crystallize a custom into legislation. Customs may not be as wise as laws, but they are always more popular.

   Benjamin Disraeli (1804–81), speech, House of Commons, 11 March 1870

4. The laws of conscience, which we

pretend to be derived from nature, proceed from custom.

Michel de Montaigne (1533–92), *Essays*, bk I, 'Of custom'

5. Custom is our nature.

   Blaise Pascal (1623–62), *Pensées*, 1670, pt I

6. The law follows custom.

   Plautus (*c*.254–*c*.184 BC), *Trinummus*, IV. iii

7. Let the law never be contradictory to custom: for if the custom be good, the law is worthless.

   Voltaire (1694–1778), *Philosophical dictionary*

47. DAMAGES

1. Injury is to be measured by malice.

   Thomas Fuller (1654–1734), *Gnomologia*, 1732, no. 3,099

2. Monster, dread our damages.
   We're the jury,
   Dread the fury!

   Sir W.S. Gilbert (1836–1911), *Trial by jury*, 1875

3. Nominal damages are a mere peg on which to hang costs.

   Maule J. (1788–1858), *Beaumont* v. *Greathead* (1846), 2 C.B. 494 at 499

48. DEBT

1. Debt rolls a man over and over, binding him hand and foot, and letting him hang upon the fatal

mesh until the long-legged interest devours him.

Henry Ward Beecher (1813–87), *Proverbs from Plymouth pulpit,* 1887

2. Debt is an inexhaustible fountain of dishonesty.

   Henry Ward Beecher (1813–87), ibid.

3. Creditor, *n.* One of a tribe of savages dwelling beyond the Financial Straits and dreaded for their desolating incursions.

   Ambrose Bierce (1842–1914?), *The devil's dictionary,* 1911

4. Debt is the prolific mother of folly and of crime.

   Benjamin Disraeli (1804–81), *Henrietta Temple,* 1837, bk II, ch. I

5. Confess debt and beg days.

   Thomas Fuller (1652–1734), *Gnomologia,* 1732

6. Debt is the worst poverty.

   Thomas Fuller (1654–1734), ibid.

7. Debtors are liars.

   George Herbert (1593–1633), *Jacula prudentum,* 1651

8. Debt: 1. A rope to your foot, cockleburs in your hair, and a clothespin on your tongue. 2. The devil in disguise.

   Frank McKinney Hubbard (1868–1930), *The Roycroft dictionary,* 1923

9. Small debts are like small shot; they are rattling on every side, and can scarcely be escaped without a wound: great debts are like cannon; of loud noise, but little danger.

   Samuel Johnson (1709–84), Letter to Joseph Simpson, 1759

10. A pound of care will not pay an ounce of debt.

    James Kelly, *Scottish proverbs,* 1721, A, no. 13

11. He begs of them that borrowed of him.

    James Kelly, ibid., H, no. 330

12. Out of debt out of danger.

    James Kelly, ibid., O, no. 13

13. Oft times the cautioner [surety] pays the debt.

    James Kelly, ibid., no. 39

14. He is my prisoner: if I let him go,
    The debt he owes will be requir'd
    of me.

    William Shakespeare (1564–1616), *The comedy of errors,* 1592–3, IV. iv

15. I will pay you some, and, as most debtors do, promise you infinitely.

    William Shakespeare (1564–1616), *Henry IV pt II,* 1597–8, Epilogue

16. To pay the petty debt twenty times over.

    William Shakespeare (1564–1616), *The merchant of Venice,* 1596–7, III. ii

17. Lending him wit that to bad debtors lends.

   William Shakespeare (1564–1616), *The rape of Lucrece*, 1593–4

18. Die in debt.

   William Shakespeare (1564–1616), *Romeo and Juliet*, 1595–6, I. i

19. He that dies, pays all debts.

   William Shakespeare (1564–1616), *The tempest*, 1611, III. ii

20. The debts may well be called desperate ones, for a madman owes 'em.

   William Shakespeare (1564–1616), *Timon of Athens*, 1607–8, III. iv

21. To contract new debts is not the way to pay old ones.

   George Washington (1732–99), Letter to James Welch, 7 April 1799

49. DECEPTION

1. Deceive not thy physician, confessor nor lawyer.

   George Herbert (1593–1633), *Jacula prudentum*, 1651

2. One may smile, and smile, and be a villain.

   William Shakespeare (1564–1616), *Hamlet*, 1599–1600, I. v

3. I like not fair terms and a villain's mind.

   William Shakespeare (1564–

1616), *The merchant of Venice*, 1596–7, I. iii

50. DEFAMATION

1. A man is not stung the less by a libel because it happens to be true.

   Lord Abinger C.B. (1769–1844), *Fraser* v. *Berkeley* (1836), 7 Car. & P. 621 at 625

2. If what they call *a libel* is all true, and can be proved to be so, instead of being the less, it is the more libellous.

   Jeremy Bentham (1748–1832), *Truth v. Ashhurst; or law as it is*, 1823

3. A good name smells sweeter than the finest ointment.

   Bible, Authorized Version, Ecclesiastes, 7: 1

4. Slander drives a wise man crazy and breaks a strong man's spirit.

   Bible, ibid., 7: 6

5. Defame, *v.t.* To lie about another. To tell the truth about another.

   Ambrose Bierce (1842–1914?), *The devil's dictionary*, 1911

6. Slander slings stones at itself.

   Thomas Fuller (1654–1734), *Gnomologia*, 1732, no. 4,183

7. Slander leaves a score behind.

   Thomas Fuller (1654–1734), ibid., no. 4,184

8. Slanderers are the devil's bellows,

to blow up contention.

Thomas Fuller (1654–1734), ibid., no. 4,185

9. Slander is a shipwreck by a dry tempest.

George Herbert (1593–1633), *Jacula prudentum*, 1651

10. Libelous: To be tactless in type.

Frank McKinney Hubbard (1868–1930), *The Roycroft dictionary*, 1923

11. Slander always leaves a slur.

James Kelly, *Scottish proverbs*, 1721, S, 13

12. Libel is such a profitable High Court casino because only rich people can play — or, those with access to taxpayers' money or trade union funds — and only big organisations can think of fighting them.

David Leigh, *Observer*, 28 April 1985

13. [His reputation] … is his property, and, if possible, more valuable than other property.

Sir R. Malins V.C. (1805–82), *Dixon* v. *Holden* (1869), 7 Eq. 488 at 492

14. What is slander? A verdict of 'guilty' pronounced in the absence of the accused, with closed doors, without defence or appeal, by an interested and prejudiced judge.

Joseph Roux (1834–1905), *Meditations of a parish priest*, trans Hapgood, 1886, ch. IV, LXVII

15. For slander lives upon succession, For ever hous'd where it once gets possession.

William Shakespeare (1564–1616), *The comedy of errors*, 1592–3, III. i

16. He that filches from me my good name,
Robs me of that, which not enriches him,
And makes me poor indeed.

William Shakespeare (1564–1616), *Othello*, 1604–5, III. ii

17. That is no slander, sir, which is a truth.

William Shakespeare (1564–1616), *Romeo and Juliet*, 1595–6, IV. i

18. What's this but libelling against the senate,
And blazoning our injustice everywhere?

William Shakespeare (1564–1616), *Titus Andronicus*, 1593–4, IV. iv

19. There is no slander in an allowed fool, though he do nothing but rail.

William Shakespeare (1564–1616), *Twelfth night*, 1599–1600, I. v

20. Slander, whose sting is sharper than the sword's.

William Shakespeare (1564–1616), *A Winter's tale*, 1610–11, II. iii

21. There is no character, howsoever good and fine, but it can be destroyed by ridicule, howsoever poor and witless. Observe the ass,

for instance: his character is about perfect, he is the choicest spirit among all the humbler animals, yet see what ridicule has brought him to. Instead of feeling complimented when we are called an ass, we are left in doubt.

Mark Twain (1835–1910), 'Pudd'nhead Wilson's calendar', *Pudd'nhead Wilson*, 1894, 'A whisper to the reader'

51. DEFENCE

1. Never make a defence or apology before you be accused.

   Charles I (1600–49), Letter to Lord Wentworth, 3 September 1636

2. Briefs for the defence are most likely to bring glory and popularity to the pleader.

   Cicero (106–43 BC), *De Officiis*, bk II, ch. XIV

3. Some men begin well, but end ill; like a certain lawyer, who on being asked why he defended so many bad causes, replied that he did so, because he had lost so many good ones.

   C.C. Colton (1780–1832), *Lacon*, 1820, vol. II, CCXLVI

4. He that defends an injury, is next to him that commits it.

   Thomas Fuller (1654–1734), *Gnomologia*, 1732, no. 2,076

5. Ignorance of the law is no excuse. (*Ignorantia juris non excusat.*)

   Legal maxim

6. A man who has no excuse for crime is indeed defenceless!

   Lord Lytton (1803–73), *The lady of Lyons*, IV. i

7. While Snatch was afraid that he would be convicted of theft, he consulted a lawyer — at a considerable price. When the lawyer had pondered, frequently and long, his mighty tomes, he said, 'Snatch, you will get off, I hope, if you run away'.

   Sir Thomas More (1478–1535), *Epigrams*

8. I have no animosity towards defence lawyers. If by getting me up on the stand and accusing me of atrocities and lies does good for them and their client, I figure that's part of their job. That's what they have to do.

   Detective Salvatore Russo, quoted in Morton M. Hunt, *The mugging*, 1972, ch. 6, III

9. Ignorance of the law excuses no man; not that all men know the law, but because 'tis an excuse every man will plead, and no man can tell how to confute him.

   John Selden (1584–1654), *Table-talk*, 1689, 'Law'

10. In defence of my lord's worthiness, I crave the benefit of law of arms.

    William Shakespeare (1564–1616), *Henry VI Pt I*, 1589–90, IV. i

52. DEMOCRACY

1. In democracies changes are mainly

due to the wanton licence of dema-
gogues.

Aristotle (384–322 BC), *The
politics*, bk V, ch. V

2. Democracies ... are commonly
more quiet, and less subject to
sedition, than where there are
stirps of nobles.

Francis Bacon (1561–1626),
Essays, 1625, 'Of nobility'

3. It is a fundamental law in
democracies, that the people
should have the sole power to
enact laws.

**Charles de Secondat, Baron de
Montesquieu** (1689–1755), *The
spirit of the laws*, 1748, bk II, 2

4. When a democracy is founded on
commerce, private people may
acquire vast riches without a corruption of morals.

**Charles de Secondat, Baron de
Montesquieu** (1689–1755), ibid.,
bk V, 6

5. In the strict sense of the term,
there never has been, and there
never will be, a real democracy. It
is against the order of nature for
the majority to govern and for the
minority to be governed.

Jean Jacques Rousseau (1712–
78), *The social contract*, 1762, bk
III, ch. IV

6. It is to be regretted I confess, that
democratical states must always
feel before they can *see*; it is this
that makes their governments slow,
but the people will be right at last.

George Washington (1732–99),
Letter to Lafayette, 25 July 1785

53. DETECTION

1. A thief myself I know the tracks of
a thief.

Callimachus (fl. 250 BC),
Epigrams, no. XLIV

2. Sherlock Holmes could not exist if
his creator and his audience did
not share the solid Dickensian
premise that 'the law is an ass'.

Alistair Cooke, *Six men*, 1977,
'Humphrey Bogart'

3. Singularity is almost invariably a
clue. The more featureless and
commonplace a crime is, the more
difficulty it is to bring it home.

Sir Arthur Conan Doyle (1859–
1930), *The adventures of Sherlock
Holmes*, 1891, 'The Boscombe
Valley mystery'

4. Detection is, or ought to be, an
exact science and should be treated
in the same cold and unemotional
manner.

Sir Arthur Conan Doyle (1859–
1930), *The sign of four*, 1890,
'The science of deduction'

5. When you have eliminated the
impossible, whatever remains,
however improbable, must be the
truth.

Sir Arthur Conan Doyle (1859–
1930), ibid., ch. 6, 'Sherlock
Holmes gives a demonstration'

6. There is no branch of detective
science which is so important and
so much neglected as the art of
tracing footsteps.

Sir Arthur Conan Doyle (1859–

1930), *A study in scarlet*, 1887, pt 2, ch. 7, 'The conclusion'

7. Set a thief to catch a thief.

   Thomas Fuller (1654–1734), *Gnomologia*, 1732, no. 4,106

8. Detectives usually worked in pairs; for obvious reasons, it was physically safer when making an arrest, and also two detectives swearing to the same lies in court always carried more weight.

   G.F. Newman, *Sir, you bastard*, 1970, ch. II

9. The *certainty* of punishment is of more consequence than the severity. Criminals do not so much flatter themselves with the lenity of the sentence, as with the hope of escaping. They are not so apt to compare what they gain by the crime with what they may suffer from the punishment, as to encourage themselves with the chance of concealment or flight.

   William Paley (1743–1805), *The principles of moral and political philosophy*, 1784, bk VI, ch. IX

10. After more than forty years I still do not know what the public expects from a detective. I am pretty sure that the public does not know itself.

    Frederick Porter Wensley (1865–1949), *Detective days*, 1931, ch. XXIX

54. DIVORCE

1. The only solid and lasting peace between a man and his wife is, doubtless, a separation.

   Lord Chesterfield (1694–1733), Letter to his son, 1 September 1763

2. Marriage to many people appears to be nothing but a necessary preliminary step towards being divorced.

   Mr Justice Darling (1849–1936), *Observer*, 'Sayings of the week', 9 May 1920

3. Women were quite ridiculous when it came to judging a man's character. No wonder so many of them ended up in the divorce courts.

   Richard Gordon, *Doctor on the boil*, 1970, ch. 5

4. Freedom to divorce is the one thing that will abolish the domestic steamroller.

   Elbert Hubbard (1856–1915), *Notebook*, p. 39

5. Divorce: 1. A legal separation of two persons of the opposite sex who desire to respect and honour each other. 2. A marital derail.

   Frank McKinney Hubbard (1868–1930), *The Roycroft dictionary*, 1923

6. Divorce: ... A female fugitive from injustice.

   Frank McKinney Hubbard (1868–1930), ibid.

7. Deadly divorce step between me and you!

   William Shakespeare (1564–1616), *All's well that ends well*, 1602–4, IV. iii

8. And from my false hand cut the
   wedding-ring,
   And break it with a deep-divorcing
   vow?

   William Shakespeare (1564–
   1616), *The comedy of errors*,
   1592–3, II. ii

55. ENFORCEMENT

1. Law cannot reach where enforcement cannot follow.

   Sir Nicholas Goodison, *The
   Times*, 16 January 1986

2. Laws do not persuade just because
   they threaten.

   Seneca (4 BC–AD 65), *Ad
   Lucilium epistulae morales*, epis.
   XCIV, 37

3. We must not make a scarecrow of
   the law,
   Setting it up to fear the birds of
   prey,
   And let it keep one shape till
   custom make it
   Their perch, and not their terror.

   William Shakespeare (1564–
   1616), *Measure for measure*,
   1604–5, II. i

4. The law hath not been dead,
   though it hath slept.

   William Shakespeare (1564–
   1616), ibid. ii

5. The brain may devise laws for the
   blood; but a hot temper leaps o'er
   a cold decree.

   William Shakespeare (1564–
   1616), *The merchant of Venice*,
   1596–7, I. ii

6. I have been often considering how
   it comes to pass, that the dexterity
   of mankind in evil, should always
   outgrow, not only the prudence
   and caution of private persons, but
   the continual expedients of the
   wisest laws contrived to prevent it.

   Jonathan Swift (1667–1745), *The
   Examiner*, no. 38, 26 April 1711

7. Laws or ordinances unobserved, or
   partially attended to, had better
   never have been made; because
   the first is a mere nihil, and the
   second is productive of much
   jealousy and discontent.

   George Washington (1732–99),
   Letter to James Madison, 31
   March 1787

8. Laws were made to be broken.

   John Wilson (1785–1854), *Noctes
   ambrosianae*, 1822, XXIV

56. EQUITY

1. If in 1815 the common law halted
   outside the bankers' door, by 1879
   equity had had the courage to lift
   the latch, walk in and examine the
   books.

   Atkin L.J. (1867–1944), *Banque
   Belge pour L'Etranger* v.
   Hambrouck, [1921] 1 K.B. 321 at
   335

2. This a finer sort of law they call
   equity — a distinction as heard-of
   out of England, as it is useless here
   to every purpose but that of delay-
   ing justice, and plundering those
   who sue for it.

   Jeremy Bentham (1748–1832),
   Truth v. Ashhurst; or, law as it is,
   1823

3. I think that common law is better than equity.

    Bowen L.J. (1835–94), *Angus* v. *Clifford* (1891), 60 L.J. Eq. 443 at 455

4. Now equity is no part of the law, but a moral virtue, which qualifies, moderates, and reforms the rigour, hardness, and edge of the law, and is an universal truth; it does also assist the law where it is defective and weak in the constitution (which is the life of the law) and defends the law from crafty evasions, delusions, and new subtleties, invented and contrived to evade and delude the common law, whereby such as have undoubted right are made remediless; and this is the office of equity, to support and protect the common law from shifts and crafty contrivances against the justice of the law. Equity therefore does not destroy the law, nor create it, but assist it.

    Lord Cowper (*c.* 1664–1723), *Dudley* v. *Dudley* (1705), Pr. Ch. 241 at 244

5. Equity, like nature, will do nothing in vain.

    Lord Cowper L.C. (*c.* 1664–1723), *Seeley* v. *Jago* (1717), 1 Peere Wms. 389

6. Every unjust decision is a reproach to the law or the judge who administers it. If the law should be in danger of doing injustice, then equity should be called in to remedy it. Equity was introduced to mitigate the rigour of the law.

    Lord Denning M.R., *Re*

    Vandervell's Trusts (No. 2), [1974] 1 Ch. 269 at 322

7. Equity is not past the age of childbearing.

    Lord Denning M.R., *Eves* v. *Eves*, [1975] 3 All E.R. 768 at 771

8. Equity abhors a beneficial vacuum.

    Diplock L.J. (1907–85), *Vandervell* v. *IRC*, [1966] 1 Ch. 261 at 291

9. Nothing would inflict on me greater pain, in quitting this place, than the recollection that I had done anything to justify the reproach that the equity of this Court varies like the Chancellor's foot.

    Lord Eldon L.C. (1751–1838), *Gee* v. *Pritchard* (1818), 2 Swans. 402 at 414. See also 56.16

10. Extravagant liberality and immoderate folly do not of themselves provide a passport to equitable relief.

    Sir Raymond Evershed M.R., *Tufton* v. *Sperni*, [1952] 2 T.L.R. 516 at 519

11. Equitable principles are, I think, perhaps rather too often bandied about in common law courts as though the Chancellor still had only the length of his own foot to measure when coming to a conclusion.

    Harman L.J. (1894–1970), *Campbell Discount Co. Ltd.* v. *Bridge*, [1961] 1 Q.B. 445 at 459. See also 56.16

12. Equity: Simply a matter of the

length of the judge's ears.

Frank McKinney Hubbard (1868–1930), *The Roycroft dictionary*, 1923

13. The rules of Courts of Equity are not ... supposed to have been established from time immemorial. It is perfectly well known that they have been established from time to time — altered, improved, and refined from time to time.

Jessel M.R. (1824–83), *Re Hallett's Estate* (1880), 13 Ch.D. 696 at 710

14. A Court of Equity can mould interests differently from a Court of Law.

Lord Kenyon C.J. (1732–1802), *Clayton* v. *Adams* (1796), 6 T.R. 604 at 605

15. Equity, in law, is the same that the spirit is in religion: what everyone pleases to make it.

John Selden (1584–1654), *Tabletalk*, 1689, 'Equity'

16. Equity is a roguish thing: for law we have a measure, know what to trust too. Equity is according to ye conscience of him that is Chancellor, and as it is larger or narrower so is equity. 'Tis all one as if they should make the standard for the measure we call a foot, a Chancellor's foot; what an uncertain measure would be this. One Chancellor has a long foot another a short foot, a third an indifferent foot; 'tis the same thing in the Chancellor's Conscience.

John Selden (1584–1654), ibid.

17. Where laws dispense with equity, equity should dispense with laws.

Sir John Vanbrugh (1664–1726), *The provok'd wife*, IV. iv

18. Equity in general mends no man's bargains.

Walton J., *Duke of Norfolk's Settlement Trusts*, [1978] 3 All E.R. 907 at 915

57. EUTHANASIA

1. It is easier to accept the principle of euthanasia than to devise satisfactory plans for putting it into effect.

Lord Devlin, *Observer*, 'Sayings of the week', 23 August 1981

58. EVIDENCE

1. The field of evidence is no other than the field of knowledge.

Jeremy Bentham (1748–1832), *An introductory view of the rationale of evidence*

2. The state of a man's mind is as much a fact as the state of his digestion.

Bowen L.J. (1835–94), *Edgington* v. *Fitzmaurice* (1885), 29 Ch.D. 459 at 483

3. Some instances of strength of memory are very surprising.

Buller J. (1746–1800), *Coleman* v. *Wathen* (1793), 5 T.R. 245

4. 'Give your evidence', said the king;

58. EVIDENCE

'and don't be nervous, or I'll have you executed on the spot.'

Lewis Carroll (1832–98), *Alice's adventures in wonderland*, 1865, ch. 11

5. The laws of evidence often prevent a person from telling the *whole* truth.

    Henry Cecil, *Hunt the slipper*, ch. 4

6. Evidence has often been termed the eye of the law.

    C.C. Colton (1780–1832), *Lacon*, 1820, vol. I, DLXXVIII

7. Take nothing on its looks; take everything on evidence. There's no better rule.

    Charles Dickens (1812–70), *Great expectations*, 1860–1, ch. XL

8. It is a capital mistake to theorize before you have all the evidence. It biases the judgement.

    Sir Arthur Conan Doyle (1859–1930), *A study in scarlet*, 1887, pt 1, ch. 3, 'The Lauriston Garden mystery'

9. I make a just complaint to the great wisdom and sagacity of our law, which refuses to admit the evidence of a wife for or against her husband. This, says a certain learned author ... would be the means of creating an eternal dissension between them. It would, indeed, be the means of perjury, and of whipping, fining, imprisoning, transporting and hanging.

    Henry Fielding (1707–54), *Tom Jones*, 1749, bk I, ch. V

10. He that proceeds on half evidence will not do quarter justice.

    Thomas Fuller (1608–61), *The holy state*, 1642, 'The good judge'

11. The facts speak for themselves. (*Res ipsa loquitur.*)

    Legal maxim

12. If I shall be condemn'd
    Upon surmises — all proofs sleep-
    ing else,
    But what your jealousies awake —
    I tell you
    'Tis rigour, and not law.

    William Shakespeare (1564–1616), *A winter's tale*, 1610–11, III. ii

13. I'll see their trial first. — Bring in
    the evidence. —
    Thou robed man of justice, take
    thy place.

    William Shakespeare (1564–1616), *King Lear*, 1605–6, III. vi

14. What is the evidence that doth
    accuse me?
    Where lawful quest have given
    their verdict up
    Unto the frowning judge?

    William Shakespeare (1564–1616), *Richard III*, 1592–3, I. iv

15. If no one were found guilty but upon such evidence as would not admit of a doubt, half the crimes in the world would be unpunished.

    Sydney Smith (1771–1845), *Counsel for prisoners*

16. Some circumstantial evidence is very strong, as when you find a

trout in the milk.

Henry D. Thoreau (1817–62), *Journal,* 11 November 1850

17. No, I don't want evidence that you can use in court. I want the truth.

John Winton, *One of our warships,* 1975, ch. IV

59. FAMILY

1. If we adjust the law to suit irresponsible parents, they will then be more irresponsible; but if we create law which requires parents to be more responsible, there is more hope that they will be.

Baroness Ewart-Biggs, House of Lords, 9 July 1984

2. In common parlance, the family consists of those who live under the same roof with the *pater familias*: those who form ... his fire-side.

Lord Kenyon C.J. (1732–1802), *R.* v. *The Inhabitants of Darlington* (1792), 4 T.R. 797 at 800

60. FEES
See also 40. Costs

1. For so long as you have five pounds in the world, no fee, no justice.

Jeremy Bentham (1748–1832), *Truth v. Ashhurst; or, law as it is,* 1823

2. A lawyer starts life giving $500 worth of law for $5, and ends giving $5 worth for $500.

Benjamin H. Brewster (1816–88), attributed

3. All thieves who could my fees afford
   Relied on my orations,
   And many a burglar I've restored
   To his friends and relations.

Sir W.S. Gilbert (1836–1911), *Trial by jury,* 1875

4. There is a New Zealand attorney just arrived in London, with 6s.8d. tattooed all over his face.

Sydney Smith (1771–1845), quoted in W. Jerrold, *Bon-Mots of Sydney Smith and R. Brinsley Sheridan,* p. 68

5. Then 'tis like the breath of an unfee'd lawyer, — you gave me nothing for 't.

William Shakespeare (1564–1616), *King Lear,* 1605–6, I. iv

6. Lawyers' fingers, who straight dream on fees.

William Shakespeare (1564–1616), *Romeo and Juliet,* 1595–6, I. iv

7. The gentlemen of the bar, are very wise indeed in all the applications of the law — because from thence arise all their fees; but in regard to the cause of the law, they very rarely consider it, for no gain can arise to them from so doing.

John Horne Tooke (1736–1812), quoted in J.H. Wigmore, *Evidence,* Preface to the first edition

8. Always remember ... that when you go into an attorney's office

door, you will have to pay for it, first or last.

Anthony Trollope (1815–82), *The last chronicle of Barset,* 1867, vol. I, ch. XX

9. That's without precedent. When did a counsel ever return his fee, pray?

William Wycherley (1640–1716), *The plain-dealer,* III. i

10. A man without money, needs no more fear a crowd of lawyers, than a crowd of pickpockets.

William Wycherley (1640–1716), ibid.

61. FINES

1. Pecuniary punishments possess this quality [frugality] in an eminent degree: nearly all the evil felt by the party paying, turns to the advantage of him who receives.

Jeremy Bentham (1748–1832), *Principles of penal law,* pt II, bk I, ch. VII, VI

2. The state by killing, mutilating, or imprisoning their members, do withall punish themselves; wherefore such punishments ought (as much as possible) to be avoided and commuted for pecuniary mulcts, which will increase labour and public wealth.

Sir William Petty (1623–87), *A treatise of taxes and contributions,* 1662, ch. X

62. FRAUD

1. Like a gun that fires at the muzzle and kicks over at the breach, a cheating transaction hurts the cheater as much as the man cheated.

Henry Ward Beecher (1813–87), *Proverbs from Plymouth pulpit,* 1887

2. There are some frauds so well conducted, that it would be stupidity *not* to be deceived by them.

C.C. Colton (1780–1832), *Lacon,* 1820, vol. I, XCVI

3. Some frauds succeed from the apparent candour, the open confidence, and the full blaze of ingenuousness that is thrown around them. The slightest mystery would excite suspicion, and ruin all. — Such stratagems may be compared to the stars, they are discoverable by *darkness,* and hidden by light.

C.C. Colton (1780–1832), ibid., LXIX

4. A charge of fraud is such a terrible thing to bring against a man that it cannot be maintained in any Court unless it is shewn that he had a wicked mind.

Lord Esher M.R. (1815–99), *Le Lievre* v. *Gould,* [1893] 1 Q.B. 491 at 498

5. He that's cheated twice by the same man, is an accomplice with the cheater.

Thomas Fuller (1654–1734), *Gnomologia,* 1732, no. 2,281

6. Fraud is infinite in variety; sometimes it is audacious and unblushing; sometimes it pays a sort of

homage to virtue, and then it is modest and retiring; it would be honesty itself if it could only afford it. But fraud is fraud all the same.

Lord Macnaghten (1830–1913), *Reddaway* v. *Banham*, [1896] A.C. 199 at 221

63. GAMBLING

1. Gaming in all its sorts, is too big an evil for the regulation of positive law.

   Lord Mansfield (1705–93), *Coote* v. *Thakerary* (1773), Lofft 151 at 152

2. Avoid Gaming. This is a vice which is productive of every possible evil; equally injurious to the morals and health of its votaries. It is the child of avarice, the brother of iniquity, and the father of mischief.

   George Washington (1732–99), Letter to Bushrod Washington, 15 January 1783

3. All Gaming, since it implies a desire to profit at the expense of another, involves a breach of the tenth Commandment.

   Richard Whately (1787–1863), *Thoughts and apothegms*, 1856, pt VI

64. GOVERNMENT

1. Fear is the foundation of most governments.

   John Adams (1735–1826), *Thoughts on government*, 1776

2. The foundation of every government is some principle or passion in the minds of the people.

   John Adams (1735–1826), ibid.

3. Good government is an empire of laws.

   John Adams (1735–1826), ibid.

4. If you want to show that crime doesn't pay, put it in the hands of the government.

   Anonymous, quoted in M.Z. Hepker, *A modern approach to tax law*, 2nd edn, 1975

5. Good laws, if they are not obeyed, do not constitute good government.

   Aristotle (384–322 BC), *Politics*, bk IV, ch. 8

6. Merciful laws are, in my opinion, the very highest testimony to any government.

   John Bright (1811–89), House of Commons, 3 May 1864

7. All government, indeed every human benefit and enjoyment, every virtue, and every prudent act, is founded on compromise and barter.

   Edmund Burke (1729–97), *Speech on conciliation with America*, 22 March 1775

8. In all forms of government the people is the true legislator.

   Edmund Burke (1719–97), *Tracts on the Popery laws*, ch. III, pt I

9. In all governments, there must of necessity be both the law and the

51

sword; laws without arms would give us not liberty, but licentiousness; and arms without laws, would produce not subjection, but slavery. The law, therefore, should be unto the sword what the handle is to the hatchet, it should direct the stroke and temper the force.

C.C. Colton (1780–1832), *Lacon*, 1820, vol. I, CLXII

10. The Government's ungirt, when justice dies.

Daniel Defoe (1660–1731), *The true-born Englishman*, 1701, pt II

11. Justice is the end of government.

Daniel Defoe (1660–1731), ibid.

12. In every government, though terrors reign,
Though tyrant kings, or tyrant laws restrain,
How small, of all that human hearts endure,
That part which laws or kings can cause or cure.

Oliver Goldsmith (1728–74), *The traveller*, 1764, 1. 427

13. The judicial power ought to be distinct from both the legislative and executive, and independent upon both, that so it may be a check upon both, as both should be checks upon that.

Thomas Jefferson (1743–1826), Letter to George Wythe, July 1776

14. A judge under the influence of government, may be honest enough in the decision of private causes, yet a traitor to the public.

Junius, *Letters*, no. I, 21 January 1769

15. Freedom of men under government is to have a standing rule to live by, common to every one of that society, and made by the legislative power erected in it; a liberty to follow my own will in all things, where the rule prescribes not; and not to be subject to the inconstant, uncertain, unknown, arbitrary will of another man.

John Locke (1632–1704), *Of civil government*, 1690, ch. IV

16. Let princes learn that from the first moment they disregard the laws and customs under which the people have lived for a great while, they begin to weaken the foundations of their authority.

Niccolo Machiavelli (1469–1527), *Discourses*, bk III, ch. VI

17. To pry into the secrets of the state.

William Shakespeare (1564–1616), *Henry VI Pt II*, 1590–1, I. i

18. As with forms of government, so with forms of law; it is the national character which decides.

Herbert Spencer (1820–1903), *Social statics*, 1870, pt III, ch. XXI, sec. 6

19. That government is best which governs not at all.

Henry D. Thoreau (1817–62), *Resistance to civil government*, 1849

20. To form a new government requires infinite care and unbounded attention; for if the foundation is badly laid, the superstructure must be bad. Too much time, therefore, cannot be

bestowed in weighing and digesting matters well.

George Washington (1732–99), Letter to John Augustine Washington, 31 May 1776

21. Candor is not a more conspicuous trait in the character of Governments than it is in individuals.

George Washington (1732–99), Letter to Timothy Pickering, 29 August 1797

22. There are a great many of us who still adhere to that ancient principle that we prefer to be governed by the power of laws, and not by the power of men.

Woodrow Wilson (1856–1924), Speech, 25 September 1912

65. GUILT

1. Penitent, *adj.* Undergoing or awaiting punishment.

Ambrose Bierce (1842–1914?), *The devil's dictionary*, 1911

2. Thank God, guilt was never a rational thing; it distorts all the faculties of the mind, it perverts them, it leaves a man no longer in the free use of his reason; it puts him into confusion. He has recourse to such miserable and absurd expedients for covering his guilt, as all those who are used to sit in the seat of judgment know have been the cause of detection of half the villanies in the world.

Edmund Burke (1729–97), *Impeachment of Warren Hastings*, 17 February 1788

3. *Clerk of the Court*: And how do you plead, guilty or not guilty? *Defendant in the Dock*: Not *very* guilty.

Sir Alun Davies QC, in *Pass the port again*, 1981, p. 48

4. Guilt has very quick ears to an accusation.

Henry Fielding (1707–54), *Amelia*, 1751, bk III, ch. XI

5. He declares himself guilty, who justifies himself before accusation.

Thomas Fuller (1654–1734), *Gnomologia*, 1732, no. 1,833

6. He that hinders not a mischief, when it is in his power, is guilty of it.

Thomas Fuller (1654–1734), ibid., no. 2,167

7. The guilty man fears the law; the innocent man fortune.

Thomas Fuller (1654–1734), ibid., no. 4,584

8. Let no guilty man escape, if it can be avoided. No personal considerations should stand in the way of performing a public duty.

Ulysses S. Grant (1822–85), Indorsement of a letter relating to the Whiskey Ring, 29 July 1875

9. Whoever secretly meditates a crime is as guilty as if he carried it out.

Juvenal (fl. AD 1st–2nd cent.), *Satires*, XIII

10. You are busy to clear yourself

when no body files you. [i.e. finds you guilty.]

James Kelly, *Scottish proverbs*, 1721, Y, no. 137

11. He that excuses the guilty, condemns the innocent.

Francis Quarles (1592–1644), *Enchyridion*, 1641, third century, XCVIII

12. A man may plead not guilty, and yet tell no lie; for by the law, no man is bound to accuse himself; so that when I say not guilty, the meaning is, as if I should say by way of paraphrase, I am not so guilty.

John Selden (1584–1654), *Tabletalk*, 1689, 'Law'

13. Who profits by crime is guilty of it.

Seneca (4 BC–AD 65), *Medea*

14. He's guilty, and he is not guilty.

William Shakespeare (1564–1616), *All's well that ends well*, 1602–4, V. iii

15. And then it started, like a guilty thing
Upon a fearful summons.

William Shakespeare (1564–1616), *Hamlet*, 1599–1600, I. i

16. In sight of God and us, your guilt is great.

William Shakespeare (1564–1616), *Henry VI Pt II*, 1590–1, II. iii

17. Who, being accus'd a crafty murderer,

His guilt should be but idly posted over
Because his purpose is not executed.

William Shakespeare (1564–1616), ibid., III. i

18. He pleaded still not guilty, and alleg'd
Many sharp reasons to defeat the law.

William Shakespeare (1564–1616), *Henry VIII*, 1612–13, II. i

19. They vanish tongue-tied in their guiltiness.

William Shakespeare (1564–1616), *Julius Caesar*, 1599–1600, I. i

20. I should be guiltier than my guiltiness.

William Shakespeare (1564–1616), *Measure for measure*, 1604–5, V. i

21. The burthen of a guilty mind.

William Shakespeare (1564–1616), *The rape of Lucrece*, 1593–4

22. But they whose guilt within their bosoms lie
Imagine every eye beholds their blame.

William Shakespeare (1564–1616), ibid.

23. Let guiltless souls be freed from guilty woe.

William Shakespeare (1564–1616), ibid.

24. My guilt be on my head, and there an end.

    William Shakespeare (1564–1616), *Richard III*, 1595–6, V. i

25. All three of them are desperate;
    their great guilt,
    Like poison given to work a great
    time after,
    Now 'gins to bite the spirits.

    William Shakespeare (1564–1616), *The tempest*, 1611, III. iii

26. Let them not speak a word, — the guilt is plain.

    William Shakespeare (1564–1616), *Titus Andronicus*, 1593–4, II. iii

27. It is better to risk saving a guilty person than to condemn an innocent one.

    Voltaire (1694–1778), *Zadig*, 1747

66. HABEAS CORPUS

1. Habeas Corpus. A writ by which a man may be taken out of jail when confined for the wrong crime.

    Ambrose Bierce (1842–1914?), *The devil's dictionary*, 1911

2. The *Habeas Corpus* act supposes, contrary to the genius of most other laws, that the lawful magistrate may see particular men with a malignant eye, and it provides for that identical case.

    Edmund Burke (1729–97), Letter to the Sheriffs of Bristol, 3 April 1777

3. I like the Habeas Corpus (when we've got it).

    Lord Byron (1788–1824), *Italy versus England*

4. Habeas Corpus Act ... the most stringent curb that ever legislation imposed on tyranny.

    Lord Macaulay (1800–59), *History of England*, 1848, ch. VI

67. HEREDITY

1. A good tree cannot bring forth evil fruit, neither can a corrupt tree bring forth good fruit.

    Bible, Authorized Version, Matthew, 7: 18

2. The idea of hereditary legislators is as inconsistent as that of hereditary judges, or hereditary juries; and as absurd as an hereditary mathematician, or an hereditary wiseman; and as ridiculous as an hereditary poet-laureate.

    Thomas Paine (1737–1809), *Rights of man*, 1791

68. HONESTY

1. What is honest is not dishonest.

    Bowen L.J. (1835–94), *Angus* v. *Clifford* (1891), 60 L.J. Eq. 443 at 456.

2. Honesty consists not in never stealing but in knowing where to stop in stealing, and how to make good use of what one does steal.

    Samuel Butler (1835–1902), *Notebooks*, ed. Festing Jones, ch. VIII

55

3. He's not honest, whom the lock only makes honest.

   Thomas Fuller (1654–1734), *Gnomologia*, 1732, no. 2,466

4. Honesty is a fine jewel; but much out of fashion.

   Thomas Fuller (1654–1734), ibid., no. 2,533

5. Honesty is the best policy.

   Thomas Fuller (1654–1734), ibid., no. 2,534

6. Knavery may serve a turn; but honesty never fails.

   Thomas Fuller (1654–1734), ibid., no. 3,131

7. A nod of an honest man is good enough.

   James Kelly, *Scottish proverbs*, 1721, A. no. 21

8. It is not true that honesty, as far as material gain is concerned, profits individuals. A clever and cruel knave will in a mixed society always be richer than an honest person can be.

   John Ruskin (1819–1900), *Munera pulveris*, 1862, IV

9. No legacy is as rich as honesty.

   William Shakespeare (1564–1616), *All's well that ends well*, 1602–4, III. v

10. If he were honester
    He were much goodlier.

    William Shakespeare (1564–1616), ibid.

11. Rich honesty dwells like a miser, sir, in a poor house; as your pearl in your foul oyster.

    William Shakespeare (1564–1616), *As you like it*, 1596–1600, V. iv

12. Ay, sir; to be honest, as this world goes, is to be one man picked out of ten thousand.

    William Shakespeare (1564–1616), *Hamlet* 1599–1600, II. ii

13. Than you are mad; which is
                enough I'll warrant,
    As this world goes, to pass for
                honest.

    William Shakespeare (1564–1616), *A winter's tale*, 1610–11, II. iii

14. Ha, ha! what a fool Honesty is! and Trust, his sworn brother, a very simple gentleman!

    William Shakespeare (1564–1616), ibid., IV. iii

15. Though I am not naturally honest, I am so sometimes by chance.

    William Shakespeare (1564–1616), ibid.

16. It is an old adage, that *honesty is the best policy*. This applies to public as well as private life, to States as well as individuals.

    George Washington (1732–99), Letter to James Madison, 30 November 1785

17. 'Honesty is the best policy;' but he who acts on that principle is not an honest man.

    Richard Whately (1787–1863), *Thoughts and apothegms*, 1856, pt II, ch. XVIII

69. ILLEGITIMACY

1. 'Good heavens! Dr Middleton, what can you mean by bringing this person here?' exclaimed Mrs. Easy. 'Not a married woman and she has a child!'
   'If you please, ma'am,' interrupted the young woman, dropping a curtsey, 'it was a very little one'.

   Frederick Marryat (1792–1848), *Mr Midshipman Easy*, 1836, ch. III

2. What, wouldst thou have me prove myself a bastard?

   William Shakespeare (1564–1616), *Titus Andronicus*, 1593–4, II. iii

3. There are no illegitimate children — only illegitimate parents.

   Judge Léon R. Yankwich, *Zipkin* v. *Mozon*, June 1928, quoted in H.L. Mencken, *Dictionary of quotations*

70. INFORMERS

1. The execution of a law cannot be enforced, unless the violation of it be denounced; the assistance of the informer is therefore altogether as necessary and as meritorious as that of the judge.

   Jeremy Bentham (1748–1832), *The rationale of reward*, 1825, bk I, ch. XIII

2. The informer vanishes when once she shares the guilt.

   Ovid (43 BC–AD 17), *Ars amatoria*, bk I

71. INJUSTICE

1. Where there is no responsibility, injustice will occasionally be committed, as long as men are men.

   Henry Peter Brougham (1778–1868), House of Commons, 7 February 1828

2. Though cheap justice was a great good, great injustice was a great evil, let it be ever so cheap and speedy.

   Henry Peter Brougham (1778–1868), ibid., 29 February 1828

3. No man can mortgage his injustice as a pawn for his fidelity.

   Edmund Burke (1729–97), *Reflections on the revolution in France*, 1790, para. 304

4. It is the feeling of *injustice* that is insupportable to all men.

   Thomas Carlyle (1795–1881), *Chartism*, 1839, ch. V

5. The very height of injustice is to seek pay for justice.

   Cicero (106–43 BC), *De legibus*, bk I, ch. XVIII

6. That which is unjust can really profit no one; that which is just can really harm no one.

   Henry George (1839–97), *The land question*, 1881, ch. XIV

7. There is such a thing as showing injustice in clamouring for justice.

   E.W. Howe (1853–1937), *Country town sayings*, 1911

8. The injustice done to an individual

is sometimes of service to the public.

Junius, *Letters*, no. XLI, 14 November 1770

9. Injustice anywhere is a threat to justice everywhere.

Martin Luther King (1929–68), *Letter from Birmingham Jail*, 16 April 1963

10. It is dangerous to tell the people that the laws are unjust, since men obey them only because they think they are just.

Blaise Pascal (1623–62), *Pensées*, 1670, pt I

11. Mankind censure injustice, fearing that they may be the victims of it and not because they shrink from committing it.

Plato (*c.*428–347 BC), *Republic*, bk I

12. Injustice all round is justice.

Persian proverb

13. Men consider some things to be unjust because they did not deserve them, some merely because they did not expect them.

Seneca (4 BC–AD 65), *De ira*, bk II, ch. XXXI

14. To chance injustice with revengeful arms:
Knights, by their oaths, should right poor ladies' harms.

William Shakespeare (1564–1616), *The rape of Lucrece*, 1593–4

15. All that have miscarried

By underhand corrupted foul injustice.

William Shakespeare (1564–1616), *Richard III*, 1592–3, V. i

16. The heavens themselves
Do strike at my injustice.

William Shakespeare (1564–1616), *A winter's tale*, 1610–11, III. ii

17. It is a true and common saying that the strictest law is often the severest injustice.

Terence (*c.*190–159 BC), *The self-tormentor*, 163 BC, IV. v

18. If the injustice is part of the necessary friction of the machine of government, let it go, let it go: perchance it will wear smooth,— certainly the machine will wear out.

Henry D. Thoreau (1817–62), *Resistance to civil government*, 1849

72. INNOCENCE

1. It is better that ten guilty persons escape, than that one innocent suffer.

Sir William Blackstone (1723–80), *Commentaries on the laws of England*, 15th edn, 1809, vol. 4, p. 358

2. Innocence is plain, direct, and simple: guilt is a crooked, intricate, inconstant, and various thing.

Edmund Burke (1729–97), *Impeachment of Warren Hastings*, 15 February 1788

3. So justice, while she winks at
   crimes,
   Stumbles on innocence sometimes.

   Samuel Butler (1612–80),
   Hudibras, pt I, canto II, 1. 1,177

4. No one who has been indicted and
   formally charged with a crime is
   really presumed innocent by anyone but his friends or well-wishers,
   or somebody who happens to
   know that the government was
   wrong.

   Charles P. Curtis, quoted in
   Morton M. Hunt, *The mugging,*
   1972, ch. 6, IV

5. I hear much of people's calling out
   to punish the guilty; but very few
   are concerned to clear the innocent.

   Daniel Defoe (1660–1731), *An
   appeal to honour and justice etc.,*
   1715

6. Innocence is its own defence.

   Benjamin Franklin (1706–90),
   Poor Richard's almanac, 1733

7. He that is innocent, may well be
   confident.

   Thomas Fuller (1654–1734),
   Gnomologia, 1732, no. 2,179

8. Innocence is no protection.

   Thomas Fuller (1654–1734),
   ibid., no. 3,100

9. The breast plate of innocence is
   not always scandal-proof.

   Thomas Fuller (1654–1734),
   ibid., no. 4,433

10. It is dreadful to be in the position

of an innocent man found guilty of
a crime through hasty judgement
and formal procedure; can the
position of the judge be worse?

La Bruyère, Jean De (1645–96),
Characters, 1688, 'Of certain
customs'

11. Innocence does not find nearly as
    much protection as crime.

    **François, Duc de La Roche-
    foucauld** (1630–80), *Maxims,*
    1678

12. The good have no need of an
    advocate.

    Phocion (*c.*402–317 BC), quoted
    in Plutarch, *Lives: Phocion*

13. Who is there who can claim inno-
    cence in the eyes of every law?

    Seneca (4 BC–AD 65), *De ira,* bk
    II, ch. XVII

14. A dumb innocent that would not
    say him nay.

    William Shakespeare (1564–
    1616), *All's well that ends well,*
    1602–4, IV. iii

15. Some innocents 'scape not the
    thunderbolt.

    William Shakespeare (1564–
    1616), *Anthony and Cleopatra,*
    1606–7, II. v

16. Gloster is as innocent
    From meaning treason to our royal
    person
    As is the sucking lamb or harmless
    dove.

    William Shakespeare (1564–
    1616), *Henry VI pt II,* 1590–1,
    III. i

17. It will help me nothing
    To plead mine innocence; for that
                    dye is on me
    Which makes my whit'st part
                        black.

    William Shakespeare (1564–
    1616), *Henry VIII*, 1612–13, I. i

18. Peace, children, peace! the king
                doth love you well:
    Incapable and shallow innocents.

    Williams Shakespeare (1564–
    1616), *Richard III*, 1592–3, II. ii

73. INSANITY

1. A madman is only punished by his
   madness.

   Sir Edward Coke (1552–1634), *A
   commentary upon Littleton (The
   first part of the institutes of the
   laws of England)*, 1628, 19th edn,
   1832, 247b

2. One mad action is not enough to
   prove a man mad.

   Thomas Fuller (1654–1734),
   Gnomologia, 1732, no. 3,767

3. Uncle Jeff Pusey, who died some
   months ago an' left considerable
   property, wuz declared insane
   t'day.

   Frank McKinney Hubbard (1868–
   1930), *New sayings by Abe Martin*,
   1917

4. Insanity vitiates all acts.

   Sir John Nicholl (1759–1838),
   Countess of Portsmouth v. *Earl of
   Portsmouth* (1828), 1 Hag. Ecc.
   355 at 359

5. Though this be madness, yet there
   is method in 't.

   William Shakespeare (1564–
   1616), *Hamlet*, 1599–1600, II. ii

6. Madness in great ones must not
   unwatch'd go.

   William Shakespeare (1564–
   1616), ibid., III. i

7. Have we eaten on the insane root
   That takes the reason prisoner?

   William Shakespeare (1564–
   1616), *Macbeth*, 1605–6, I. iii

8. If a man is not too mad to intend
   what he does, he is not too mad to
   be punished for it.

   Richard Whately (1787–1863),
   Thoughts and apothegms, 1856, pt
   VI

74. INSOLVENCY
See also 14. Bankruptcy

1. Insolvency is not a very thrilling or
   amusing subject.

   Lord Mishcon, House of Lords, 15
   January 1985

75. INSURANCE

1. The underwriter knows nothing
   and the man who comes to him to
   ask him to insure knows everything.

   Scrutton L.J. (1856–1934),
   Rozanes v. *Bowen* (1928), 32 Ll.
   L. Rep. 98 at 102

2. An insurance policy is like old

under-wear. The gaps in its cover are only shown by accident.

David Yates, quoted in the *Sunday Times*, 21 October 1984, p. 26

76. INTERNATIONAL LAW

1. I do not know the method of drawing up an indictment against a whole people.

   Edmund Burke (1729–97), *Speech on conciliation with America*, 22 March 1775

2. Only when the world is civilized enough to keep promises will we get any kind of international law.

   Julius Henry Cohen, 'Rent control after World War I — recollections', *New York University Law Quarterly Review*, 1946, p. 271

77. INTOXICATION

1. Hee that kilth a man when he is
   drunke,
   Shal be hangd when he is sober.

   John Heywood (1506–65), *Proverbs*, 1546, pt I, ch. X

2. What you do when you're drunk, you must pay for when you are dry.

   James Kelly, *Scottish proverbs*, 1721, W, no. 40

3. If all the tears and misery that are caused by alcohol could be rained down on this earth, I am sure that the whole of mankind would drown in the deluge.

   Justice Lee, *Sydney Morning Herald*, 'Sayings of the week', 5 April 1986

4. Men intoxicated are sometimes stunned into sobriety.

   Lord Mansfield (1705–93), *R.* v. *Wilkes* (1770), 4 Burr. 2527 at 2563

5. Drunkeness is his best virtue, for he will be swine-drunk; and in his sleep does little harm, save to his bedclothes about him; but they know his conditions and lay him in straw.

   William Shakespeare (1564–1616), *All's well that ends well*, 1602–4, IV, iii

6. O God, that men should put an enemy in their mouths to steal away their brains! that we should with joy, pleasance, revel, and applause, transform ourselves into beasts.

   William Shakespeare (1564–1616), *Othello*, 1604–5, II. iii

78. JUDGEMENT

1. Sir Roger heard them both upon a round trot; and having paused some time, told them, with the air of a man who would not give his judgement rashly, that *much might be said on both sides.*

   Joseph Addison (1672–1719), *Spectator*, no. 122, 20 July 1711

2. I confess, that the character of

judge in my own cause is a thing that frightens me.

Edmund Burke (1729–97), *Speech on conciliation with America*, 22 March 1775

3. A judicial decision is based on reason and is known to be so because it is supported by reasons. An arbitrary decision ... may be based on personal feelings, or even on whims, caprice or prejudice.

Lord Denning, *Freedom under the law*, 1949, pp. 91–2

4. Every man is blind in his own cause.

James Kelly, *Scottish proverbs*, 1721, E, no. 61

5. No man can be judge in his own cause. (*Nemo debet esse judex in propia sua causa.*)

Legal maxim

6. He that judges without informing himself to the utmost that he is capable, cannot acquit himself of judging amiss.

John Locke (1632–1704), *Essay concerning human understanding*, 1690, bk II, ch. XXI, 67

7. The constitution does not allow reasons of State to influence our judgements: God forbid it should! We must not regard political consequences; how formidable soever they might be: if rebellion was the certain consequence, we are bound to say *Fiat justitia, ruat caelum.*

Lord Mansfield (1705–93), *R.* v. *Wilkes* (1770), 4 Burr. 2527 at 2561–2

8. Never did two men make the same judgement of the same thing.

Michel de Montaigne (1533–92), *Essays*, bk III, 1595, 'Of experience'

9. No just judge will pronounce one type of judgement in his own case and a different one in the case of others.

Seneca (4 BC–AD 65), *De ira*, bk I, ch. XIV

10. He who decides a case without hearing the other side, may decide justly, but is himself unjust.

Seneca (4 BC–AD 65), *Medea*

11. Struck me in the very seat of judgement.

William Shakespeare (1564–1616), *Henry IV pt II*, 1597–8, V. ii

12. Under heavy judgement.

William Shakespeare (1564–1616), *Macbeth*, 1605–6, I. iii

13. What judgement shall I dread, doing no wrong?

William Shakespeare (1564–1616), *The merchant of Venice*, 1596–7, IV. i

79. JUDGES

1. That judges of important causes should hold office for life is not a good thing, for the mind grows old as well as the body.

Aristotle (384–322 BC), *Politics*, trans. Jowett, bk II, ch. 9

2. It is best, we may observe, where the laws are enacted upon right principles, that everything should, as far as possible, be determined absolutely by the laws, and as little as possible left to the discretion of the judges.

Aristotle (384–322 BC), *The rhetoric*, trans. Welldon, bk I, ch. I

3. Judges ought to be more learned than witty, more reverend than plausible, and more advised than confident.

Francis Bacon (1561–1626), *Essays*, 1625, LVI, 'Of judicature'

4. The principle duty of a judge is to suppress force and fraud; whereof force is the more pernicious when it is open, and fraud when it is close and disguised. Add thereto contentious suits, which ought to be spewed out, as the surfeit of courts.

Francis Bacon (1561–1626), ibid.

5. Judges must beware of hard constructions and strained inferences: for there is no worse torture than the torture of the laws.

Francis Bacon (1561–1626), ibid.

6. The parts of a judge in hearing are four: to direct the evidence; to moderate length, repetition, or impertinency of speech; to recapitulate, select, and collate the material points of that which hath been said; and to give the rule or sentence.

Francis Bacon (1561–1626), ibid.

7. The worst judge, they say, is a deaf judge.

Walter Bagehot (1826–77), *The English constitution*, 1867, ch. IV

8. [Judges are] ... the depositaries of the laws, the living oracles, who must decide in all cases of doubt, and who are bound by an oath to decide according to the law of the land.

Sir William Blackstone (1723–80), *Commentaries on the laws of England*, 15th edn, 1809, vol. 1, p. 69

9. You can't exactly say to a judge: 'Buzz off'.

Louis Blom-Cooper QC, *The Times*, 3 September 1985

10. Judges, like Caesar's wife should be above suspicion.

Bowen L.J. (1835–94), *Leeson* v. *General Council of Medical Education & Registration* (1890), 43 Ch.D. 366 at 385

11. Every amelioration of the criminal code of this country has been carried against the opinion of the majority of the judges.

John Bright (1811–89), House of Commons, 3 May 1864

12. Judges are but men.

John Bright (1811–89), ibid.

13. A man who is a judge one half the year, and a barrister the other, is not likely to make either a good judge or a good barrister.

Henry Peter Brougham (1778–1868), House of Commons, 7 February 1828

14. It is said, that the magistracy ought

not to be responsible, because it is not paid; but we ought not to forget, that as gold itself may be bought too dear, so may economy; money may be saved at too high a cost.

Henry Peter Brougham (1778–1868), ibid.

15. The cold neutrality of an impartial judge.

Edmund Burke (1729–97), Preface to the Address of M. Brissot, 1794

16. Justices of the peace must judge all pieces.

Lord Byron (1788–1824), *Don Juan*, canto XVI, st. LXIII

17. It must feel very like contempt of Court to think of a judge indulging in the ordinary daily routine of life — to visualize the terrible red-robed figure getting into the bath — quite naked.

Henry Cecil, *Sober as a Judge*, 1958, ch. 6

18. Amongst twelve judges may not
   one be found
(On bare, bare possibility I ground
This wholesome doubt) who may
   enlarge, retrench,
Create and uncreate, and from the
   bench,
With winks, smiles, nods, and such
   like paltry arts,
May work and worm into a jury's
   hearts?

Charles Churchill (1731–64), *The farewell*, 1764

19. For as the law governs the magistrate, so the magistrate governs the people. Therefore, it may be said that the magistrate is a speaking law, and the law is a silent magistrate.

Cicero (106–43 BC), *De legibus*, bk III, ch. I

20. It is always the business of the judge in a trial to find out the truth.

Cicero (106–43 BC), *De officiis*, bk II, ch. XIV

21. A fool with judges, amongst fools a judge.

William Cowper (1731–1800), *Conversation*, 1782

22. One must be careful, even now, to give no cause to be classed with Lord Jeffreys.

Darling J. (1849–1936), *Gould & Co. Ltd.* v. *Houghton*, [1921] 1 K.B. 509 at 521

23. It is the judges who are the guardians of justice in this land.

Lord Denning M.R., *Re Grosvenor Hotel, London*, [1965] 1 Ch. 1210 at 1246

24. Faced with glaring injustice, the judges are, it is said, impotent, incapable and sterile. Not so with us in this court.

Lord Denning M.R., *Nothman* v. *Barnet London Borough Council*, [1978] 1 W.L.R. 220 at 228

25. [Hard cases make bad law] ... is a maxim which is quite misleading. It should be deleted from our vocabulary. It comes to this: 'Unjust decisions make good law': whereas they do nothing of the kind. Every

unjust decision is a reproach to the law or to the judge who administers it.

Lord Denning M.R., *Re Vandervell's Trusts (No. 2),* [1974] 3 All E.R. 205 at 213

26. The judges are too often inclined to fold their hands and blame the legislature, when really they ought to set to work and give the words a reasonable meaning, even if this does involve a departure from the letter of them. By so doing they are more likely to find the truth.

Lord Denning, 'The influence of religion', in *The changing law,* 1953, p. 106

27. My root belief is that the proper role of a judge is to do justice between the parties before him. If there is any rule of law which impairs the doing of justice, then it is the province of the judge to do all he legitimately can to avoid that rule — or even to change it — so as to do justice in the instant case before him.

Lord Denning, *The family story,* 1981, p. 174

28. One thing a judge must never do. He must never lose his temper. However sorely tried.

Lord Denning, ibid., p. 206

29. Every Judge on his appointment discards all politics and all prejudices. You need have no fear. The Judges of England have always in the past — and always will — be vigilant in guarding our freedoms. Someone must be trusted. Let it be the judges.

Lord Denning, ibid., p. 251

30. They will not be diverted from their duty by any extraneous influences; not by hope of reward nor by the fear of penalties; not by flattering praise nor by indignant reproach. It is the sure knowledge of this that gives the people their confidence in the judges.

Lord Denning, *What next in the law,* 1982, p. 310

31. A judge should be *sans peur et sans reproche.*

Lord Denning, *Sunday Times,* 25 August 1982

32. The silence awoke Mr. Justice Stareleigh, who immediately wrote down something with a pen without any ink in it, and looked unusually profound to impress the jury with the belief that he always thought most deeply with his eyes shut.

Charles Dickens (1812–70), *The Pickwick papers,* 1837, ch. XXXIV

33. Hard cases offer a strong temptation to let them have their proverbial consequences. It is a temptation that the judicial mind must be vigilant to resist.

Lord Diplock (1907–85), *Gibson v. Manchester City Council,* [1979] 1 All E.R. 972 at 976

34. My Lords, this is a hard case, and we all know where hard cases can take a judge.

Lord Edmund-Davies, *Gibson v. Manchester City Council,* [1979] 1 All E.R. 972 at 976

35. The judge weighs the arguments, and puts a brave face on the

matter, and, since there must be a decision, decides as he can, and hopes he has done justice, and given satisfaction to the community.

Ralph Waldo Emerson (1803–82), *The conduct of life*, 1860, 'Considerations by the way'

36. I am as sober as a judge.

Henry Fielding (1707–54), *Don Quixote in England*, 1734, III. xiv

37. Judges can be the very epitome of charm when it suits them.

Jack Fingleton, *Batting from memory*, 1981

38. Magistrates are to obey as well as execute laws.

Thomas Fuller (1654–1734), *Gnomologia*, 1732, no. 3,305

39. The judge is condemn'd when the criminal is absolved.

Thomas Fuller (1654–1734), ibid., no. 4,610.

40. All hail great Judge!
    To your bright rays
    We never grudge
    Ecstatic praise.
                All hail!
    May each decree
    As statute rank
    And never be
    Reversed in banc.
                All hail!

Sir W.S. Gilbert (1836–1911), *Trial by jury*, 1875

41. Though all my law is fudge,
    Yet I'll never, never budge,

But I'll live and die a Judge!

Sir W.S. Gilbert (1836–1911), ibid.

42. I said that virtue was the weakness of strong generals, and the strength of weak magistrates.

Jean Giraudoux (1882–1944), *Duel of angels*, I

43. I do not want to appoint judges who are not up to snuff.

Lord Hailsham, *Observer*, 'Sayings of the week', 8 April 1984

44. It needs a good deal of experience to tell what's going to happen to a good advocate when he gets on the bench.

Lord Hailsham, *Sunday Times*, 25 August 1985, p. 29

45. Judges are perhaps more apt than legislators to take a long view.

Learned Hand (1872–1961), *The bill of rights*, 1958, III

46. The judges are just like any other human beings.

Sir Michael Havers, *Observer*, 'Sayings of the week', 2 February 1982

47. Art thou a magistrate? then be severe:
    If studious, copy fair, what time hath blurr'd;
    Redeem truth from his jaws.

George Herbert (1593–1633), *The temple*, 1633, 'The church porch', st. 15

48. A good judge conceives quickly,

judges slowly.

George Herbert (1593–1633), *Jacula prudentum,* 1651

49. All the sentences of precedent judges that have ever been, cannot all together make a law contrary to natural equity.

Thomas Hobbes (1588–1679), *Leviathan,* 1651, pt II, ch. XXVI

50. I recognize without hesitation that judges do and must legislate, but they can do so only interstitially; they are confined from molar to molecular motions.

Holmes J. (1841–1935), *Southern Pacific Co.* v. *Jensen* (1917), 244 U.S. 205 at 221

51. The good and upright magistrate has preferred the honourable to the profitable.

Horace (65–8 BC), *Odes,* trans. C. Smart, bk IV, ode IX

52. The wide experience of a judge dealing with humanity is in every phase, makes him slow to condemn.

Elbert Hubbard (1856–1915), *Notebook,* p. 120

53. Judges ... should always be men of learning and experience in the laws, of exemplary morals, great patience, calmness and attention; their minds should not be distracted with jarring interests; they should not be dependent upon any man or body of men.

Thomas Jefferson (1743–1826), Letter to George Wythe, July 1776

54. An argument which does not convince yourself, may convince the judge to whom you urge it: and if it does convince him, why, then Sir, you are wrong, and he is right. It is his business to judge.

Samuel Johnson (1709–84), *Boswell's life,* Spring 1768

55. Whereas in Britain the judge acts as a kind of referee in what is largely a test of debating skills between counsel, in France it is the presiding judge who does all the questioning.

Ludovic Kennedy, *Observer,* 5 May 1985

56. In the hurry of business ... the most able Judges are liable to err.

Lord Kenyon C.J. (1732–1802), *Cotton* v. *Thurland* (1793), 5 T.R. 405 at 409

57. The duty of judges is to deal out justice; their profession is to delay it. Some know their duty and practice their profession.

La Bruyère, Jean De (1645–96), *Characters,* 1688, 'Of certain customs'

58. Be this, ye rural magistrates, your plan,
Firm be your justice, but be friend to man.

John Langhorne (1735–79), *The country justice*

59. I think that a judge should be looked on rather as a sphinx than a person — you shouldn't be able to imagine a judge having a bath.

Mr Justice Leon, *Observer,* 'Sayings of the week', 21 December 1975

60. The reason that judges are appointed is, that even a good man cannot be trusted to decide a cause in which he is himself concerned. Not a day passes on which an honest prosecutor does not ask for what none but a dishonest tribunal would grant.

Lord Macaulay (1800–59), *Warren Hastings*, October 1841

61. There should be many judges, because a few will always favour the few.

Niccolo Machiavelli (1469–1527), *The discourses*, bk I, ch. VII

62. I never give a judicial opinion upon any point, until I think I am master of every material argument and authority relative to it. It is not only a justice done to the Crown and the party, in every criminal cause where doubts arise, to weigh well the grounds and reasons of the judgment; but it is of great consequence, to explain them with accuracy and precision, in open Court; especially if the questions be of a general tendency, and upon topics never before fully considered and settled; that the criminal law of the land may be certain and known.

Lord Mansfield (1705–93), *R.* v. *Wilkes* (1770), 4 Burr. 2527 at 2549

63. I will not do that which my conscience tells me is wrong, upon this occasion; to gain the huzzas of thousands, or the daily praise of all the papers which come from the press: I will not avoid doing what I think is right; though it should draw on me the whole artillery of libels; all that falsehood and malice can invent, or the credulity of a deluded populace can swallow ... Once for all, let it be understood, 'that no endeavours of this kind will influence any man who at present sits here'.

Lord Mansfield (1705–93), *R.* v. *Wilkes* (1770), 4 Burr. 2527 at 2562

64. Who's to doom, when the judge himself is dragged to the bar?

Herman Melville (1819–91), *Moby-Dick*, 1851, ch. 132

65. Judge — A law student who marks his own examination papers.

H.L. Mencken (1880–1956), *Sententiae*

66. Nothing shocks your Old Bailey Judge more than a bent copper.

John Mortimer, *Rumpole for the defence*, 1981, 'Rumpole and the rotten apple'

67. A judge is not supposed to know anything about the facts of life until they have been presented in evidence and explained to him at least three times.

Lord Chief Justice Parker, *Observer*, 'Sayings of the week', 12 March 1961

68. Thank heaven, the English bench is rich in judges with a sense of humour.

Arthur W. Pinero (1855–1934), *A wife without a smile*, II

69. The judge should not be young; he should have learned to know evil, not from his own soul, but from

late and long observation of the nature of evil in others: knowledge should be his guide, not personal experience.

Plato (*c.*428–347 BC), *Republic,* bk III

70. A magistrate who watches for the good of the community should in his actions always prefer right to popular measures, and in his speeches know how to make those right measures agreeable, by separating from them whatever may offend.

Plutarch (46–120 AD), *Lives: Cicero*

71. Judges are philologists of the highest order.

Pollock C.B. (1783–1870), *Ex parte William Davis* (1857), 21 J.P. 280

72. When I was at the Bar I'm bound to say that I found some judges extraordinarily wooden headed. I had to say the same thing over and over again to them. And, now I'm on the Bench, I can't understand why counsel are always repeating themselves.

Mr Justice Salter, quoted in Henry Cecil, *Sober as a judge,* 1958, ch. 13

73. In the field of statute law the judge must be obedient to the will of Parliament as expressed in its enactments. In this field Parliament makes, and un-makes, the law: the judge's duty is to interpret and to apply the law, not to change it to meet the judge's idea of what

justice requires.

Lord Scarman, *Duport Steels Ltd. v. Sirs,* [1980] I.C.R. 161 at 189

74. When one is considering law in the hands of the judges, law means the body of rules and guidelines within which society requires its judges to administer justice. Legal systems differ in the width of the discretionary power granted to judges: but in developed societies limits are invariably set, beyond which the judges may not go. Justice in such societies is not left to the unguided, even if experienced, sage sitting under the spreading oak tree.

Lord Scarman, ibid.

75. Great judges are in their different way judicial activists.

Lord Scarman, ibid., at 190

76. If people and Parliament come to think that the judicial power is to be confined to nothing other than the judge's sense of what is right ... confidence in the judicial system will be replaced by fear of it becoming uncertain and arbitrary in its application. Society will then be ready for Parliament to cut the power of the judges. Their power to do justice will become more restricted by law than it need be, or is today.

Lord Scarman, ibid., at 190

77. To vindicate the policy of the law is no necessary part of the office of a judge.

Sir William Scott (1745–1836), *Evans* v. *Evans* (1790), 1 Hag. Con. 35 at 36

78. For as anger does not become a Judge, so neither doth pity, for one is the mark of a foolish woman, as the other is of a passionate man.

Scroggs C.J. (1623?–83), *R.* v. *Johnson* (1678), 2 Show, K.B. 1 at 4

79. The upright judge condemns crimes but he does not hate the criminals.

Seneca (4 BC–AD 65), *De ira*, bk I, ch. XVI

80. I'll be a brave judge.

William Shakespeare (1564–1616), *Henry IV Pt I*, 1597–8, I. ii

81. Heaven is above all yet; there sits a Judge
That no king can corrupt.

William Shakespeare (1564–1616), *Henry VIII*, 1612–13, III. i

82. To offend and judge are distinct offices
And of opposed natures.

William Shakespeare, (1564–1616), *The merchant of Venice*, 1596–7, II. ix

83. It doth appear you are a worthy judge;
You know the law; your exposition Hath been most sound: I charge you by the law,
Whereof you are a well-deserving pillar,
Proceed to judgement.

William Shakespeare (1564–1616), ibid., IV. i

84. O wise and upright judge,
How much more elder art thou than thy looks!

William Shakespeare (1564–1616), ibid.

85. *Judge Willis*: Mr. Smith have you ever heard of a saying by Bacon — the great Bacon — that youth and discretion are ill-wed companions.
F.E. Smith: Indeed I have, Your Honour; and has Your Honour ever heard of a saying by Bacon — the great Bacon — that a much talking judge is like an ill-tuned cymbal?

F.E. Smith (1872–1930), quoted in *The Life of F.E. Smith, by his son*, 1959, ch. IX. See 83.10

86. *Judge Willis*: What do you suppose I am on the Bench for Mr. Smith?
F.E. Smith: It is not for me, Your Honour, to attempt to fathom the inscrutable workings of Providence.

F.E. Smith (1872–1930), ibid.

87. *Judge*: I have heard your case, Mr. Smith, and I am no wiser now than I was when I started.
F.E. Smith: Possibly not, My Lord, but far better informed.

F.E. Smith (1872–1930), ibid.

88. Nothing can be more unjust than to speak of judges, as if they were of one standard, and one heart and head pattern.

Sydney Smith (1771–1845), *Counsel for prisoners*

89. Of all false and foolish *dicta*, the most trite and the most absurd is that which averts that the Judge is counsel for the prisoner.

Sydney Smith (1771–1845), ibid.

90. How awful it is when the right judge judges wrongly.

   Sophocles (496–406 BC), *Antigone*

91. Judges are persons appointed to decide all controversies of property, as well as for the trial of criminals; and picked out from the most dextrous lawyers who are grown old or lazy.

   Jonathan Swift (1667–1745), *Gulliver's travels*, 1726, pt IV, ch. V

92. Our magistrates mostly do better at the beginning, and fall off towards the end.

   Tacitus (*c.*55–*c.*117), *Annals*, bk XV, sec. 21

93. If thou be a severe, sour-complexioned man, then I here disallow thee to be a competent judge.

   Izaak Walton (1593–1683), *The compleat angler*, 1653, 'To all readers of this discourse'

94. Judges and all executive officers should be made as much as possible, independent of the will of the people at large.

   Noah Webster (1758–1843), *A collection of essays*, no. II. 1788, p. 39

95. He only judges right who weighs, compares,
And, in the sternest sentence which his voice
Pronounces, ne'er abandons charity.

   William Wordsworth (1770–

1850), *Ecclesiastical sonnets*, pt II, no. I, 1845

96. I shall no more mind you, than a hungry judge does a cause, after the clock has struck one.

   William Wycherley (1640–1716), *The plain-dealer*, I. i

80. JURIES
See also 82. Jurors

1. The facts will eventually test all our theories, and they form, after all, the only impartial jury to which we can appeal.

   Jean Louis Rodolphe Agassiz (1807–86), *Geological sketches*, 1870, ch. 9

2. After the jury had been charged, one of its members asked the court whether the word 'statute' used throughout the case, meant a human being. The judge explained that the word meant written law.

   Anonymous: report of a court case in Detroit, quoted in H.L. Mencken, *America*, 1925, 'Michigan'

3. Juries are the touchstone of common sense.

   Anonymous

4. [Trial by jury] ... has been the bulwark of liberty, the shield of the poor from the oppression of the rich and powerful.

   Atkin L.J. (1867–1944), *Ford* v. *Blurton* (1922), 38 T.L.R. 801 at 805

5. By whom should the members of

a jury be appointed? Answer: By no man, but by fortune. Man has sinister interests; fortune has no sinister interests. Under man's appointment, justice would have no even chance; under fortune's appointment, she will have an even chance, and that is the best chance that can be given to her.

Jeremy Bentham (1748–1832), *Principles of judicial procedure*, ch. XXIII

6. I consider the method of Juries a most wholesome, wise, and perfect invention, for the purpose of judicial inquiry ... it supplies that knowledge of the world, and that sympathy with its tastes and feelings, which judges seldom possess, and which, from their habits and station in society, it is not decent that they should possess, in a large measure, upon all subjects.

Henry Peter Brougham (1778–1868), House of Commons, 7 February 1828

7. The whole machinery of the state, all the apparatus of the system, and its varied workings, end in simply bringing twelve good men into a box.

Henry Peter Brougham (1778–1868), *The state of the law*, 1828, introductory matter

8. 'Write that down,' the king said to the jury, and the jury eagerly wrote down all three dates on their slates, and then added them up, and reduced the answer to shillings and pence.

Lewis Carroll (1832–98), *Alice's adventures in wonderland*, 1865, ch. 11

9. We often witness the jury ... resorting to falsehood and contradiction, from an amiable determination to adhere to that which is merciful, rather than that which is legal.

C.C. Colton (1780–1832), *Lacon*, 1820, vol. II, CXXXIX

10. Hanging Jury
Justice was suspended at the Old Bailey yesterday when a jury was stuck for half an hour between floors.

Daily Mirror, report, 5 August 1981

11. Trial by jury, instead of being a security to persons who are accused, will be a delusion, a mockery, and a snare.

Lord Denman (1779–1854), *O'Connell* v. *R.* (1844), 11 Cl. & Fin. 155 at 351

12. Whenever a man is on trial for serious crime, or when in a civil case a man's honour or integrity is at stake, or when one or other party must be deliberately lying, then trial by jury has no equal.

Lord Denning M.R., *Ward* v. *James*, [1966] 1 Q.B. 273 at 295

13. It's how a jury should be selected that's the problem. It used to be said that juries were entirely composed of middle-aged, middle-class men. That was true, but they came to some very reliable decisions.

Lord Denning, *Sunday Times*, 1 August 1982

14. [A modern jury] ... is pre-

dominately male, middle-aged, middle-minded and middle class.

Lord Devlin, *Trial by jury*, 1956, p. 20

15. The first object of any tyrant in Whitehall would be to make Parliament utterly subservient to his will; and the next to overthrow or diminish trial by jury, for no tyrant could afford to leave a subject's freedom in the hands of twelve of his countrymen. So that trial by jury is more than an instrument of justice and more than one wheel of the constitution, it is the lamp that shows that freedom lives.

Lord Devlin, ibid., p. 164

16. Juries are not good at distinguishing between good and bad policemen.

Lord Devlin, *Observer*, 'Sayings of the week', July 1980

17. What makes juries worthwhile is that they see things differently from the judges ... trial by jury is the lamp that shows that freedom lives.

Lord Devlin, *Sunday Times*, 18 April 1982

18. It amounted to positive certainty that the cause of truth and justice, or, in other words, the cause of his much-injured and most oppressed client, must prevail with the high-minded and intelligent dozen of men whom he now saw in that box before him.

   Counsel usually begin in this way, because it puts the jury on the very best terms with themselves, and makes them think what sharp fellows they must be.

Charles Dickens (1812–70), *The Pickwick papers*, 1837, ch. XXXIV

19. If juries through sympathy do occasionally acquit a defendant whom the judge, applying the law strictly, would have convicted, it may be that that is one of the things that juries are for.

Lord Diplock (1907–85), *R.* v. *Lemon*, [1979] 2 W.L.R. 281 at 290

20. Grand juries, gentlemen, are, in reality, the only censors of this Nation.

Henry Fielding (1707–54), *A charge delivered to the grand jury*, 1749

21. A jury is 12 people brought together to decide which side has the best lawyer.

Robert Frost (1874–1963), quoted in the *Observer*, 12 January 1986

22. A fox should not be of the jury at a goose's trial.

Thomas Fuller (1654–1734), *Gnomologia*, 1732, no. 116

23. A *Kentish* jury; hang half, save half.

Thomas Fuller (1654–1734), ibid., no. 231

24. Now, Jurymen, hear my advice —
All kinds of vulgar prejudice
I pray you set aside:
With stern judicial frame of mind
From bias free of every kind,

73

This trial must be tried.

Sir W.S. Gilbert (1836–1911), *Trial by jury*, 1875

25. No one has ever yet been able to find a way of depriving a British jury of its privilege of returning a perverse verdict.

Lord Chief Justice Goddard (1877–1971), *Observer*, 'Sayings of the week', 20 February 1955

26. Jury ... The stupidity of one brain multiplied by twelve.

Frank McKinney Hubbard (1868–1930), *The Roycroft dictionary*, 1923

27. If deciding guilt or innocence were identical with ascertaining the factual truth, the jury would be an outlandishly inefficient mechanism.

Morton M. Hunt, *The mugging*, 1972, ch. 5, II

28. Juries ... are not qualified to *judge* questions of *law*, but they are very capable of judging questions of *fact*.

Thomas Jefferson (1743–1826), Letter to M. L'Abbé Arnoud, 19 July 1789

29. The most extraordinary thing about the jury system is that it has lasted so long.
Justice of the Peace Review, 19 August 1972

30. A jury never looks at a defendant it has convicted.

Harper Lee, *To kill a mockingbird*, 1960, ch. 21

31. The public's confidence in our present system of trial by jury is essentially a matter of faith. It is based on practically no evidence whatever.

Sir Robert Mark, Dimbleby lecture, November 1973

32. If the jury system survives, it will be because the public is never made aware of how badly it does its job.

Paul Matthews, *Observer*, 30 August 1981, p. 21

33. A trial without a jury is like an operation without anaesthetic, or a luncheon without a glass of wine.

John Mortimer, *Rumpole for the defence*, 1981, 'Rumpole and the dear departed'

34. Juries are like Almighty God ... totally unpredictable.

John Mortimer, *The trials of Rumpole*, 1979, 'Rumpole and the man of God'

35. Trial by jury has been under a long, insidious attack by our rulers. Juries are supposed to be too slow, or to let off too many people, or be unsuitable in Ireland.

John Mortimer, *Sunday Times*, 4 March 1984

36. Since twelve honest men have decided the cause
And were judges of fact, though not judges of laws.

Sir William Pulteney (1684–1764), *The honest jury*

37. The jury, passing on the prisoner's life,

May, in the sworn twelve, have a
thief or two
Guiltier than him they try.

William Shakespeare (1564–
1616), *Measure for measure*,
1604–5, II. i

38. The man that is not prejudiced
against a horse-thief is not fit to sit
on a jury in this town.

George Bernard Shaw (1856–
1950), *The shewing-up of Blanco
Posnet*, 1909

39. Juries are generally composed of
illiterate plebians, apt to be
mistaken, easily misled, and open
to sinister influence.

Tobias Smollett (1721–71), *The
expedition of Humphry Clinker*,
1771, vol. II

40. A jury is a group of twelve people
of average ignorance.

Herbert Spencer (1820–1903),
Attributed

41. It is not trial by jury that produces
justice, but it is the sentiment of
justice that produces trial by jury,
as the organ through which it is to
act; and the organ will be inert
unless the sentiment is there.

Herbert Spencer (1820–1903),
Social statics, 1870, pt III, ch.
XXI, sec. 6

42. The jury box is where the people
come into court. The jury attends
in judgement, not only upon the
accused, but also upon the justice
and humanity of the law.

E.P. Thomson, *Sunday Times*, 18
April 1982

43. Jury trial, fine as it is, has a good
deal to answer for.

John Henry Wigmore (1863–
1943), *Evidence*, 3rd edn, 1940,
vol. I, p. 279

44. [Members of the Bar] ... have
been known to wrest from
reluctant juries triumphant verdicts
of acquittal for their clients, even
when those clients, as often happens, were clearly and unmistake-
ably innocent.

Oscar Wilde (1854–1900), *The
decay of lying*

81. JURISPRUDENCE

1. The science of jurisprudence, the
pride of the human intellect, —
which, with all its defects, redun-
dancies, and errors, is the collected
reason of ages, combining the
principles of original justice with
the infinite of human concerns, —
as a heap of old exploded errors,
would be no longer studied.

Edmund Burke (1729–97),
*Reflexions on the revolution in
France*, 1790, para. 267

2. The gladsome light of Jurisprudence.

Sir Edward Coke (1552–1634),
*The first part of the institutes of the
laws of England*, 1628, Epilogue

3. Almost all of the problems of jurisprudence come down to a fundamental one of rule and discretion,
of administration of justice by law
and administration of justice by the

more or less trained intuition of experienced magistrates.

Roscoe Pound (1870–1964), *Introduction to the philosophy of law*, 1922, ch. 3

4. Criminal jurisprudence, the choicest of conversation to an old lawyer.

Sir Walter Scott (1771–1832), *Journal*, 11 April 1829

5. The lawless science of our law,
That codeless myriad of precedent,
That wilderness of single instances.

Alfred, Lord Tennyson (1809–92), *Aylmer's field*, 1864, 1. 435

6. The good judge ... in him jurisprudence seems impersonated, and his opinions are authorities.

Edwin P. Whipple (1819–86), *Character and characteristic men*, 1866, ch. III, p. 72

82. JURORS
See also 80. Juries

1. Jurymen, though but ephemeral judges, are not the less judges.

Jeremy Bentham (1748–1832), *Principles of judicial procedure*, ch. XXIII

2. I do not mean that [jurors] often deliberately disregard the law. But if they think it is too stringent, they sometimes take a very merciful view of the facts.

Lord Devlin, quoted in Morton M. Hunt, *The mugging*, 1972, ch. 6, VI

3. A good, contented, well-breakfasted juryman, is a capital thing to get hold of. Discontented or hungry jurymen, my dear sir, always find for the plaintiff.

Charles Dickens (1812–70), *The Pickwick papers*, 1837, ch. XXXIV

4. To expect that twelve men, taken by lot out of a promiscuous multitude, should agree in their opinion upon points confessedly dubious, and upon which oftentimes the wisest judgements might be holden in suspense; or to suppose that any real *unanimity*, or change of opinion, in the dissenting jurors, could be procured by confining them until they all consented to the same verdict; bespeakes more of the conceit of a barbarous age, than of the policy which could dictate such an institution as that of juries.

William Paley (1743–1805), *The principles of moral and political philosophy*, 1784, bk. VI, ch. VIII

5. Criminals and lunatics, like clergymen and lawyers, are automatically disqualified from jury service. But the same does not go for those who are stone-deaf, half-blind, illiterate, unable to understand English, or a brother-in-law of the accused person's alleged victim.

John Spencer, *The Times*, 1 August 1986

6. Jurors are sometimes wiser, even if less logical, than lawyers. They have kind hearts as well as common sense.

Stephenson L.J., *R.* v. *Bruce*, [1975] 3 All E.R. 277 at 279

7. Judges, by long custom, become hardened in the business of condemning, and may sometimes pronounce sentence, which, even when legal, may be unnecessary. Jurors, less accustomed to the cruel task, retain those feelings which sometimes plead against evidence in favour of humanity, and soften the rigour of penal laws.

Noah Webster (1758–1843), *A collection of essays*, no. XXIII, 1789, p. 291

8. [It is] a strange, wild jurisdiction; where the jurors are judges both of law and of fact, and ignorant country fellows are to determine the nicest point of law.

Wilmot J. (1709–92), *Doe* v. *Roe* (1760), 2 Burr. 1046 at 1047

83. JUSTICE

1. Convenience and justice are often not on speaking terms.

Lord Justice Ackner, *Observer*, 'Sayings of the week', 25 October 1981

2. The law, on the one hand is inexorable to the cries and lamentations of the prisoners. On the other it is deaf, deaf as an adder to the clamors of the population.

John Adams (1735–1826), quoted by Catherine Drinker Brown, *John Adams and the American Revolution*, 1949, ch. 22

3. It is strange to see how completely justice is forgotton in the presence of great international struggles.

Henri-Frédéric Amiel (1821–81), *Journal*, trans. Ward, 28 October 1870

4. Justice is the right to the maximum of individual independence compatible with the same liberty for others.

Henri-Frédéric Amiel (1821–81), ibid.

5. Justice must not only be done. It must be seen to be believed.

Anonymous, quoted in *Private Eye*, no. 513, 14 August 1981

6. Man, when perfected, is the best of animals, but, when separated from law and justice, he is the worst of all.

Aristotle (384–322 BC), *Politics*, trans. Jowett, bk I, ch. 2

7. Justice is not a cloistered virtue: she must be allowed to suffer the scrutiny and respectful, even though outspoken, comments of ordinary men.

Lord Atkin (1867–1944), *Ambard* v. *A.G. for Trinidad and Tobago*, [1936] A.C. 322 at 335

8. When these ghosts of the past stand in the path of justice clanking their mediaeval chains the proper course for the judge is to pass through them undeterred.

Lord Atkin (1867–1944), *United Australia Ltd.* v. *Barclays Bank Ltd.*, [1941] A.C. 1 at 29

9. So when any of the four pillars of government are mainly shaken or weakened (which are Religion,

Justice, Counsel and Treasure), men had need to pray for fair weather.

Francis Bacon (1561–1626), *Essays*, 1625, XV, 'Of seditions and troubles'

10. Patience and gravity of hearing is an essential part of justice and an overspeaking judge is no well-tuned cymbal.

Francis Bacon (1561–1626), ibid., LVI, 'Of judicature'

11. The place of justice is an hallowed place.

Francis Bacon (1561–1626), ibid.

12. There are not more meshes in a net than there are in the administration of human justice.

Henry Ward Beecher (1813–87), *Proverbs from Plymouth pulpit*, 1887

13. Justice, *n.* A commodity which in a more or less adulterated condition the state sells to the citizen as a reward for his allegience, taxes and personal service.

Ambrose Bierce (1842–1914?), *The devil's dictionary*, 1911

14. Redress, *n.* Reparation without satisfaction.
Ambrose Bierce (1842–1914?), ibid.

15. It is always undesirable to draw a hard and fast line limiting the power of the Court to do justice.

Bowen L.J. (1835–94), *Re Onward Building Society*, [1891] 2 Q.B. 463 at 479

16. Cheap justice, Sir, is a very good thing; but costly justice is very much better than cheap injustice.

Henry Peter Brougham (1778–1868), House of Commons, 7 February 1828

17. To see so many lawyers, advocates, so many tribunals, so little justice; so many magistrates, so little care of the common good; so many laws, yet never more disorders.

Robert Burton (1577–1640), *The anatomy of melancholy*, 'Democritus to the reader'

18. For justice, tho' she's painted blind,
Is to the weaker side inclin'd,
Like charity; else right and wrong
Could never hold it out so long.

Samuel Butler (1612–80), *Hudibras*, pt. III, canto III, 1. 709

19. Justice must not only be done but must appear to be done and, may I add, must be paid for being done.

Henry Cecil, *Brothers in law*, 1955, ch. 5, 'Around and about the law'

20. The foundation of justice is good faith.

Cicero (106–43 BC), *De officiis*, bk I, ch. VII

21. Not even those who live by wickedness and crime can get on without some small element of justice.

Cicero (106–43 BC), ibid., bk II, ch. XI

22. In truth justice is the daughter of

the law, for the law bringeth her forth.

Sir Edward Coke (1552–1634), *A commentary upon Littleton (the first part of the institutes of the laws of England)*, 1628, 19th ed, 1832, 142a

23. Justice is always violence to the party offending, for every man is innocent in his own eyes.

Daniel Defoe (1660–1731), *The shortest way with dissenters*, 1703

24. Justice is truth in action.

Benjamin Disraeli (1804–81), House of Commons, 11 February 1851

25. Hogan's r-right whin he says: 'Justice is blind'. Blind she is, an' deef an' dumb an' has a wooden leg.

Finley Peter Dunne (1867–1936), *Mr Dooley's opinions*, 1900

26. One man's justice is another's injustice.

Ralph Waldo Emerson (1803–82), *Essays, first series*, 1841, 'Circles'

27. Whoever fights, whoever falls, Justice conquers evermore.

Ralph Waldo Emerson (1803–82), *Voluntaries*, IV

28. Because justice is not executed speedily men persuade themselves that there is no such thing as justice.

James Anthony Froude (1818–94), *Short studies on great subject*, 1871, 'Calvinism'

29. He that buyeth magistracy, must sell justice.

Thomas Fuller (1654–1734), *Gnomologia*, 1732, no. 2,055

30. It is the justice's clerk, that makes the justice.

Thomas Fuller (1654–1734), ibid., no. 3,024

31. Justice needs not injury to assist it, in getting its own.

Thomas Fuller (1654–1734), ibid., no. 3,115

32. Justice will not condemn even the devil himself wrongfully.

Thomas Fuller (1654–1734), ibid., no. 3,116

33. Rigid justice, is the greatest injustice.

Thomas Fuller (1654–1734), ibid., no. 4,055

34. Justice is a machine that, when someone has once given it the starting push, rolls on of itself.

John Galsworthy (1867–1933), *Justice*, 1910, II

35. That justice is the highest quality in the moral hierarchy I do not say; but that it is the first. That which is above justice must be based on justice, and include justice, and be reached through justice.

Henry George (1839–97), *Social problems*, 1883, ch. IX

36. Justice, I think, is the tolerable accommodation of the conflicting interests of society, and I don't

believe there is any royal road to attain such accommodations.

Learned Hand (1872–1961), Attributed

37. I have always looked upon the processes for getting justice, and the machinery for getting it, as a series of sieves.

Lord Harmar Nicholls, House of Lords, 11 July 1984

38. What makes it so difficult to do justice to others is, that we are hardly sensible of merit, unless it falls in with our own views and line of pursuit; and where this is the case, it interferes with our own pretentions.

William Hazlitt (1778–1830), *Characteristics*, 1823, IV

39. Justice pleases few in their own home.

George Herbert (1593–1633), *Jacula prudentum*, 1651

40. It ... is of fundamental importance that justice should not only be done, but should manifestly and undoubtedly be seen to be done.

Lord Hewart C.J. (1870–1943), *R.* v *Sussex Justices*, [1924] 1 K.B. 256 at 259

41. All the justice we know is man's justice.

Elbert Hubbard (1856–1915), *Notebook*, p. 161

42. The reason why the Goddess is blindfolded is so she can not see what the lawyers and judges do.

Frank McKinney Hubbard (1868–1930), *Epigrams*, 1923

43. Justice: A system of revenge where the state imitates the criminal.

Frank McKinney Hubbard (1868–1930), *The Roycroft dictionary*, 1923

44. Justice is the arm of the law.

Luther A. Huston, *The department of justice*, 1967, ch. I

45. To embarrass justice by multiplicity of laws, or to hazard it by confidence in judges, seem to be the opposite rocks on which all civil institutions have been wrecked, and between which legislative wisdom has never yet found an open passage.

Samuel Johnson (1709–84), 'Memoirs of the King of Prussia', *Literary Magazine*, 15 November to 15 December 1756

46. For most of mankind the love of justice is the fear of suffering injustice.

François, Duc de La Rochefoucauld (1630–80), *Maxims*, 1678

47. There is no grievance that is a fit object of redress by mob law.

Abraham Lincoln (1809–65), Speech, Young Men's Lyceum, Springfield, Illinois, 27 January 1838

48. Justice, and with it 'natural justice', is in truth an elaborate and artificial product of civilisation which varies with different civilisations.

Megarry V.C., *McInnes* v. *Onslow-Fane*, [1978] 1 W.L.R. 1520 at 1530

49. The suitability of the term 'fairness' ... is increased by the curiosities of the expression 'natural justice'. Justice is far from being a 'natural' concept. The closer one goes to a state of nature, the less justice does one find.

    Megarry V.C., ibid.

50. Justice should rule at all times and everywhere. Everyone who comes along should make this his concern, because it is a common interest for us all.

    Menander (*c*.342–292 BC), *The arbitration*, II

51.   Justice, indeed,
    Should be close-eared and open-mouthed,
    That is, to hear little and speak much.

    Thomas Middleton (1580–1627), *The old law*, 1618, V. i

52. Even the laws of justice themselves cannot subsist without a mixture of injustice.

    Michel de Montaigne (1533–92), *Essays*, bk II, 'We taste nothing pure'

53. I don't think anyone would dispute that lots and lots of people are denied justice.

    Sir David Napley, *Observer*, 'Sayings of the week', 31 October 1982

54. Who, indeed, can hope to obtain justice while living?

    Napoleon I (1769–1821), *Table talk and opinions*, 1868, p. 40

55. Blood is thicker than justice.

    Louis Nizer, *The jury returns*, 1966, 'Divorce'

56. As fashion makes what is agreeable, so it makes what is just.

    Blaise Pascal (1623–62), *Pensées*, 1670, pt I

57. Justice without power produces no result, power without justice is tyrannical.

    Blaise Pascal (1623–62), ibid.

58. Justice is nothing other than the interest of the stronger.

    Plato (*c*.428–347 B.C.), *Republic*, bk I

59. Poetic justice, with her lifted scale;
    Where in nice balance, truth with gold she weighs,
    And solid pudding against empty praise.

    Alexander Pope (1688–1744), *The dunciad*, 1728, bk I, 1. 52

60. Justice sums up all virtues in itself.

    Proverb, quoted by Aristotle, *Nichomachean ethics*, bk V, ch. 1

61. We love justice greatly, and just men but little.

    Joseph Roux (1834–1905), *Meditations of a parish priest*, trans. Hapgood, 1886, ch. IV, x

62. Humanity is the second virtue of Courts, but undoubtedly the first is Justice.

    Sir William Scott (1745–1836), *Evans* v. *Evans* (1790), 1 Hag. Con. 35 at 35–6

63. To pluck down justice from your awful bench.

   William Shakespeare (1564–1616), *Henry IV pt II*, 1597–8, V. ii

64. And praise the cause in justice'
   equal scales,
   Whose beam stands sure, whose
   rightful cause prevails.

   William Shakespeare (1564–1616), *Henry VI pt II*, 1590–1, II. i

65. A man may see how this world goes, with no eyes. Look with thine ears: see how yond justice rails upon yond simple thief. Hark, in thine ear: change places; and, handy-dandy, which is the justice, which is the thief?

   William Shakespeare (1564–1616), *King Lear*, 1605–6, IV. vi

66. Justice always whirls in equal measure.

   William Shakespeare (1564–1616), *Love's labour's lost*, 1594–5, IV, iii

67. This even-handed justice
   Commends the ingredients of our poison'd chalice
   To our own lips.

   William Shakespeare (1564–1616), *Macbeth*, 1605–6, I. vii

68. Thyself shalt see the act:
   For, as thou urgest justice, be assur'd
   Thou shalt have justice, more than thou desir'st.

   William Shakespeare (1564–1616), *The merchant of Venice*, 1596–7, IV. i

69. Justice is feasting while the widow weeps.

   William Shakespeare (1564–1616), *The rape of Lucrece*, 1593–4)

70. Sparing justice feeds iniquity.

   William Shakespeare (1564–1616), ibid.

71. Justices come and go, but justice itself should endure.

   Shearman J. (1857–1930), *Marsland* v. *Taggart*, [1928] 2 K.B. 447 at 450

72. There is a point at which even justice brings harm with it.

   Sophocles (496–406 B.C.), *Electra*

73. Fill the seats of justice
   With good men not so absolute in
   goodness,
   As to forget what human frailty is.

   Sir Thomas Noon Talfourd (1795–1854), *Ion*, V. iii

74. The acquittal of a guilty person constitutes a miscarriage of justice just as much as the conviction of the innocent.

   Margaret Thatcher, *Observer*, 'Sayings of the week', 21 July 1985

75. The administration of justice is the firmest pillar of government.

   George Washington (1732–99), Letter to Edmund Randolph, 27 September 1789

76. Justice, sir, is the great interest of man on earth.

   Daniel Webster (1782–1852), *On Mr Justice Story*, 1845

77. Most men are admirers of justice, — when justice happens to be on their side.

    Richard Whately (1787–1863), *Thoughts and apothegms*, 1856, pt VI

78. The weaker the man, as a dispenser of justice, the more the rule is exalted and the stiffer its bonds become.

    John Henry Wigmore (1863–1943), *Evidence*, 3rd edn, 1940, vol. I, p. 263

79. For Man's grim Justice goes its
    way
    And will not swerve aside:
    It slays the weak, it slays the
    strong,
    It has a deadly stride.

    Oscar Wilde (1854–1900), *The ballad of Reading Gaol*, 1898, III, XXXII

80. Justice, and only justice, shall always be our motto.

    Woodrow Wilson (1856–1924), First inaugural address, 4 March 1913

81. I respect the ancient processes of justice; and I would be too proud not to see them done justice, however wrong they are.

    Woodrow Wilson (1856–1924), Speech, 12 November 1917

84. LAND

1. The land shall not be sold forever: for the land is mine; for ye are strangers and sojourners with me.

    Bible, Authorized Version, Leviticus, 25: 23

2. Land, *n.* A part of the earth's surface, considered as property. The theory that land is property subject to private ownership and control is the foundation of modern society, and is eminently worthy of the superstructure. Carried to its logical conclusion, it means that some have the right to prevent others from living; for the right to own implies the right exclusively to occupy; and in fact laws of trespass are enacted wherever property in land is recognised. It follows that if the whole area of *terra firma* is owned by A, B and C, there will be no place for D, E, F and G to be born, or, born as trespassers, to exist.

    Ambrose Bierce (1842–1914?), *The devil's dictionary*, 1911

3. All classes and individuals in a State subsist or are enriched at the expense of the proprietors of the land.

    Richard Cantillion (1680–1734), *Essai sur la nature du commerce en générale*, 1775

4. No land is bad, but land is worse. If a man owns land, the land owns him. Now let him leave home, if he dare.

    Ralph Waldo Emerson (1803–82), *The conduct of life*, 1860, 'Wealth'

5. To permit one man to monopolise the land from which the support of others is to be drawn is to permit him to appropriate their labour, and, in so far as he is permitted to

do this, to appropriate them. It is to institute slavery.

Henry George (1839–97), *Our land and land policy*, 1871, in *Works*, 1904, vol. VIII, p. 86

6. What is necesary for the use of land is not its private ownership, but the security of improvements. It is not necessary to say to a man, 'this land is yours', in order to induce him to cultivate or improve it. It is only necessary to say to him, 'whatever your labour or capital produces on this land shall be yours.' Give a man security that he may reap, and he will sow.

    Henry George (1839–97), *Progress and poverty*, bk. VIII, ch. I

7. Private property in land is an obstacle to the investment of capital on land ... The possibilities of free investment of capital in land, free competition in agriculture, are much greater under the system of free renting than under the system of private property in land. Nationalisation of the land, is as it were, landlordism without the landlord.

    V.I. Lenin (1870–1924), *Selected works*, vol. I, p. 211

8. No man made the land. It is the original inheritance of the whole species. Its appropriation is wholly a question of general expediency. When private property in land is not expedient, it is unjust.

    John Stuart Mill (1806–73), *Principles of political economy*, bk. II, ch. II, 6

9. You may buy land now as cheap as stinking mackerel.

William Shakespeare (1564–1616), *Henry IV pt I*, 1597-8, II. iv

10. Now would I give a thousand furlongs of sea for an acre of barren ground: long heath, brown furze, any thing.

    William Shakespeare (1564–1616), *The tempest*, 1611–12, I. ii

11. No one supposes, that the owner of urban land, performs *qua* owner, any function. He has a right of private taxation; that is all.

    R.H. Tawney (1880–1962), *The acquisitive society*, 1921, ch. III

85. LAW
See also 25. Civil Law; 28. Common Law; 76. International Law; 81. Jurisprudence; 92. Legislation

1. The law I think would be an unwise law, if it did not make allowance for human infirmities.

    Lord Abinger C.B. (1769–1844), *Fraser* v. *Berkeley* (1836), 7 Car. & P. 621 at 624

2. Ethics precede laws as man precedes society.

    Jason Alexander, *Philosophy for investors*, 1979

3. Law alone is eternal.

    Henri-Frédéric Amiel (1821–81), *Journal*, trans. Ward, 13 January 1879

4. Every law has its loophole.

    Anonymous

5. Law has nothing to do with justice.

   Anonymous

6. The law is often said to be what the judges had for breakfast.

   Anonymous

7. Law is the crystallized prejudices of the community.

   Anonymous quoted in Ian Fleming, *Goldfinger*

8. Law is a bottomless pit, it is a cormorant, a harpy, that devours everything.

   John Arbuthnot (1667–1735), *Law is a bottomless pit*, 1712, pt I, ch. VI

9. Whereas the law is passionless, passion must ever sway the heart of man.

   Aristotle (384–322 BC), *Politics*, trans. Jowett, bk III, ch. 15

10. It makes no difference whether a good man defrauds a bad one, nor whether a man who commits an adultery be a good or a bad man; the law looks only to the difference created by the injury.

    Aristotle (384–322 BC), *Nicomachean ethics*, trans. Peters, bk. V, ch. 4

11. The philosophers, they make imaginery laws for imaginary commonwealths, and their discourses are on the stars, which give little light because they are so high.

    Francis Bacon (1561–1626), *The advancement of learning*, bk II, XXIII, 49

12. It were better live where nothing is lawful, than where all things are lawful.

    Francis Bacon (1561–1626), *Apothegms*, 1624

13. One of the Seven was wont to say 'that laws were like cobwebs; where the small flies are caught, and the great break through'.

    Francis Bacon (1561–1626), ibid.

14. The law does not act vindictively.

    Bacon V.C. (1798–1895), *Barrett v. Hammond* (1879), 10 Ch.D. 285 at 289

15. The laws of a nation suit its life.

    Walter Bagehot (1826–77), *The English constitution*, 1867, ch. IV

16. The law is of as much interest to the layman as it is to the lawyer.

    Lord Balfour (1848–1930), attributed

17. Laws are not masters but servants, and he rules them who obeys them.

    Henry Ward Beecher (1813–87), *Proverbs from Plymouth pulpit*, 1887

18. The law is a battery, which protects all that is behind it, but sweeps with destruction all that is outside.

    Henry Ward Beecher (1813–87), ibid.

19. A code of laws is like a vast forest; the more it is divided, the better it is known.

    Jeremy Bentham (1748–1832), *A*

general view on a complete code of laws, ch. I

20. The general object which all laws have, or ought to have, is to augment the total happiness of the community.

    Jeremy Bentham (1748–1832), *Principles of morals and legislation*, 1789, ch. XV

21. The law of England will not sanction what is inconsistent with humanity.

    Best J. (1767–1845), *Ilott* v. *Wilkes* (1820), 3 B. & A. 304 at 319

22. The law has respect to human infirmity.

    Best C.J. (1767–1845), *Robertson* v. *McDougall* (1828), 4 Bing. 670 at 679.

23. Ye shall have one manner of law, as well for the stranger, as for one of your own country.

    Bible, Authorized Version, Leviticus, 24: 22

24. The law is light.

    Bible, Authorized Version, Proverbs, 6: 23

25. Now, O king, establish the decree, and sign the writing, that it be not changed, according to the law of the Medes and Persians, which altereth not.

    Bible, Authorized Version, Daniel, 6: 8

26. The law is open.

    Bible, Authorized Version, Acts, 19: 38

27. These, having not the law, are a law unto themselves.

    Bible, Authorized Version, Romans, 2: 14

28. Where no law is, there is no transgression.

    Bible, Authorized Version, ibid., 4:15

29. But now we are delivered from the law, that being dead wherein we were held; that we should serve in newness of spirit, and not in the oldness of the letter.

    Bible, Authorized Version, ibid., 7:6

30. Is the law sin? God forbid. Nay, I had not known sin, but by the law.

    Bible, Authorized Version, ibid., 7: 7

31. Love worketh no ill to his neighbour: therefore love is the fulfilling of the law.

    Bible, Authorized Version, ibid., 13: 10

32. All things are lawful for me, but all things are not expedient: all things are lawful for me, but all things edify not.

    Bible, Authorized Version, I Corinthians, 10: 23

33. The law is good, if a man use it lawfully.

    Bible, Authorized Version, I Timothy, 1: 8

34. The law is not made for a righteous man, but for the lawless and disobedient, for the ungodly and for

sinners, for the unholy and pro-fane, for murderers, for mans-layers.

Bible, Authorized Version, ibid., 1: 9

35. Lawful, *adj.* Compatible with the will of a judge having jurisdiction.

Ambrose Bierce (1842–1914?), *The devil's dictionary*, 1911

36. [Law is] ... a species of knowledge in which the gentlemen of England have been more remarkably deficient than those of all Europe besides.

Sir William Blackstone (1723–80), *Commentaries on the laws of England*, 15th edn, 1809, vol. 1, p. 4

37. Law, in its most general and com-prehensive sense, signifies a rule of action; and is applied indiscrim-inately to all kinds of action, whether animate or inanimate, rational or irrational. Thus we may say, the laws of motion, of gravi-tation, of optics, of mechanics, as well as the laws of nature and of nations. And it is that rule of action which is prescribed by some superior, and which the inferior is bound to obey.

Sir William Blackstone (1723–80) ibid., p. 38

38. The law is a causeway upon which so long as he keeps to it a citizen may walk safely.

Robert Bolt, *A man for all seasons*, 1960

39. The American attitude toward time is the same as the American attitude to the law. That means we can take it and we can leave it alone.

Malcolm Bradbury, *Stepping westward*, 1965, bk. II, ch. IV

40. How much nobler will be our Soverign's boast, when he shall have it to say, that he found the law dear, and left it cheap; found it a sealed book — left it a living letter; found it the patrimony of the rich — left it the inheritance of the poor; found it the two-edged sword of craft and oppression — left it the staff of honesty and the shield of innocence.

Henry Peter Brougham (1778–1868), House of Commons, 7 February 1828

41. The laws reach but a very little way.

Edmund Burke (1729–97), Thoughts on the causes of the present discontents, 1770

42. People crushed by law have no hopes but from power. If laws are their enemies, they will be enemies to laws; and those who have much to hope and nothing to lose will always be dangerous more or less.

Edmund Burke (1729–97), Letter to Charles James Fox, 8 October 1777

43. Laws are commanded to hold their tongues amongst arms; and tri-bunals fall to the ground with the peace they are no longer able to uphold.

Edmund Burke (1729–97), *Reflections on the revolution in France*, 1790, para. 76

44. If civil society be the offspring of convention, that convention must be its law.

   Edmund Burke (1729–97), ibid., para. 161

45. No certain laws, establishing invariable grounds of hope and fear, would keep the actions of men in a certain course, or direct them to a certain end.

   Edmund Burke (1729–97), ibid., para. 268

46. Laws, like houses, lean on one another.

   Edmund Burke (1729–97), *Tracts on the popery laws*, ch. III, pt I

47. There are two and only two, foundations of law; and they are both of them conditions without which nothing can give it any force; I mean equity and utility.

   Edmund Burke (1729–97), ibid.

48. Turn your eye next to the labyrinth of the law, and the iniquity conceived in its intricate processes.

   Edmund Burke (1729–97), *A vindication of natural society*

49. It is a matter of deep study to be exact in the law.

   Gilbert Burnet (1643–1715), *History of his own times*, 1724

50. That which is law to-day is none to-morrow.

   Robert Burton (1577–1640), *The anatomy of melancholy*, 'Democritus to the reader'

51. The true laws of God are the laws of our own well-being.

   Samuel Butler (1835–1902), *Notebooks*, ed. Festing Jones, ch. II

52. The written law is binding, but the unwritten law is much more so. You may break the written law at a pinch and on the sly if you can, but the unwritten law — which often comprises the written — must not be broken. Not being written, it is not always easy to know what it is, but this has got to be done.

   Samuel Butler (1835–1902), ibid., ch. VII

53. A legal broom's a chimney-sweeper,
   And that's the reason he himself is so dirty.

   Lord Byron (1788–1824), *Don Juan*, canto X, st. XV

54. He who holds no laws in awe,
   He must perish by the law.

   Lord Byron (1788–1824), *A very mournful ballad on the seige and conquest of Alhama*, 1818, st. 12

55. All Law is but a tamed furrow-field, slowly worked out and rendered arable from the waste jungle.

   Thomas Carlyle (1795–1881), quoted by J.H. Wigmore, *Evidence*, Preface to the first edition

56. 'In my youth,' said his father, 'I took to the law,
   And argued each case with my wife;
   And the muscular strength, which it gave to my jaw,

Has lasted the rest of my life.'

Lewis Carroll (1832–98), *Alice's adventures in wonderland*, 1865, ch. V

57. Who to himself is law, no law doth need,
Offends no law and is a king indeed.

George Chapman (*c*.1559–1634), *Bussy D'Ambois*, 1641, II. i.

58. I am ashamed the law is such an ass.

George Chapman (*c*.1559–1634), *Revenge for honour*, 1654, III. ii

59. The law, as manipulated by clever and highly respected rascals, still remains the best avenue for a career of honourable and leisurely plunder.

Gabriel Chevalier, *Clochmerle*, 1936, ch. 14

60. The good of the people shall be the highest law.

Cicero (106–43 BC), *De legibus*, bk III, ch. III

61. Reason is the life of the law, nay the common law itself is nothing else but reason; which is to be understood of an artificial perfection of reason, gotten by long study, observation, and experience, and not of every man's natural reason; for *Nemo nascitur artifex*. [Nobody is born an artificer.]

Sir Edward Coke (1552–1634), *A commentary upon Littleton (the first part of the institutes of the laws of England)*, 1628, 19th edn, 1832, 97b

62. England, with a criminal code the most bloody, and a civil code the most expensive in Europe, can, notwithstanding, boast of more happiness and freedom than any other country under heaven. The reason is, that despotism, and all its minor ramifications of discretionary power, lodged in the hands of individuals, is utterly unknown. The laws are supreme.

C.C Colton (1780–1832), *Lacon*, 1820, vol. I, CXXXIX

63. Law and equity are two things which God hath joined, but which man hath put asunder.

C.C Colton (1780–1832), ibid., CCCLXXXI

64. A law overcharged with severity, like a blunderbuss overloaded with powder, will each of them grow rusty by disuse, and neither will be resorted to from the shock and the recoil that must inevitably follow their explosion.

C.C Colton (1780–1832), ibid., vol. II, CXXXIX

65. One with the law is a majority.

Calvin Coolidge (1872–1933), Speech, 27 July 1920

66. Law is but an heathen word for power.

Daniel Defoe (1660–1731), *History of the Kentish petition*, 1701

67. The meanest *English* plow-man studies law,
And keeps thereby magistrates in awe;
Will boldly tell them what they

ought to do,
And sometimes punish their
omissions too.

Daniel Defoe (1660–1731), *The true-born Englishman*, 1701, pt II

68. The voice of nations, and the
course of things,
Allow that laws superior are to
kings.

Daniel Defoe (1660–1731), ibid.

69. Even if chaos should result, still the law must be obeyed.

Lord Denning M.R., *Bradbury* v. *Enfield London Borough Council*, [1967] 1 W.L.R. 1311 at 1324

70. Anyone who breaks a bad law by his own private authority authorizes everyone else to break the good ones.

Denis Diderot (1713–84), *Supplement of Bougainville's 'Voyage'*, IV

71. The law exists to protect us all, whether we are union members, union leaders, employers or merely long-suffering members of the public. We cannot do without it. But the law is not a one-way street. Part goes our way, part goes against us. We have either to accept it all or else to opt for anarchy.

Sir John Donaldson, *Con-Mech (Engineers) Ltd.* v. *AUEW*, [1973] I.C.R. 620 at 623–4

72. Laws are vain, by which we right enjoy,
If kings unquestioned can those laws destroy.

John Dryden (1631–1700), *Absalom and Achitophel*, 1681

73. For lawful power is still superior
found,
When long driven back, at length it
stands the ground.

John Dryden (1631–1700), ibid.

74. No written laws can be so plain, so
pure,
But wit may gloss, and malice may
obscure.

John Dryden (1631–1700), *The hind and the panther*, 1687, pt. II

75. The law's made to take care o' raskills.

George Eliot (1819–80), *The mill on the Floss*, 1860, bk III, ch. 4

76. They have but one law, to seize the power and keep it.

T.S. Eliot (1888–1965), *Murder in the cathedral*, 1935, pt I

77. Law reformers have to be as adventurous as possible, but practice the art of the possible.

Robert Ellicott, *Sydney Morning Herald*, 'Sayings of the week', 14 September 1985

78. Let a man keep the law, — any law, — and his way will be strown with satisfaction.

Ralph Waldo Emerson (1803–82), *Essays, first series*, 1841, 'Prudence'

79. The law is only a memorandum.

Ralph Waldo Emerson (1803–82), *Essays, second series*, 1844, 'Politics'

80. Any laws but those which men

make for themselves are laughable.

Ralph Waldo Emerson (1803–82), ibid.

81. The law is a sort of god or divine man to men, being the sense of equity or conscience applied, as close as men can, to the action of men.

Ralph Waldo Emerson (1803–82), *Journals*, 10 November 1830

82. The laws find their root in the credence of the people.

Ralph Waldo Emerson (1803–82), ibid.

83. Law makes long spokes of the short stakes of men.

William Empson, *Legal fiction*, 1928

84. The law is for the protection of the weak more than the strong.

Erle J. (1793–1880), *R.* v. *Woolley* (1850), 4 Cox C.C. 193 at 196

85. Where there is hunger, law is not regarded; and where the law is not regarded, there will be hunger.

Benjamin Franklin (1706–90), *Poor Richard's almanac*, 1755

86. Laws *too gentle* are seldom *obeyed*; *too severe*, seldom *executed.*

Benjamin Franklin (1706–90), ibid., 1756

87. Our human laws are but the copies, more or less imperfect, of the eternal laws so far as we can read them.

James Anthony Froude (1818–94), *Short studies on great subjects*, 'Calvinism', 1871

88. Just laws are no restraint upon the freedom of the good, for the good man desires nothing which a just law will interfere with.

James Anthony Froude (1818–94), ibid., 'Reciprocal duties of state and subject', 1894

89. Good men want the laws for nothing but to defend themselves.

Thomas Fuller (1654–1734), *Gnomologia*, 1732, no. 1,720

90. Humane laws reach not thoughts.

Thomas Fuller (1654–1734), ibid., no. 2,562

91. *Lidford* law; first hang and draw, then hear the cause.

Thomas Fuller (1654–1734), ibid., no. 3,206

92. Much law, but little justice.

Thomas Fuller (1654–1734), ibid., no. 3,482

93. The more laws, the more offenders.

Thomas Fuller (1654–1734), ibid., no. 4,663

94. Where there are many laws, there are many enormities.

Thomas Fuller (1654–1734), ibid., no. 5,672

95. *The Law, is what it is* — a majestic edifice, sheltering all of us, each

stone of which rests on another.

John Galsworthy (1867–1933), *Justice*, 1910, II

96. The Law is the true embodiment
Of everything that's excellent.
It has no kind of fault or flaw,
And I, my Lords, embody the
Law.

    Sir W.S. Gilbert (1836–1911), *Iolanthe*, 1882, I, 'Lord Chancellor's song'

97. I know of no method to secure the repeal of bad or obnoxious laws so effective as their stringent execution.

    Ulysses S. Grant (1822–85), Inaugural address, 4 March 1869

98. Law, licensed breaking of the peace.

    Matthew Green (1696–1737), *The spleen*, 1. 286

99. With all the law's faults it had one great virtue. It was there.

    Arthur Hailey, *In high places*, 1962, ch. 6, 2

100. Men seldom understand any laws but those they feel.

    Lord Halifax (1633–95), *Political thoughts and reflections*

101. The law hath so many contradictions, and varyings from itself that the law may not improperly be called a lawbreaker.

    Lord Halifax (1633–95), ibid.

102. No man can imagine, not Swift himself, things more shameful, absurd and grotesque than the things which do take place daily in the Law.

    Sir Arthur Helps (1813–75), *Companions of my solitude*, 1851, ch. 1

103. Law affords a notable example of loss of time, of heart, of love, of leisure.

    Sir Arthur Helps (1813–75), ibid.

104. Fear the beadle of the law.

    George Herbert (1593–1633), *Jacula prudentum*, 1651

105. That whom he could not by the sword destroy, he might supplant by the law.

    Hobart C.J. (?–1625), *Sheffield v. Ratcliffe* (1615), Hob. 334 at 335

106. All laws, written and unwritten, have need of interpretation.

    Thomas Hobbes (1588–1679), *Leviathan*, 1651, pt II, ch. XXVI

107. Unnecessary laws are not good laws, but traps for money.

    Thomas Hobbes (1588–1679), ibid., ch. XXX

108. Except in extreme emergencies, the rule of law excludes self-help.

    Quintin Hogg, *The case for conservatism*, 1947, pt II, ch. 13

109. The life of the law has not been logic: it has been experience ... The law embodies the story of a nation's development through many centuries, and it cannot be dealt with as if it contained only

the axioms and corrollaries of a book of mathematics.

Oliver Wendell Holmes (1841–1935), *The common law*, 1881, lecture I

110. The Law, wherein, as in a magic mirror, we see reflected not only our own lives, but the lives of all men that have been! When I think of this majestic theme, my eyes dazzle.

Oliver Wendell Holmes (1841–1935), *To the Suffolk Bar Association*, 1885

111. Keep we must, if keep we can,
These foreign laws of God and
man.

A.E. Housman (1859–1936), *Last poems*, 1922, XII

112. That ignorant, blundering, blind thing, the law.

Elbert Hubbard (1856–1915), *Notebook*, p. 128

113. The law, for most people, is a great, mysterious, malevolent engine of wrath.

Elbert Hubbard (1856–1915), ibid., p. 193

114. Statute: The proof, record and final justification of the infallibility of Ignorance.

Frank McKinney Hubbard (1868–1930), *The Roycroft dictionary*, 1923

115. It is the will of the nation which makes the law obligatory.

Thomas Jefferson (1743–1826), Letter to E. Randolph, 18 August 1799

116. A strict observance of the written laws is doubtless *one* of the high duties of a good citizen, but it is not *the highest*. The laws of necessity, of self-preservation, of saving our country when in danger, are of higher obligation. To lose *our* country by a scrupulous adherence to written law, would be to lose the law itself.

Thomas Jefferson (1743–1826), Letter to J.B. Colvin, 20 September 1810

117. Nature has given women so much power that the law has very wisely given them little.

Samuel Johnson (1709–84), Letter to John Taylor, 18 August 1763

118. Laws are not made for particular cases, but for men in general.

Samuel Johnson (1709–84), *Boswell's life*, 7 April 1776

119. The Norman conquest was not complete, until Norman lawyers had introduced their laws, and reduced slavery to a system.

Junius, *Letters*, no. XLI, 14 November 1770

120. A penny-weight of love is worth a pound-weight of law.

James Kelly, *Scottish proverbs*, 1721, A, no. 95

121. Abundance of law breaks no law.

James Kelly, ibid.

122. He that loves law, will get his fill of it.

James Kelly, ibid.

123. We must not, by any whimsical conceits supposed to be adapted to the altering fashions of the times, overturn the established law of the land: it descended to us as a sacred charge, and it is our duty to preserve it.

Lord Kenyon C.J. (1732–1802), *Clayton* v. *Adams* (1796), 6 T.R. 604 at 605

124. I submit that an individual who breaks a law that conscience tells him is unjust, and who willingly accepts the penalty of imprisonment in order to arouse the conscience of the community over its injustice, is in reality expressing the highest respect for the law.

Martin Luther King (1929–68), *Letter from Birmingham Jail*, 16 April 1963

125. Now this is the Law of the jungle — as old and as true as the sky.

Rudyard Kipling (1865–1936), *The law of the jungle*

126. There was an Old Man with a gong,
Who bumped at it all the day long;
But they called out, 'O law!
You're a horrid old bore!'
So they smashed that Old Man with a gong.

Edward Lear (1812–88), *The book of nonsense*

127. Extreme law, extreme injustice. (*Summum ius summa iniuria.*)

Legal maxim, quoted by Cicero, *De officiis*, bk I, ch. X

128. The law does not concern itself with trifles. (*De minimis non curat lex.*)
Legal maxim

129. The laws are adapted to those cases which most frequently arise. (*Ad ea quae frequentius accidunt jura adaptantur.*)

Legal maxim

130. When Romulus had worshipped the gods, he called the people together and issued the rules of law because nothing but law could unite them into a single body politic.

Livy (59 BC–AD 17), *History of Rome*, bk I, VII

131. No law is equally convenient for everyone; the only question is whether it is beneficial on the whole and good for the majority.

Livy (59 BC–AD 17), ibid., bk XXXIV

132. What duty is, cannot be understood without a law; nor a law be known, or supposed without a law-maker, or without reward and punishment.

John Locke (1632–1704), *Essay concerning human understanding*, 1690, bk. I, ch. III, 12

133. Without a notion of a law-maker, it is impossible to have a notion of a law, and an obligation to observe it.

John Locke (1632–1704), ibid., ch. IV, 8

134. There are few Englishmen who will not admit that the English law, in spite of modern improve-

ments, is neither so cheap nor so speedy as might be wished. Still it is a system which has grown up among us. In some points, it has been fashioned to suit our feelings; in others, it has gradually fashioned our feelings to suit itself.

Lord Macaulay (1800–59), *Warren Hastings*, October 1841

135. The law, when enacted, furnishes its own reason.

E. McQuillin, quoted in M.R. Lett, *Rent control*, p. 51

136. Old law rests not on contract but on status.

Sir Henry Maine (1822–88), quoted by Walter Bagehot, *Physics and politics*, p. 157

137. Very happily, the more the law is looked into, the more it appears founded in equity, reason, and good sense.

Lord Mansfield (1705–93), *James* v. *Price* (n.d.), Lofft 219 at 221

138. However harmless a thing is, if the law forbids it most people will think it wrong.

W. Somerset Maugham (1874–1966), *A writer's notebook*, 1896

139. The law is blind and speaks in general terms
She cannot pity where occasion serves.

Thomas May (1595–1650), *The heir*, IV

140. England, it may be said, is not a country where everything is forbidden except what is expressly permitted: it is a country where everything is permitted except what is expressly forbidden.

Megarry V.C., *Malone* v. *Metropolitan Police Commissioner*, [1979] 2 W.L.R. 700 at 711

141. Whoso loves the law dies either mad or poor.

Thomas Middleton (1570?–1627), *The phoenix*, 1607

142. The Law ... can be civil to you or downright criminal.

Keith Miles, *The finest swordsman in all France*, 1984

143. The laws of most countries are far worse than the people who execute them, and many of them are only able to remain laws by being seldom or never carried into effect.

John Stuart Mill (1806–93), *The subjection of women*, 1869, ch. II

144. Laws and institutions require to be adapted, not to good men, but to bad.

John Stuart Mill (1806–73), ibid.

145. Law can discover sin, but not remove
Save by those shadowy expiations weak.

John Milton (1608–74), *Paradise lost*, bk XII, 1. 290

146. It is the rule of rules, the general law of laws, that every one

observe those of the place where he lives.

Michel de Montaigne (1533–92), *Essays*, bk I, 'Of custom'

147. I am of the opinion that it would be better to have no laws at all than to have as many as we do.

Michel de Montaigne (1533–92), ibid., bk. III, 1595, 'Of experience'

148. The laws keep up their credit, not for being just, but because they are laws; it is the mystic foundation of their authority.

Michel de Montaigne (1533–92), ibid.

149. The laws do not undertake to punish anything other than overt acts.

Charles de Secondat, Baron de Montesquieu (1689–1755), *The spirit of the laws*, bk XII, 11

150. I have always believed that the law, and indeed the administration of the law, is far too important a subject to be left to the experts.

Lord Morris, House of Lords, 14 January 1985

151. To me the law seems like a sort of maze through which a client must be led to safety, a collection of reefs, rocks and underwater hazards through which he or she must be piloted.

John Mortimer, *Clinging to the wreckage*, 1982, ch. 7

152. Laws were made to prevent the

strong from always having their way.

Ovid (43 BC–AD 17), *Fasti*, bk III, 1. 279

153. A law not repealed continues in force, not because it *cannot* be repealed, but because it *is not* repealed; and the non-repealing passes for consent.

Thomas Paine (1737–1809), *Rights of man*, 1791

154. Too many matters have been regulated by laws, which nature, long custom and general consent, ought only to have governed.

Sir William Petty (1623–87), *Political arithmetic*, 1690, Preface

155. [Law is] ... the greatest, most interesting, and in one word, the most humane of the political sciences.

Sir Fredrick Pollock (1835–1937), *Oxford lectures*, 1890, p. 94

156. The effective power of law is not only the work but the test of a civilised commonwealth.

Sir Fredrick Pollock (1845–1937), ibid., p. 100

157. The law is a living science.

Sir Fredrick Pollock (1845–1937), ibid., p. 105

158. Curse on all laws but those which love has made!

Alexander Pope (1688–1744), *Eloisa to Abelard*, 1717, 1. 74

159. Mark what unvary'd laws pre-

serve each state,
Laws wise as nature, and as fixed
as fate.
In vain thy reason finer webs
shall draw,
Entangle justice in her net of law,
And right, too rigid, harden into
wrong;
Still for the strong too weak, the
weak too strong.

Alexander Pope (1688–1744),
An essay on man, 1733, epistle
III, 1. 189

160. The law must be stable, but it
must not stand still.

Roscoe Pound (1870–1964), *An
introduction to the philosophy of
law*, 1922

161. Law is a practical matter.

Roscoe Pound (1870–1964),
Social control through law, 1968,
IV

162. For nothing is law that is not reason.

Powell J. (1645–1713), *Coggs* v.
Bernard (1703), 2 Ld. Ray. 909
at 911

163. The more laws, the less justice.

German proverb

164. Laws describe constraint. Their
purpose is to control, not to create.

Tom Robbins, *Still life with
woodpecker*, 1980, ch. 71

165. Him the same laws, the same
protection yield,

Who ploughs the furrow, as who
owns the field.

Richard Savage (?–1743), *Of
public spirit*, 1736

166. Unpalatable statute law may not
be disregarded or rejected,
merely because it is unpalatable.

Lord Scarman, *Duport Steels
Ltd.* v. *Sirs*, [1980] I.C.R. 161 at
190

167. The law is a great power in our
lives. It can be a power for good
or for evil.

Lord Scarman, *Sunday Times*,
12 January 1986

168. I'm a romantic optimist about the
law. I believe it can always be
reformed to make it better.

Lord Scarman, ibid

169. If they take the sword of the Law
I must lay hold of the shield.

Sir Walter Scott (1771–1832),
Journal, 16 February 1826

170. Law and Devotion must loose
some of their dignity as often as
they adopt new fashions.

Sir Walter Scott (1771–1832),
Ibid., 28 May 1829

171. Every law is a contract between
the king and the people, and
therefore to be kept.

John Selden (1584–1654),
Table-talk, 1689, 'Law'

172. He hath resisted law,
And therefore law shall scorn
him any further trial

Than the severity of the public power.

William Shakespeare (1564–1616), *Coriolanus,* 1607–8, III. i

173. The law's delay.

William Shakespeare (1564–1616), *Hamlet,* 1599–1600, III. i

174. But, I pr'ythee, sweet wag, shall there be gallows standing in England when thou art king? and resolution thus fobbed as it is with the rusty curb of old father antic the law?

William Shakespeare (1564–1616), *Henry IV Pt I,* 1597–8, I. ii

175. I have, perhaps, some shallow spirit of judgement: But in these nice sharp quillets of the law, Good faith, I am no wiser than a daw.

William Shakespeare (1564–1616), *Henry VI, Pt I,* 1589–90, II. iv

176. Faith, I have been a truant in the law, And never yet could frame my will to it; And, therefore, from the law unto my will.

William Shakespeare (1564–1616), ibid.

177. Let him have all the rigour of the law.

William Shakespeare (1564–1616), *Henry VI Pt II,* 1590–1, I. iii

178. The law, thou seest, hath judged thee: I cannot justify whom the law condemns.

William Shakespeare (1564–1616), ibid., II. iii

179. Press not a falling man too far; 'tis virtue: His faults lie open to the laws; let them, Not you, correct him.

William Shakespeare (1564–1616), *Henry VIII,* 1612–13, III. ii

180. When law can do no right, Let it be lawful that law bar no wrong: Law cannot give my child his kingdom here; For he that holds his kingdom holds the law: Therefore, since law itself is perfect wrong, How can the law forbid my tongue to curse?

William Shakespeare (1564–1616), *King John,* 1596–7, III. i

181. O just but severe law!

William Shakespeare (1564–1616), *Measure for measure,* 1604–5, II. i

182. Bidding the law make court'sy to their will.

William Shakespeare (1564–1616), ibid., II. iv

183. The manacles of the all-binding law.

William Shakespeare (1564–1616), ibid.

184. Laws for all faults,

But faults so countenanc'd that
the strong statutes
Stand like the forfeits in a
barber's shop,
As much in mock as mark.

William Shakespeare (1564–
1616), ibid., V. i

185. In law, what plea so tainted and
corrupt,
But, being season'd with a gra-
cious voice.
Obscure the show of evil?

William Shakespeare (1564–
1616), *The merchant of Venice*,
1596–7., III. ii

186. Wrest once the law to your
authority:
To do a great right, do a little
wrong.

William Shakespeare (1564–
1616), ibid., IV. i

187. The bloody book of law.

William Shakespeare (1564–
1616), *Othello*, 1604–5, I. iii

188. The state of law is bondslave to
the law.

William Shakespeare (1564–
1616), *Richard II*, 1595–6, II. i

189. Still you keep o' the windy side
of the law.

William Shakespeare (1564–
1616), *Twelfth night*, 1599–
1600, III. iv

190. Let the law go whistle.

William Shakespeare (1564–
1616), *The winter's tale*, 1610–
11, IV. iii

191. Most laws are, and all laws ought
to be, stronger than the strongest
individual.

George Bernard Shaw (1856–
1950), *Getting married*, 1908,
Preface

192. The law may be only the intolerance of the community; but it is
a defined and limited tolerance.

George Bernard Shaw (1856–
1950), *The shewing-up of Blanco
Posnet*, 1909, 'The rejected state-
ment', pt. I

193. Laws are generally found to be
nets of such a texture, as the little
creep through, the great break
through, and the middle-sized
are alone entangled in.

William Shenstone (1714–63),
*Essays on men, manners and
things*

194. Blind, unquestioning obedience
is the law of tyrants and of slaves:
it does not yet flourish on English
soil.

Lord Simonds (1881–1971),
Christie v. *Leachinsky*, [1947]
A.C. 573 at 591

195. The law must be related to the
changing standards of life, not
yielding to every shifting impulse
of the popular will but having
regard to fundamental assess-
ments of human values and the
purposes of society.

Viscount Simonds (1881–1971),
Shaw v. *D.P.P.*, [1962] A.C. 220
at 268

196. Nothing can be done in any
discussion upon any point of law

in England without quoting Mr. Justice Blackstone. Mr. Justice Blackstone, we believe, generally wrote his Commentaries late in the evening with a bottle of wine before him; and little did he think, as each sentence fell from the glass and pen, of the immense influence it might hereafter exercise upon the law and usage of his country.

Sydney Smith (1771–1845), *Counsel for prisoners*

197. The great object of all law is, that the guilty should be punished, and that the innocent should be acquitted.

Sydney Smith (1771–1845), ibid.

198. The unwritten laws of God do not change.

Sophocles (496–406 BC), *Antigone*

199. It is not true that once upon a time men said — 'Let there be law;' and there was law. Administration of justice was originally impracticable, Utopian; and has become more and more practicable only as men have become less savage.

Herbert Spencer (1820–1903), *Social statics*, 1870, pt. III, ch. XXI, sec. 6

200. There is no such thing as 'natural law'. The expression is nothing but old nonsense. Prior to laws, what is natural is only the strength of the lion, or the need of the creature suffering from

hunger or cold, in short, need.

Stendhal (1783–1842), *The red and the black*, 1831

201. I will not say with Lord Hale, that 'The Law will admit of no rival' ... but I will say that it is a jealous mistress and requires a long and constant courtship. It is not to be won by trifling favours, but by lavish homage.

Joseph Story (1779–1845), *The value and importance of legal studies, miscellaneous writings*

202. If there be no law, there is no transgression.

Jonathan Swift (1667–1745), *Seasonable advice to the grand jury*, 1724

203. If books and laws continue to increase as they have done for fifty years past; I am in some concern for future ages, how any man will be learned, or any man a lawyer.

Jonathan Swift (1667–1745), *Thoughts on various subjects*, 1711

204. Nothing is that errs from law.

Alfred, Lord Tennyson (1809–92), *In memoriam*, 1850, LXXIII, 1. 8

205. What the law requires, let it have of your own free will.

Terence (c.190–159 BC), *Adelphi*, III. iv. 44

206. Law has never made men a whit more just.

Henry D. Thoreau (1817–62),

Resistance to civil government,
1849

207. Those who violate the law must
not apply to the law for protection.

Lord Truro L.C. (1782–1855),
Benyon v. *Nettlefold* (1850), 3
Mac. & G. 94 at 102

208. Some persons seem to submit to
the laws of their country in the
same manner as they do to the
changes of the seasons, and the
rising and setting of the sun,
merely because they cannot help
it.

Richard Whately (1787–1863),
Thoughts and apothegms, 1856,
pt. VI

209. Judicial knowledge is the knowledge of the ordinary wide-awake
man, used by one who is trained
to express it in terms of precision.

Lord Wilberforce, *Brisbane City
Council* v. *AG for Queensland,*
[1978] 3 W.L.R. 299 at 306

210. He [Blackstone] it was that first
gave to the law the air of a
science. He found it a skeleton,
and clothed it with life, colour
and complexion; he embraced
the cold statue and by his touch it
grew into youth, health and
beauty.

**Barry Yelverton, First Viscount
Avonmore** (1736–1805), attributed

86. LAW AND ORDER

1. An unjust society causes and
defines crime; and an aggressive

social structure which is unjust
and must create aggressive social
disruption, receives the moral
sanction of being 'law and order'.
Law and order is one of the steps
taken to maintain injustice.

Edward Bond, *Lear,* 1972,
Author's preface

2. They are very strict about law
and order these days. You must
not beat anyone for nothing, only
for the sake of order.

Maxim Gorki (1868–1936), *The
lower depths,* I

3. If at the bottom of law and order
there is only a man armed to the
teeth, a man without a heart,
without a conscience, then law
and order are meaningless.

Henry Miller (1891–1980), *The
air-conditioned nightmare,* 1945,
'The soul of anaesthesia'

4. In primitive law the end is simply
to keep the peace.

Roscoe Pound (1870–1964),
The spirit of the common law,
1921, IV

5. Law is not merely an instrument
of order, but may frequently be
its adversary.

Jerome H. Skolnick, *Justice
without trial,* 1966, ch. 1

6. Those who dread a dead-level of
income or wealth ... do not dread,
it seems, a dead-level of law and
order, and of security of life and
property. They do not complain
that persons endowed by nature
with unusual qualities of strength,
audacity, or cunning are prevented

from reaping the full fruits of these powers.

R.H. Tawney (1880–1962), *Equality*, 4th ed, p. 85

87. LAW SOCIETY

1. The restraining influence of the Law Society in a profession which once had a proverbial bad name is obvious.

   Gilbert Russell, *Nuntius*, 1926

88. LAWYERS

1. The body of the law is no less incumbered with superfluous members, that are like Virgil's army, which he tells us was so crowded, many of them had not room to use their weapons.

   Joseph Addison (1672–1719), *Spectator*, no. 21, 24 March 1711

2. If you ask two barristers you will get two or three opinions.

   Anonymous barrister

3. For the lawyers, they write according to the states where they live what is received law, and not what ought to be law: for the wisdom of a lawmaker is one, and of a lawyer is another.

   Francis Bacon (1561–1626), *The advancement of learning*, bk II, XXIII, 49

4. When Mr Justice was a counsellor, he would never take less than a guinea for doing anything, nor less than half a one for doing nothing. He durst not if he would: among

lawyers, moderation would be infamy.

Jeremy Bentham (1748–1832), *Truth v. Ashhurst; or, law as it is,* 1823

5. Woe unto you also, ye lawyers! for ye lade men with burdens grievous to be borne, and ye yourselves touch not the burdens with one of your fingers.

   Bible, Authorized Version, St Luke, 11: 46

6. Woe unto you, lawyers! for ye have taken away the key of knowledge: ye entered not in yourselves, and them that were entering in ye hindered.

   Bible, Authorized Version, ibid., 11: 52

7. Lawyer, *n.* One skilled in circumvention of the law.

   Ambrose Bierce (1842–1914?), *The devil's dictionary*, 1911

8. LL.D. Letters indicating the degree of *Legumptionorum Doctor*, one learned in the laws, gifted with legal gumption. Some suspicion is cast upon this derivation by the fact that the title was formerly ££.d., and conferred only upon gentlemen distinguished for their wealth.

   Ambrose Bierce (1842–1914?), ibid

9. I believe that an experienced lawyer may be, as it were, instinctively right without at the moment being able to give a good reason for his opinion.

   Lord Bramwell (1808–92), *Mills*

v. *Armstrong* (1888), 13 App. Cas. 1 at 12

10. The lawyer has his forms, and his positive institutions too, and he adheres to them with a veneration altogether as religious. The worst cause cannot be so prejudicial to the litigant, as his advocate's or attorney's ignorance of these forms.

Edmund Burke (1729–97), *A vindication of natural society*

11. A man must not think he can save himself the trouble of being a sensible man and a gentleman by going to his solicitor, any more than he can get himself a sound constitution by going to his doctor; but a solicitor can do more to keep a tolerably well-meaning fool straight than a doctor can do for an invalid. Money is to the solicitor what souls are to the parson or life to the physician. He is our money-doctor.

Samuel Butler (1835–1902), *Notebooks*, ed. Festing Jones, ch. II

12. The lawyer's brief is like the surgeon's knife,
Dissecting the whole inside of a question,
And with it all the process of digestion.

Lord Byron (1788–1824), *Don Juan*, canto X, st. XIV

13. Sometimes even lawyers need lawyers.

Billy Carter, *Observer*, 'Sayings of the week', 27 July 1980

14. The laws I love, the lawyers I suspect.

Charles Churchill (1731–64), *The farewell*, 1764

15. A lawyer who has a varied practice is constantly improving his education.

Julius Henry Cohen, 'Rent control after World War I — recollections', *New York University Law Quarterly Review*, 1946, p. 277

16. The trouble with law is lawyers.

Clarence Darrow (1857–1938), Attributed

17. Next bring some lawyers to thy bar,
By innuendo they might all stand there;
There let them expiate their guilt,
And pay for all that blood their tongues ha'spilt,
These are the mountebanks of state.
Who by the slight of tongue can crimes create,
And dress up trifles in the robes of fate.

Daniel Defoe (1660–1731), *A hymn to the pillory*, 1703

18. Lawyers run the world.

Len Deighton, *Berlin game*, 1983, ch. 21

19. As an advocate he [a barrister] is a minister of justice equally with the judge.

Lord Denning M.R., *Rondel* v. *Worsley*, [1967] 1 Q.B. 443 at 502

20. A barrister cannot pick or choose his clients. He is bound to accept a

brief for any man who comes before the courts. No matter how great a rascal the man may be. No matter how given to complaining. No matter how undeserving or unpopular his cause. The barrister must defend him to the end.

Lord Denning M.R., ibid

21. It is a mistake to suppose that he [the barrister] is the mouthpiece of his client to say what he wants: or his tool to do what he directs. He is none of these things. He owes allegiance to a higher cause. It is the cause of truth and justice.

Lord Denning M.R., ibid.

22. Words are the lawyer's tools of trade.

Lord Denning, *The discipline of law*, 1979, p. 5

23. Most lawyers are conservative. That's what's wrong with them. They seem to have a vested interest in not changing the law.

Lord Denning, *Sunday Times*, 1 August 1982

24. When I was Master of the Rolls I had a great deal to do with solicitors. I admitted 35,000 of them. I signed all their admission certificates by hand myself. They called me the father-in-law of all solicitors.

Lord Denning, House of Lords, 14 January 1985

25. If there were no bad people, there would be no good lawyers.

Charles Dickens (1812–70), *The old curiosity shop*, 1841, ch. LVI

26. It is ... entirely unreasonable that the closed solicitors' shop should remain closed when one considers that the bulk of legal advice is nowadays given outside that shop.

Lord Donaldson, House of Lords, 5 July 1984

27. As a result of her experience she formed the view that all the solicitors whom she had consulted were conspiring together to stifle her justified complaints. Whilst it is inherently unlikely that she is correct, this is not an uncommon reaction by a dissatisfied client. If this were itself a justification for compulsory detention, the mental hospitals would be over-full.

Sir John Donaldson M.R., *Winch v. Jones*, [1985] 3 All E.R. 98 at 99

28. The good lawyer is not the man who has an eye to every side and angle of contingency, and qualifies all his qualifications, but who throws himself on your part so heartily, that he can get you out of a scrape.

Ralph Waldo Emerson (1803–82), *The conduct of life*, 1860, 'Power'

29. The old woman hesitated, then cast a quick eye at a certain open box beside her roll-top desk and apparently decided that even lawyers can be thieves — a possibility few who have had to meet their fees would dispute.

John Fowles, *The French lieutenant's woman*, 1977, ch. 46

30. Commonly physicians, like beer, are best when they are old, and

lawyers, like bread, when they are young and new.

Thomas Fuller (1608–61), *The holy state*, 1642, 'The good advocate'

31. Lawyers don't love beggars.

Thomas Fuller (1654–1734), *Gnomologia*, 1732, no. 3,151

32. Sure, he's a lawyer: for he makes indentures as he goes.

Thomas Fuller (1654–1734), ibid., no. 4,289

33. I know you lawyers can, with ease,
Twist words and meanings as you please;
That language, by your skill made pliant,
Will bend to favour ev'ry client.

John Gay (1685–1732), *Fables*, vol. II, 1738, fable I, 'The dog and the fox'

34. There is usually a decency about counsel which prevents them from pressing that to a conclusion which can never be concluded.

Gibbs C.J. (1751–1820), *Tomkins v. Willshear* (1814), 5 Taunt. 431

35. When I, good friends, was called to the bar,
I'd an appetite fresh and hearty,
But I was, as many young barristers are,
An impecunious party.

Sir W.S. Gilbert (1836–1911), *Trial by jury*, 1875

36. That whether you're an honest man or whether you're a thief
Depends on whose solicitor has

given me my brief.

Sir W.S. Gilbert (1836–1911), *Utopia limited*, 1893, I

37. There's no better way of using the imagination than the study of law. No poet ever interpreted nature as freely as a lawyer interprets truth.

Jean Giraudoux (1882–1944), *Tiger at the gates*

38. Lawyers are always more ready to get a man into troubles, than out of them.

Oliver Goldsmith (1728–74), *The good natur'd man*, 1768, III

39. Lawyers do not take law reform seriously — there is no reason why they should. They think the law exists as the atmosphere exists, and the notion that it could be improved is too startling to entertain.

Lord Goodman, *Sydney Morning Herald*, 17 July 1982, p. 38

40. Well, I know'd he was near-sighted, was lawyer, and couldn't see a pint clear of his nose, unless it was pint o'law.

Thomas Chandler Haliburton (1796–1865), *The attaché; or Sam Slick in England*, 1843, vol. I, ch. XI

41. If the laws could speak for themselves they would complain of the lawyers in the first place.

Lord Halifax (1633–95), *Political thoughts and reflexions*

42. I do not know a meaner or sadder portion of a man's existence, or one more likely to be full of

impatient sorrow, than that which he spends in waiting at the offices of lawyers.

Sir Arthur Helps (1813–75), *Companions of my solitude*, 1851, ch. 1

43. Lawyer's houses are built on the heads of fools.

George Herbert (1593–1633), *Jacula prudentum*, 1651

44. A British lawyer would like to think of himself as part of that mysterious entity called The Law; an American lawyer would like a swimming pool and two houses.

Simon Hoggart, *Observer*, 10 August 1986

45. The lawyers are a picked lot, 'first scholars' and the like, but their business is as unsympathetic as Jack Ketch's.

Oliver Wendell Holmes (1809–94), *The poet at the breakfast-table*, 1872

46. Every lawyer should be a conciliator.

Elbert Hubbard (1856–1915), *Notebook*, p. 120

47. Seventy per cent of the members of all our law-making bodies are lawyers. Very naturally, lawyers making laws favour laws that make lawyers a necessity. If that were not so, lawyers would not be human.

Elbert Hubbard (1856–1915), ibid., p. 193

48. Lawyer ... An unnecessary evil ... The only man in whom ignorance of the law is not punished.

Frank McKinney Hubbard (1868–1930), *The Roycroft dictionary*, 1923

49. Johnson observed, that 'he did not care to speak ill of any man behind his back, but he believed the gentleman was an *attorney*.'

Samuel Johnson (1709–84), *Boswell's life*, 1770

50. A lawyer has no business with the justice or injustice of the cause which he undertakes, unless his client asks his opinion, and then he is bound to give it honestly. The justice or injustice of the cause is to be decided by the judge ... If lawyers were to undertake no causes till they were sure they were just, a man might be precluded altogether from a trial of his claim, though were it judicially examined, it might be found to be a very just claim.

Samuel Johnson (1709–84), ibid., 15 August 1773

51. As it rarely happens that a man is fit to plead his own cause, lawyers are a class of the community, who, by study and experience, have acquired the art and power of arranging evidence, and of applying to the points at issue what the law has settled. A lawyer is to do for his client all that his client might fairly do for himself, if he could.

Samuel Johnson (1709–84), ibid.,

52. I have ne'er been in a chamber with a lawyer when I did not wish either to scream with desperation or else fall into the deepest of

sleeps, e'en when the matter concern'd my own future most profoundly.

Erica Jong, *Fanny*, bk. III, ch. XVI

53. Lawyers Can Seriously Damage Your Health.

Michael Joseph, title of book

54. There are limits to permissible misrepresentation, even at the hands of a lawyer.

John Maynard Keynes (1883–1946), *The shadow of Keynes*, 1978, ch. 3, p. 33

55. Lawyers generally prefer not to rush things.

Justice Kirby, Australian Law Reform Commission, on the 52 years it has taken for lawyers to join scientists as ANZAAS, *Sydney Morning Herald*, 'Sayings of the week', 15 May 1982

56. I think lawyers are the narrowest section of society. They bury their heads in their lawbooks and know nothing about life. They're the dullest section of the community — you can't have a conversation with them.

Jim McClelland (former judge), *Sydney Morning Herald*, 'Sayings of the week', 22 March 1986

57. The law, by any standards, is an extraordinary profession. Its practitioners are always anxious to voice the highest principles of fairness and impartiality in relation to everyone but themselves.

Sir Robert Mark, *In the office of constable*, 1978, ch. 22

58. A certain young lawyer is said to criticise my verses. I do not know his name, but if I find out, lawyer, woe to you!

Martial (AD *c*.40–*c*.104), *Epigrams*, bk V, epig. XXXIII

59. [Lawyers] ... men that hire out words and anger.

Martial (AD *c*.40–*c*.104), quoted by Joseph Addison, *Spectator*, no. 21

60. He had the prosperous look of a lawyer.

W. Somerset Maugham (1874–1966), *A writer's notebook*, 1917

61. It is the curse, as well as the fascination of the law, that lawyers get to know more than is good for them about their fellow human beings.

John Mortimer, *The trials of Rumpole*, 1979, 'Rumpole and the man of God'

62. The lawyer's is a manifold art.

Sir Frederick Pollock (1845–1937), *Oxford lectures*, 1890, p. 2

63. The practice of the law is a perfectly distinct art.

Sir Frederick Pollock (1845–1937), ibid.

64. The lawyer has not reached the height of his vocation who does not find therein ... scope for a peculiar but genuine artistic function.

Sir Frederick Pollock (1845–1937), ibid., p. 100

65. 'It is the act of lawyers', answered

Pantagruel, 'to sell words'.

François Rabelais (*c*.1494–1553), *Panatgruel*, 1532, bk. IV, ch. LVI

66. Lawyers are brought up with an exaggerated reverence for their system and, apart from a few, they don't see what's wrong with it.

Tom Sargant, *Observer*, 26 September 1982

67. An English lawyer ignores history at his peril.

Lord Scarman, *Williams and Glyn's Bank* v. *Boland*, [1981] A.C. 487 at 511

68. A barrister of extended practice if he has any talents at all is the best companion in the world.

Sir Walter Scott (1771–1832), *Journal*, 30 April 1828

69. I may be partial but the conversation of intelligent barristers amuses me more than that of other professional persons.

Sir Walter Scott (1771–1832), ibid., 22 May 1828

70. The law is not a profession so easily acquired.

Sir Walter Scott (1771–1832), ibid., 24 March 1831

71. With lawyers in the vacation; for they sleep between term and term, and then they perceive not how time moves.

William Shakespeare (1564–1616), *As you like it*, 1596–1600, III. ii

72. I will make

One of her women lawyer to me:
for
I yet not understand the case
myself.

William Shakespeare (1564–1616), *Cymbeline*, 1609–10, II. iii

73. Why may not that be the skull of a lawyer? Where be his quiddits now, his quillets, his cases, his tenures, his tricks?

William Shakespeare (1564–1616), *Hamlet*, 1599–1600, V. i

74. *Dick*: The first thing we do, let's kill all the lawyers.
Cade: Nay, that I mean to do. Is not this a lamentable thing, that of the skin of an innocent lamb should be made parchment? that parchment being scribbled o'er, should undo a man? Some say the bee stings; but I saw 'tis the bee's wax; for I did but seal once to a thing, and I was never mine own man since.

William Shakespeare (1564–1616), *Henry VI Pt II*, 1597–8, IV. ii

75. O perilous mouths,
That bear in them one and the self-
same tongue,
Either of condemnation or
approof!
Bidding the law make court'sy to
their will
Hooking both right and wrong to
the appetite,
To follow as it draws!

William Shakespeare (1564–1616), *Measure for measure*, 1604–5, II. iv

76. Do as adversaries do in law, —
Strive mightily, but eat and drink

as friends.

William Shakespeare (1564–1616), *The taming of the shrew*, 1593-4, I. ii

77. A lawyer's a man well trained in
                                memory
   Of cases, precedent, repartee,
                                speeches.

Stephen Spender, *Trial of a judge*, 1938, I

78. There was a society of men [lawyers] among us, bred up from their youth in the art of proving by words multiplied for the purpose, that *white* is *black*, and *black* is *white*, according as they are paid. To this society all the rest of the people are slaves.

Jonathan Swift (1667–1745), *Gulliver's travels*, 1726, pt IV, ch. V

79. I never heard a finer piece of satire against *lawyers*, than that of *astrologers*; when they pretend by rule of art to foretell in what time a suit will end, and whether to the advantage of the plaintiff or defendant: thus making the matter depend entirely upon the influence of the stars, without the least regard to the merits of the cause.

Jonathan Swift (1667–1745), *Thoughts on various subjects*, 1711

80. A woman with a good jointure is a doosid deal easier a profession than the law, let me tell you.

William Makepeace Thackeray (1811–63), *The history of Pendennis*, ch. XXVIII

81. I have undertaken the duty of constituting myself one of the attorneys for the people in any court to which I can get entrance. I don't mean as a lawyer, for while I was a lawyer, I have repented.

Woodrow Wilson (1856–1924), Speech, 2 September 1912

82. These are those lawyers who, by being in all causes, are in none.

William Wycherley (1640–1716), *The plain-dealer*, III. i

89. LEGAL AID

1. One has to remember that legal aid can be used most oppressively against innocent people.

Lord Denning, House of Lords, 14 January 1985

2. The man of moderate means, who is faced with large expenditure in protection of his legal rights, is just as deserving of help as the man who is penniless and is faced with smaller expenditure.

Sir John Donaldson, Law Society Annual Conference, Bournemouth, 18 October 1984

90. LEGAL EDUCATION

1. When I was a lad I served a term
   As office boy to an Attorney's
                                firm.
   I cleaned the windows and I swept
                                the floor,
   And I polished up the handle of
                                the big front door ...

I polished up that handle so care-
fullee,
That now I am the Ruler of the
Queen's Navee!

Sir W.S. Gilbert (1836–1911),
HMS Pinafore, 1878, I

2. Almost the wisest-looking thing in
the world is a country boy who has
been boarding in town three or
four months, studying law.

E. W. Howe (1853–1937), *Country town sayings*, 1911

3. The law may be studied as well in
one place as another: because it is
a study of books alone, at least till
near the close of it.

Thomas Jefferson (1743–1826),
Letter to Colonel T.M. Randolph,
11 August 1787

4. The study of the law is useful in a
variety of points of view. It qualifies a man to be useful to himself,
to his neighbours, and to the
public.

Thomas Jefferson (1743–1826),
Letter to T.M. Randolph, 30 May
1790

5. The study of laws, on condition
they are good laws, is unrivalled in
its ability to improve the student.

Plato (*c.*428–347 BC) *The laws*,
bk. XII

6. The law schools in Britain have
been traditionally concerned in the
main with the lawyer's view of the
law, meaning by that the professional lawyer.

William Robson, *Man and the
social sciences*, 1972, p. xii

91. LEGALITY

1. Just to the windward of the law.

Charles Churchill (1731–64), *The
ghost*, 1763, bk III

2. I walk within the purlieus of the
law.

Sir George Etheredge (1636–94),
Love in a tub, I. iii

3. I am not partial to infringe our
laws.

William Shakespeare (1564–
1616), *Comedy of errors*, 1592–3,
I. i

4. I'll be no breaker of the law.

William Shakespeare (1564–
1616), *Henry VI pt I*, 1589–90, I.
iii

5. Listen to the chattings of men
about their affairs; examine into
trade practices; read over business
correspondence; or get a solicitor
to detail his conversations with his
clients: — you will find that in
most cases conduct depends not
upon what is right, but what is
legal.

Herbert Spencer (1820–1903),
Social statics, 1870, pt IV, ch.
XXX, sec. 7

92. LEGISLATION

1. The habit of lightly changing the
laws is an evil ... For the law has
no power to command obedience
except that of habit, which can
only be given by time, so that a
readiness to change from old to

new laws enfeebles the power of the law.

Aristotle (384–322 BC), *Politics*, trans. Jowett, bk II, ch. 8

2. It usually takes a hundred years to make a law, and then, after it has done its work, it usually takes a hundred years to get rid of it.

Henry Ward Beecher (1813–87), *Proverbs from Plymouth pulpit*, 1887

3. Legislators and judges have often thought like the vulgar: they have applied unpolished rules to what demanded a delicate discernment.

Jeremy Bentham (1748–1832), *Principles of penal law*, pt I, ch. XII

4. All lawyers know how easy it could be in this place to raise a smile, at the least, by recounting the little fooleries of our draftsmen.

Henry Peter Brougham (1778–1868), House of Commons, 7 February 1828

5. A true lawgiver ought to have a heart full of sensibility. He ought to love and respect his kind, and to fear himself.

Edmund Burke (1729–97), *Reflections on the revolution in France*, 1790, para. 483.

6. Any law, however well meant as a law, which has become a bounty on unthrift, idleness, bastardy and beer-drinking, must be put an end to.

Thomas Carlyle (1795–1881), *Chartism*, 1839, ch. III

7. 'Tis easier to make certain things legal than to make them legitimate.

Sébastian Roch Nicolas Chamfort (1741–94), attributed

8. History must be replete with instances where the stated intentions of legislative actions have diverged from the actual effects.

Steven N.S. Cheung. 'Roofs or stars: the stated intents and actual effects of a rents ordinance', *Economic Inquiry*, vol. XIII, March 1975, p. 1

9. Changes in the law come more or less like changes in automobiles, radios or bombers — we learn by experience — by trial and error.

Julius Henry Cohen, 'Rent control after World War I — recollections', *New York University Law Quarterly Review*, 1946, p. 272

10. The science of legislation, is like that of medicine; in one respect, that it is far more easy to point out what will do harm, than what will do good.

C.C Colton (1780–1832), *Lacon*, 1820, vol. I, DXXIX

11. Men would be great criminals did they need as many laws as they make.

Charles John Darling (1849–1936), *Scintillæ juris*, 1877

12. But when we come to matters with a European element, the Treaty [of Rome] is like an incoming tide. It flows into the estuaries and up the rivers. It cannot be held back. Parliament has decreed that the Treaty is henceforward to be part

of our law. It is equal in force to any statute.

Lord Denning M.R., *H.P. Bulmer Ltd.* v. *J. Bollinger SA*, [1974] 4 Ch. 401 at 418

13. The wise know that foolish legislation is a rope of sand, which perishes in the twisting.

    Ralph Waldo Emerson (1803–82), *Essays, second series*, 1844, 'Politics'

14. Ill kings make many good laws.

    Thomas Fuller (1654–1734), *Gnomologia*, 1732, no. 3,072

15. New lords, new laws.

    Thomas Fuller (1654–1734), ibid., no. 3,536

16. One of the truly great tragedies of some social legislation is that it labours under assumptions which might have been true in the past, but which are not applicable to the present.

    Allen Gibboney, 'Residential rent control: Stoneridge Apartments v. Lindsay', *University of Pittsburgh Law Review*, 1970, pp. 473–4

17. One result of the institution of law, is, that the institution, once begun, can never be brought to a close. Edict is heaped on edict, and volume upon volume.

    William Godwin (1756–1836), *Enquiry concerning political justice*, 1798, vol. II, bk VII, ch. VIII

18. Shiny new laws do not deter criminals if they are just as content to break the new laws as they were to break the old ones.

    Sir Nicholas Goodison, *The Times*, 16 January 1986

19. An Act of Parliament can do no wrong, though it may do several things that look pretty odd.

    Holt C.J. (1642–1710), *City of London* v. *Wood* (1701), 12 Mod. 669 at 687–8

20. This country [USA] is suffering from over-legislation. Our reformers seem to have small faith in natural law ... This country is all right — or will be as soon as we repeal a few silly laws.

    Elbert Hubbard (1856–1915), *Notebook*, p. 70

21. Any law that can easily be broken is a bad law.

    Elbert Hubbard (1856–1915), ibid., p. 121

22. It is really more questionable, than may at first be thought, whether Bonaparte's dumb legislature, which said nothing, and did much, may not be preferable to one which talks much, and does nothing.

    Thomas Jefferson (1743–1826), *Autobiography*

23. It is rather difficult to get legislation on to the statute book. It is even more difficult to remove it.

    Lord Jenkins, House of Lords, 27 June 1984

24. Laws are formed by the manners and exigencies of particular times, and it is but accidental that they

last longer than their causes.

Samuel Johnson (1709–84), Letter to James Boswell, 3 February February 1776

25. The legislature is never so well employed as when they look to the interests of those who are at a distance from them in the ranks of society. It is their duty to do so: religion calls for it; humanity calls for it; and if there are hearts who are not awake to either of those feelings, their own interests would dictate it.

Lord Kenyon (1732–1802), *R.* v. *Rusby* (1800), Pea. (2) 189 at 192

26. Many laws certainly make men bad, as bad men make many laws.

Walter Savage Landor (1775–1864), *Imaginary conversations*, 1824–9, 'Diogenes and Plato'

27. Those who lay the foundations of a state and give it laws must assume that all men are bad and will always show their evil nature when they are given a chance.

Niccolo Machiavelli (1469–1527), *Discourses*, bk I, ch. III

28. No arbitrary regulation, no act of the legislature, can add anything to the capital of the country; it can only force it into artificial channels.

J.R. McCulloch (1789–1864) *Principles of political economy*, new edn, pt I, ch. VII

29. Even if every woman were a wife, and if every wife ought to be a slave, all the more would these slaves stand in need of legal pro-

tection: and we know what legal protection the slaves have, where the laws are made by their masters.

John Stuart Mill (1806–73), *The subjection of women*, 1869, ch. III

30. [Laws] are often made by fools, still oftener by men who, out of hatred to equality, fail in equity; but always by men, vain and irresolute authors. There is nothing so much, nor so grossly, nor so ordinarily faulty, as the laws.

Michel de Montaigne (1533–92), *Essays*, bk. III, 1595 'Of experience'

31. It is the job of the legislature to follow the spirit of the nation, provided it is not contrary to the principles of government.

Charles de Secondat, Baron de Montesquieu (1689–1755), *The spirit of the laws*, 1748, bk XIX, 5

32. What is enjoined by law should be practicable, if the legislator desires to punish a few to some good purpose, and not many to no purpose.

Plutarch (46–120), *Lives: Solon*

33. One of the greatest delusions in the world is the hope that the evils of this world can be cured by legislation.

Thomas B. Reed (1839–1902), attributed

34. Sometimes we need to pause and think about the extent to which we legislate on purely administrative matters.

Lord Renton, House of Lords, 21 January 1985

35. Good laws cause better laws to be made, while bad ones lead to worse.

    Jean Jacques Rousseau (1712–78), *The social contract*, 1762, bk. III, ch. XV

36. Among the defects of the bill, which were numerous, one provision was conspicuous by its presence and another by its absence.

    Lord John Russell (1792–1878), attributed

37. Official acceptance of women's equality through legislation like the Equal Pay and Anti-Discrimination Acts can produce a false sense of accomplishment and victory, and therefore apathy.

    Sue Sharpe, *Just like a girl*, 1976, ch. IX

38. To judge whether [a workman] is fit to be employed, may surely be trusted to the discretion of the employers whose interest it so much concerns. The affected anxiety of the law-giver lest they should employ an improper person, is evidently as impertinent as it is oppressive.

    Adam Smith (1723–90), *Wealth of nations*, 1776, vol. I bk I, ch. X

39. Every man who makes laws says, 'This may be my case:' but it requires the repeated efforts of humane men ... to awaken the attention of law-makers to evils from which they are exempt.

    Sydney Smith (1771–1845), *Counsel for Prisoners*

40. When I hear any man talk of an unalterable law, the only effect it produces on me is to convince me that he is an unalterable fool.

    Sydney Smith (1771–1845), *The Peter Plymley letters*, 1807, IV

41. Every law which orginated in ignorance and malice, and gratifies the passions from whence it sprang, we call the wisdom of our ancestors.

    Sydney Smith (1771–1845), ibid., V

42. The Scottish legislation is founded, in a great measure, on the civil law; consequently, their proceedings vary from those of the English tribunals; but, I think, they have the advantage of us in their method of examining witnesses apart, and in the constitution of their jury.

    Tobias Smollett (1721–71), *The expedition of Humphry Clinker*, 1771, vol. II

43. Is not our government as busy still as though the work of law-making commenced but yesterday? ... Nearly every parliamentary proceeding is a tacit confession of incompetency. There is scarely a bill introduced but is entitled 'An Act to amend an Act'. The 'Whereas' of almost every preamble heralds an account of the miscarriage of previous legislation.

    Herbert Spencer (1820–1903), *Social statics*, 1870, introduction

44. There is this perennial delusion, common to Radical and Tory, that legislation is omnipotent, and that things will be done because laws

are passed to do them.

Herbert Spencer (1820–1903), *The study of sociology*, 1880, ch. XI

45. A populist law passed in haste is usually repented at leisure.

Sunday Times, 24 January 1982

46. As the aggressor is said to have generally the advantage of the defender; so, the makers of the law, which is to defend our rights, have usually not so much industry or vigour, as those whose interest leads them to attack it.

Jonathan Swift (1667–1745), *The examiner*, no. 38, 26 April 1711

47. If my neighbour hath a mind to my cow, he hires a lawyer to prove that he ought to have my cow from me. I must then hire another to defend my right; it being against all rules of law that any man should be allowed to speak for himself.

Jonathan Swift (1667–1745), *Gulliver's travels* 1726, pt IV, ch. V

48. Laws penned with the utmost care and exactness, and in the vulgar language, are often perverted to wrong meanings.

Jonathan Swift (1667–1745), *Thoughts on various subjects*, 1711

49. There is no worse legislator than the one whose spirit was molded applying the laws.

Miguel Unamuno (1864–1937), *Perplexities and paradoxes*, 'Civilization is civism', trans. S. Gross

50. New laws are too apt to be voluminous, and so perplexed and mutable, from whence proceeds neglect, contempt and ignorance.

William Warburton (1698–1779), *The causes of podigies and miracles*, I

51. There never was a law yet made ... that hit the taste *exactly* of every man, or every part of the community.

George Washington (1732–99), Letter to Daniel Morgan, 8 October 1794

52. Since 1889, if not before, 'man' has embraced 'woman'.

Glanville Williams, *Learning the law*, 9th edn, 1973, p. 93

93. LIBERTY

1. Liberty, next to religion, has been the motive of good deeds and the pretext of crime.

Lord Acton (1834–1902), 'The history of freedom in antiquity', Address given on 26 February 1877

2. In this country, amid the clash of arms, the laws are not silent. They may be changed, but they speak the same language in war as in peace. It has always been one of the pillars of freedom, one of the principles of liberty for which on recent authority we are now fighting, that the judges are no respecters of persons and stand between the subject and any

attempted encroachment on his liberty by the executive, alert to see that any coercive action is justified in law.

Lord Atkin (1867–1944), *Liversidge* v. *Anderson*, [1942] A.C. 206 at 244

3. Liberty is the soul's right to breathe, and when it cannot take a long breath laws are girdled too tight. Without liberty man is a syncope.

Henry Ward Beecher (1813–87), *Proverbs from Plymouth pulpit*, 1887

4. There are multitudes of persons whose idea of liberty is the right to do what they please, instead of the right of doing that which is lawful and best.

Henry Ward Beecher (1813–87), ibid.

5. Abstract liberty, like other mere abstractions, is not to be found.

Edmund Burke (1729–97), *Speech on conciliation with America*, 22 March 1775

6. As we must give away some natural liberty, to enjoy civil advantages; so we must sacrifice some civil liberties, for the advantages to be derived from the communion and fellowship of a great empire.

Edmund Burke (1729–97), ibid.

7. A fig for those by the law protected!
Liberty's a glorious feast!
Courts for cowards were erected,

Churches built to please the priest.

Robert Burns (1759–96), *The jolly beggars*

8. A man's liberty of movement is regarded so highly by the law of England that it is not to be hindered or prevented except on the surest grounds.

Lord Denning M.R., *Ghani* v. *Jones*, [1970] 1 Q.B. 693 at 709

9. It is better to have too much freedom than too much control: but it is better still to strike the happy mean.

Lord Denning, 'The free press' in *The road to justice*, 1955, p. 87

10. Lean liberty is better than fat slavery.

Thomas Fuller (1654–1734), *Gnomologia*, 1732, no. 3,158

11. Extremism in the defence of liberty is no vice. And ... moderation in the pursuit of justice is no virtue.

Barry Goldwater, Speech, 16 July 1964

12. Liberty: 1. A password in universal use, and hence of no value. 2. The slogan of a party or sect that seeks to enslave some other party or sect.

Frank McKinney Hubbard (1868–1930), *The Roycroft dictionary*, 1923

13. Liberty 'tis plain consists in a power to do, or not to do; to do, or forbear doing as we *will*.

John Locke (1632–1704), *Essay*

concerning human understanding,
1690, bk II, ch. XXI, 56

14. The last end that can happen to any man, never comes too soon, if he falls in support of the law and liberty of his country: (for liberty is synonymous to law and government).

Lord Mansfield (1705–93), *R.* v. *Wilkes* (1770), 4 Burr. 2527 at 2563

15. All that makes existence valuable to any one, depends on the enforcement of restraints upon the actions of other people. Some rules of conduct, therefore, must be imposed, by law in the first place, and by opinion on many things which are not fit subjects for the operation of the law.

John Stuart Mill (1806–73), *On liberty*, 1859, ch. 1

16. Liberty is the right to do whatever the laws permit.

Charles de Secondat, Baron de Montesquieu (1689–1755), *The spirit of the laws*, 1748, bk XI, 3

17. To do what we will, is natural liberty: to do what we will, consistent with the interest of the community to which we belong, is civil liberty.

William Paley (1743–1805), *The principles of moral and political philosophy*, 1784, bk VI, ch. V

18. Let it be, let it pass. (*Laissez faire, laissez passer.*)

François Quesnay (1694–1774), attributed

19. All laws impinge on individual freedom.

W. Duncan Reekie, *The economics of advertising*, 1981, ch. 8, sec. 5, 'Legislation'

20. O liberty! O liberty! what crimes are committed in your name.

Madame Roland (1754–93), remark from the scaffold on seeing a Statue of Liberty

21. Man is born free, and everywhere he is in chains.

Jean Jacques Rousseau (1712–78), *The social contract*, 1762, bk I, ch. I

22. Liberty plucks justice by the nose.

William Shakespeare (1564–1616), *Measure for measure*, 1604–5, I. iii

23. If a nation could not prosper without the enjoyment of perfect liberty and perfect justice, there is not in the world a nation which could ever have prospered.

Adam Smith (1723–90), *Wealth of nations*, 1776, vol. II, bk IV, ch. IX

24. The Judge is intrusted with the liberties of the people, and his saying is the law.

Twisden J. (1602–83), *R.* v. *Wagstaffe* (1665), Sir T. Ray. 138

25. [Freedom is] a blessing, on which all the good and evil of life depends.

George Washington (1732–99), Letter to George Mason, 5 April 1769

26. To love both Power and Liberty is not very consistent.

    Richard Whately (1787–1863), *Thoughts and apothegms*, 1856, pt VI

27. Our political institutions ... are but the body of which liberty is the soul.

    Edwin P. Whipple (1819–86), *Character and characteristic men*, 1866, ch. XII, 'Washington and the principles of the revolution', p. 323

28. The shallow ... consider liberty a release from all law, from every constraint. The wise see in it, on the contrary, the potent Law of Laws.

    Walt Whitman (1819–91), 'Notes left over', *Democratic Vistas*, 1881

29. Free speech does not mean free speech; it means speech hedged in by all the laws against defamation, blasphemy, sedition and so forth; it means freedom governed by law.

    Lord Wright M.R. (1869–1964), *James* v. *Commonwealth of Australia*, [1936] A.C. 578 at 627

94. LIES

1. Liars are not believed even when they tell the truth.

    Aesop (fl. *c*.550 BC)

2. Tell a lie and find a truth.

    Francis Bacon (1561–1626), *The advancement of learning*, bk II, XXIII, 18

3. A lie always needs a truth for a handle to it. The worst lies are those whose blade is false, but whose handle is true.

    Henry Ward Beecher (1813–87), *Proverbs from Plymouth pulpit*, 1887

4. If you are a defendant, and tell lies, you are punished for it; if you are plaintiff, and will *not* tell lies, you lose your cause.

    Jeremy Bentham (1748–1832), *Truth v. Ashhurst; or, law as it is*, 1823

5. Liar, *n.* A lawyer with a roving commission.

    Ambrose Bierce (1842–1914?), *The devil's dictionary*, 1911

6. A man may tell a lie about the state of his own mind just as much as he can tell a lie about the state of the weather or about the state of his own digestion.

    Bowen L.J. (1835–94), *Angus* v. *Clifford*, (1891), 60 L.J. Eq. 443 at 455

7. Any fool can tell the truth but it requires a man of some sense to know how to lie well.

    Samuel Butler (1835–1902), *Notebooks*, ed. Festing Jones, ch. XIX

8. A lie begets a lie.

    Thomas Fuller (1654–1734), *Gnomologia*, 1732

9. One lie calls for many.

    Thomas Fuller (1654–1734), ibid., no. 3,766

10. Tell a lie, and find out the truth.

    Thomas Fuller (1654–1734), ibid., no. 4,324

11. Show me a liar, and I'll show you a thief.

    George Herbert (1593–1633), *Jacula prudentum*, 1651

12. Liar: ... An expert witness on the side of the Prosecution, or any witness called by the Defence.

    Frank McKinney Hubbard (1868–1930), *The Roycroft dictionary*, 1923

13. A good liar should have a good memory.

    James Kelly, *Scottish proverbs*, 1721, A, no. 323

14. A lie is a breach of promise: for whoever seriously addresses his discourse to another, tacitly promises to speak the truth, because he knows that the truth is expected.

    William Paley (1743–1805), *The principles of moral and political philosophy*, 1784, bk III, pt I, ch. XV

15. He will lie, sir, with such volubility that you would think truth were a fool.

    William Shakespeare (1564–1616), *All's well that ends well*, 1602–4, IV. iii

16. *Jacques*: Can you nominate in order now the degrees of the lie.
    Touchstone: ... The first, the Retort courteous; the second, the Quip modest; the third, the Reply churlish; the fourth, the Reproof valiant; the fifth, the Countercheck quarrelsome; the sixth, the Lie with circumstance; the seventh, the Lie direct. All these you may avoid but the lie direct; and you may avoid that too with an *If*. I knew when seven justices could not take up a quarrel; but when the parties were met themselves, one of them thought but of an *If*, as *If you said so, then I said so*; and they shook hands, and swore brothers. Your *If* is the only peace-maker: — much virtue in *If*.

    William Shakespeare (1564–1616), *As you like it*, 1596–1600, V. iv

17. Will poor folks lie,
    That have afflictions on them,
    knowing 'tis
    A punishment or trial? Yes, no
    wonder,
    When rich ones scarce tell true: to
    lapse in fulness
    Is sorer than to lie for need; and
    falsehood
    Is worse in kings than beggars.

    William Shakespeare (1564–1616), *Cymbeline*, 1609–10, III. vi

18. 'Tis as easy as lying.

    William Shakespeare (1564–1616), *Hamlet*, 1599–1600, III. ii

19. How this world is given to lying!

    William Shakespeare (1564–1616), *Henry IV pt I*, 1597–8, V. iv

20. Tells a lie and swears it.

    William Shakespeare (1564–1616), *Much ado about nothing*, 1598–9, IV. i

21. With lies well steel'd with weighty arguments.

    William Shakespeare (1564–1616), *Richard III*, 1592–3, I. i

22. One of the most striking differences between a cat and a lie is that a cat has only nine lives.

    Mark Twain (1835–1910), 'Pudd'nhead Wilson's calendar', *Pudd'nhead Wilson*, 1894, ch. 7

23. What is a fine lie? Simply that which is its own evidence.

    Oscar Wilde (1854–1900), *The decay of lying*

95. LITIGATION

1. Were women permitted to plead in courts of judicature, I am persuaded they would carry the eloquence of the bar to greater heights than it has yet arrived at. If any one doubt this, let him but be present at those debates which frequently arise among the ladies of the British fishery.

   Joseph Addison (1672–1719), *Spectator*, no. 247, 13 December 1711

2. May you have a lawsuit in which you know you are in the right.

   Anonymous — gypsy curse, quoted in W.H. Auden and L. Kronenberger, *The Faber book of aphorisms*

3. A law-suit is a suit for life.

   John Arbuthnot (1667–1735), *Law is a bottomless pit*, 1712, pt I, ch. XII

4. Litigation, *n*. A machine which you go into as a pig and come out of as a sausage.

   Ambrose Bierce (1842–1914?), *The devil's dictionary*, 1911

5. Litigant, *n*. A person about to give up his skin for the hope of retaining his bones.

   Ambrose Bierce (1842–1914?), ibid.

6. Englishmen may have been law-abiding, but they have not been unlitigious.

   Brett L.J. (1815–99), *Martin* v. *Mackonochie* (1879), 4 Q.B.D. 697 at 749

7. Lopping off needless litigation, by measures calculated to lessen the expense of procedure in all its branches, would greatly increase the number of lawsuits — real suits, which ought to be encouraged, as necessary to justice, but which at present are kept out of Court, by the double tax of cost and delay.

   Henry Peter Brougham (1778–1868), House of Commons, 7 February 1828

8. A law-suit is like an ill-managed dispute, in which the first object is soon out of sight, and the parties end upon a matter wholly foreign to that on which they began.

   Edmund Burke (1729–97), *A vindication of natural society*, 1756

9. The law of England is the greatest grievance of the nation, very expensive and dilatory: there is no

end to suits, especially when they are brought into chancery.

Gilbert Burnet (1643–1715), *History of his own times*, 1724

10. But what his common sense came
    short,
    He eked out wi' law, man.

Robert Burns (1759–96), *Extempore in the Court of Session*

11. We may justly tax our wrangling lawyers, they do *consenescere in litibus* [grow old in lawsuits], are so litigious and busy here on earth, that I think they will plead their clients' causes hereafter, some of them in hell.

Robert Burton (1577–1640), *Anatomy of melancholy*, 'Democritus to the reader'

12. So he that goes to law, as the proverb is, holds a wolf by the ears, or, as a sheep in a storm runs for shelter to a briar.

Robert Burton (1577–1640), ibid.

13. There's only one motto I know of that's any good. 'Never go to law.'

Henry Cecil, *Brothers in law*, 1955, ch. 5

14. It is ignorance of the law rather than knowledge of it that leads to litigation.

Cicero (106–43 BC), *De legibus*, bk I, ch. VI

15. *The benefit of going to law*
    Two beggars travelling along,
        One blind, the other lame,
    Pick'd up an oyster on the way
        To which they both lay
        claim:

The matter rose so high, that they
    Resolv'd to go to law,
As often richer fools have done,
    Who quarrel for a straw.
A lawyer took it straight in hand,
    Who knew his business was,
To mind nor one nor t'other side,
    But make the best o' th'
    cause;
As always in the law's the case
    So he his judgement gave,
And lawyer-like he thus resolv'd
    What each of them should
    have
*Blind plaintiff, lame defendant,
    share
The friendly law's impartial care,
A shell for him, a shell for thee,
The middle is the lawyer's fee.*

Benjamin Franklin (1706–90), *Poor Richard's almanac*, 1733. See also 95.32 and 95.33

16. A petitioner at court that spares his purse, angles without a bait.

Thomas Fuller (1654–1734), *Gnomologia*, 1732, no. 347

17. An indifferent agreement, is better than carrying a cause at law.

Thomas Fuller (1654–1734); ibid., no. 637

18. Fools and obstinate men make lawyers rich.

Thomas Fuller (1654–1734), ibid., no. 1,565

19. He that would thrive by law, must see his enemy's counsel as well as his own.

Thomas Fuller (1654–1734), ibid., no. 2,370

20. Sue a beggar, and catch a louse.

    Thomas Fuller (1654–1734), ibid., no. 4,285

21. I demand, said Dennis, I demand an unsuit.

    Thomas Chandler Haliburton (1786–1865), *The Clockmaker*, 4th edn. 1838, ch. V, 'Justice Pettifog'

22. Avoid litigation. You never know where you are.

    Sir A.P. Herbert (1890–1971), *Rex v. Bopple: avoid litigation*, 1948

23. Lawsuits consume time and money, and rest and friends.

    George Herbert (1593–1633), *Jacula prudentum*, 1651

24. The worst of the law is, that one suit breeds twenty.

    George Herbert (1593–1633), ibid.

25. Litigation: A form of hell whereby money is transferred from the pockets of the proletariat to that of lawyers.

    Frank McKinney Hubbard (1868–1930), *The Roycroft dictionary*, 1923

26. It is wrong to stir up law-suits; but when once it is certain that a lawsuit is to go on, there is nothing wrong in a lawyer's endeavouring that he shall have the benefit, rather than another.

    Samuel Johnson (1709–84), *Boswell's life*, 16 March 1776

27. There has hardly been a court case in which the litigation was not started by a woman.

    Juvenal (fl. AD 1st–2nd cent.), *Satires*, VI

28. It is not completely out of the question that a person in high favour could lose a lawsuit.

    La Bruyère Jean De (1645–96), *Characters*, 1688, 'Of certain customs'

29. 'Lawsuit mania' ... a continual craving to go to law against others, while considering themselves the injured party.

    Cesare Lombroso (1836–1909), *The man of genius*, 1891, pt III, ch. 3

30. Your lawsuit has been through three courts, has lasted twenty years, and is wearing you out. Idiot! does anyone carry on a lawsuit for twenty years if he could have given up? [The courts were the Old Roman Court, and those of Julius Caesar and Augustus.]

    Martial (AD c.40–c.104), *Epigrams*, bk VII, epig. LXV

31. Miscarriage of justice — we lost the case.

    Keith Miles, *The finest swordsman in all France*, 1984

32. Once (says an author, where, I
    need not say)
    Two travellers found an oyster in
    their way;
    Both fierce, both hungry, the dis-
    pute grew strong,
    While, scale in hand, Dame Justice
    past along.

Before her each with clamour
    pleads the laws,
Explained the matter, and would
    win the cause;
Dame Justice, weighing long the
    doubtful right,
Takes, opens, swallows it, before
    their sight.
The cause of strife removed so
    rarely well,
There, take (says Justice) take ye
    each a shell.
We thrive at Westminster on fools
    like you,
'Twas a fat oyster — live in peace
    — adieu.

Alexander Pope (1688–1744),
'Verbatim from Boileau', *The
publick register*, 10 January 1741.
See also 95.15 and 95.33

33. Blind plaintiff, lame defendent
        share
    The friendly law's impartial care,
    A shell for him a shell for thee
    The middle is the lawyer's fee.

    Matthew Prior (1664–1721), *The
    lame and the blind disputing the
    right to an oyster found; the lawyer
    decides the controversy*, 1720

34. There is something sickening in
    seeing poor devils drawn into great
    expense about trifles by interested
    attorneys. But too cheap an access
    to litigation has its evils on the
    other hand, for the proneness of
    the lower classes to gratify spite
    and revenge in this way would be a
    dreadful evil were they able to
    endure the expense.

    Sir Walter Scott (1771–1832),
    Journal, 12 December 1825

35. The silence often of pure inno-
    cence

Persuades, when speaking fails.

William   Shakespeare   (1564–
1616), *The winter's tale*, 1610–11,
II. ii

36. You never, but never, go to liti-
    gation if there is another way out
    ... Litigation only makes lawyers
    fat.

    Wilbur Smith, *Hungry as the sea*,
    1979, p. 214

37. An artful legislature will take away
    some of the causes of litigation.

    Noah Webster (1758–1843), *A
    collection of essays*, no. VII, 1787,
    p. 117

96. MAGNA CARTA

1. Magna Carta is such a fellow that
   he will have no sovereign.

   Sir Edward Coke (1552–1634),
   House of Commons, 17 May 1628

2. Good is a good doctor, but Bad is
   sometimes   better.   'Tis   the
   oppression   of   William   the
   Norman, savage forest-laws, and
   crushing despotism, that made
   possible the inspirations of *Magna
   Charta* under John.

   Ralph Waldo Emerson (1803–
   82), *The conduct of life*, 1860,
   'Consideration by the way'

97. MARRIAGE

1. Marriage is bound to be a failure if
   a woman can only have one husband at a time.

   Anonymous

2. The common law does not regulate the form of agreements between spouses. Their promises are not sealed with seals and sealing wax. The consideration that really obtains for them is that natural love and affection which counts for so little in these cold Courts.

   Atkin L.J. (1867–1944), *Balfour* v. *Balfour*, [1919] 2 K.B. 571 at 579.

3. Marriage in my experience was a ring drawn around a man's life by the radius of his natural limitations. On marrying him you went inside and stayed there, forswearing all limitations of your own.

   Mary Austin (1868–1934), *A woman of genius*, 1912, bk IV, ch. IX

4. Marriage, considered as a contract, has drawn women from the hardest and most humiliating servitude; it has distributed the mass of the community into distinct families; it has created a domestic Magistracy.

   Jeremy Bentham (1748–1832), *Principles of the civil code*, pt III, ch. V

5. Marriage, *n.* The state or condition of a community consisting of a master, a mistress and two slaves, making in all, two.

   Ambrose Bierce (1842–1914?), *The devil's dictionary*, 1911

6. By marriage, the husband and wife are one person in law: that is, the very being or legal existence of the woman is suspended during the marriage, or at least is incorporated and consolidated into that of the husband: under whose wing, protection, and cover, she performs every thing.

   Sir William Blackstone (1723–80), *Commentaries on the laws of England*, 15th edn, 1809, vol. 1, p. 442

7. Even in present times, when there was a movement by women for equality with men, a sensible wife, certainly in a united family, did not generally make the major decisions. Most wives sensibly left such decisions to their husbands. A solicitor should not take instruction from a wife when a husband was also available.

   Caulfield J., *Morris* v. *Duke-Cohan & Co.*, *The Times*, 21 November 1975

8. Marriage is a duel to the death, which no man of honour should decline.

   G.K. Chesterton (1874–1936), *Manalive*, 1912, ch. IV

9. The two extremes appear like man
   and wife,
   Coupled together for the sake of
   strife.

   Charles Churchill (1731–64), *The rosciad*, 1750, 1. 1,005

10. Sir Sampson is enraged, and talks desperately of committing matrimony himself.

    William Congreve (1670–1729), *Love for love*, 1695, IV. iii

11. *Sharper*:Thus grief still treads
    upon the heels of pleasure;
    Married in haste, we may
    repent at leisure.

Setter: Some by experience find
those words misplaced
At leisure married, they
repent in haste.

William Congreve (1670–1729),
The old bachelor, 1693, V. iii

12. 'The law supposes that your wife
acts under your direction.'
'If the law supposes that,' said Mr.
Bumble, squeezing his hat empha-
tically in both hands, 'the law is a
ass — a idiot. If that's the eye of
the law, the law is a bachelor; and
the worst I wish the law is, that his
eye may be opened by experience
— by experience.'

Charles Dickens (1812–70),
Oliver Twist, 1838, ch. LI

13. Matrimony is a great 'limitation of
action'.

Thomas Chancellor Haliburton
(1786–1865), *The letter bag of the
Great Western*, 1840, no. X,
'Letter from a lawyer's clerk'

14. The contract of marriage is a very
simple one, which does not require
a high degree of intelligence to
comprehend.

Sir J. Hannen (1821–94),
Durham v. *Durham* (1885), 10
P.D. 80 at 82

15. Wedding is destiny, and hanging
likewise.

John Heywood (1506–65),
Proverbs, 1546, pt I, ch. III

16. When folkes will needes wed,
Moe thinges belong then foure
bare legges in a bed.

John Heywood (1506–65), ibid.,
ch. VIII

17. Marriage: ... A legal or religious
ceremony by which two persons of
the opposite sex solemnly agree to
harass and spy on each other for
ninety-nine years, or until death do
them join.

Frank McKinney Hubbard (1868–
1930), *The Roycroft dictionary*,
1923

18. Men are always doomed to be
duped ... They are always wooing
goddesses, and marrying mere
mortals.

Washington Irving (1783–1859),
Bracebridge Hall, 1822

19. [Marriage is] like signing a 356-
page contract without knowing
what's in it.

Mick Jagger, *Observer*, 'Sayings of
the week', 20 January 1985

20. A gentleman who had been very
unhappy in marriage, married
immediately after his wife died:
Johnson said, it was the triumph of
hope over experience.

Samuel Johnson (1709–84),
Boswell's life of Johnson, 1770

21. [Marriage is] the most valuable
consideration imaginable.

Kay L.J. (1822–97), *A.G.* v.
Jacobs Smith, [1895] 2 Q.B. 341
at 354

22. He that marries a maiden, marries
a pokeful of pleasure,
He that marries a widow, marries a
pokeful of pleas sure.
[Pleas = lawsuits]

James Kelly, *Scottish proverbs*,
1721, H, nos. 298 and 299

23. By the old laws of England, the husband was called the *lord* of the wife; he was literally regarded as her sovereign, inasmuch that the murder of a man by his wife was called treason (*petty* as distinguished from *high* treason).

    John Stuart Mill (1806–73), *The subjection of women*, 1869, ch. II

24. 'Twas a happy marriage betwixt a blind wife and a deaf husband.

    Michel de Montaigne (1533–92), *Essays*, bk III, 1595, 'Of experience', ch. V

25. Matrimony and murder both carry a mandatory life sentence.

    John Mortimer, *Rumpole for the defence*, 1981, 'Rumpole and the boat people'

26. I ought now to tell the unwary.
    That into the noose they'll be led,
    By giving a promise to marry,
    And acting as if they were wed.
    But if, when the promise you're plighting,
    To keep it you think you'd be loath, —
    Just see that it isn't in writing,
    And then it must come to your oath.

    Lord Charles Neaves (1800–76), *Songs and verses*, 1868, 'The tourist's matrimonial guide'

27. In olden times sacrifices were made at the altar — a custom which is still continued.

    Helen Rowland (1876–1950), quoted in B. House, *From Eve on*

28. Marriage is nothing but a civil contract.

    John Selden (1584–1654), *Tabletalk*, 1689, 'Marriage'

29. I do marry that I may repent.

    William Shakespeare (1564–1616), *All's well that ends well*, 1602–4, I. iii

30. Quoth she, before you tumbled me,
    You promis'd me to wed.

    William Shakespeare (1564–1616), *Hamlet*, 1599–1600, IV. v

31. Marriage is a matter of more worth Than to be dealt with in by attorneyship.

    William Shakespeare (1564–1616), *Henry VI, Pt I*, 1589–90, V. v

32. The one point on which all women are in furious secret rebellion against the existing law is the saddling of the right to a child with the obligation to become the servant of a man.

    George Bernard Shaw (1856–1950), *Getting married*, 1908, Preface

33. Marriage resembles a pair of shears, so joined that they cannot be separated; often moving in opposite directions, yet always punishing anyone who comes between them.

    Sydney Smith (1771–1845), W. Jerrold, *Bon-mots of Sydney Smith and R. Brinsley Sheridan*, p. 49

34. The reason why so few marriages are happy, is, because young ladies spend their time in making *nets*, and not in making *cages*.

    Jonathan Swift (1667–1745), *Thoughts on various subjects*, 1711

35. Marriage is a bribe to make a housekeeper think she's a householder.

    Thornton Wilder (1897–1975), *The matchmaker*, 1954, I

36. Man and wife are one — but the man is the one.

    Glanville Williams, *The legal unity of husband and wife* (1947), 10 M.L.R. 16 at 17

37. The laws respecting woman ... make an absurd unit of a man and his wife; and then, by the easy transition of only considering him as responsible, she is reduced to a mere cipher.

    Mary Wollstonecraft (1759–97), *A vindication of the rights of woman*, 1792, ch. IX

38. I may be told that a number of women are not slaves in the marriage state. True, but then they become tyrants; for it is not rational freedom, but a lawless kind of power, resembling the authority exercised by the favourites of absolute monarchs.

    Mary Wollstonecraft (1759–97), ibid., ch. XI

98. MERCY

1. A miscarriage of mercy is as bad as a miscarriage of justice.

   Anonymous

2. Mercy, *n.* An attribute beloved of detected offenders.

   Ambrose Bierce (1842–1914?), *The devil's dictionary*, 1911

3. Reason to rule, but mercy to forgive:
   The first is law, the last prerogative.

   John Dryden (1631–1700), *The hind and the panther*, 1687, pt I

4. Thwackum was for doing justice, and leaving mercy to heaven.

   Henry Fielding (1707–54), *Tom Jones*, 1749, bk III, ch. 10

5. All are not hanged that are condemned.

   Thomas Fuller (1654–1734), *Gnomologia*, 1732, no. 501

6. Cruelty deserves no mercy.

   Thomas Fuller (1654–1734), ibid., no. 1,212

7. A spirit of mercy breathes through the laws of England.

   Oliver Goldsmith (1728–74), *Citizen of the world*, 1762, letter LXXX

8. Mercy is not what every criminal is entitled to. What he is entitled to is justice.

   Lord Hailsham, *Observer*, 'Sayings of the week', 14 February 1975

9.　　　　　Yet I shall temper so Justice with mercy.

John Milton (1608–74), *Paradise lost*, bk X, 1. 77

10. Save a thief from the gallows, and he'll cut your throat.

Proverb, quoted in Tobias Smollett, *The expedition of Humphry Clinker*, 1771, vol. I

11. Mercy has freedom and sentences not in accordance with the letter of the law but in accordance with what is fair.

Seneca (4 BC–AD 65), *De clementia*, bk II, ch. III

12. Now, trust me, were it not against our laws,
Against my crown, my oath, my dignity,
Which princes, would they, may not disannul,
My soul should sue as advocate for thee.

William Shakespeare (1564–1616), *The comedy of errors*, 1592–3, I. i

13. There is no more mercy in him than there is milk in a male tiger.

William Shakespeare (1564–1616), *Coriolanus*, 1607–8, V. iv

14. Whereto serves mercy
But to confront the visage of the offence?

William Shakespeare (1564–1616), *Hamlet*, 1599–1600, III. iii

15. They have dealt with me like thieves of mercy.

William Shakespeare (1564–1616), ibid., IV. vi

16. The gates of mercy shall be all shut up.

William Shakespeare (1564–1616), *Henry V*, 1598–9, III. ii

17. And what makes robbers bold but too much lenity?

William Shakespeare (1564–1616), *Henry VI pt III*, 1590–1, II. vi

18. My pity hath been balm to heal their wounds,
My mildness hath allay'd their swelling griefs,
My mercy dried their water-flowing tears.

William Shakespeare (1564–1616), ibid., IV. viii

19. There's no hop'd-for mercy with the brothers,
More than with ruthless waves, with sands, and rocks.

William Shakespeare (1564–1616), ibid., V. iv

20. If I talk to him, with his innocent prate
He will awake my mercy, which lies dead.

William Shakespeare (1564–1616), *King John*, 1596–7, IV. i

21. Now mercy goes to kill,
And shooting well is then accounted ill.

William Shakespeare (1564–1616), *Love's labour's lost*, 1594–5, IV. i

22. Mercy is not itself, that oft looks so;

Pardon is still the nurse of second
woe.

William Shakespeare (1564–1616), *Measure for measure*, 1604–5, II. i

23. No ceremony that to great ones
'longs,
Not the king's crown, nor the
deputed sword,
The marshall's truncheon, nor the
judge's robe,
Become them with one half so
good a grace
As mercy does.

William Shakespeare (1564–1616), ibid., II. ii

24. Ignominy in ransom and free pardon
Are of two houses; lawful mercy is
Nothing akin to foul redemption.

William Shakespeare (1564–1616), ibid., II. iv

25. There is a devilish mercy in the
judge,
If you'll implore it, that will free
your life,
But fetter you till death.

William Shakespeare (1564–1616), ibid., III. i

26. The quality of mercy is not strain'd
It droppeth as the gentle rain from
heaven
Upon the place beneath: it is twice
bless'd;
It blesseth him that gives and him
that takes:
'Tis mightiest in the mightiest; it
becomes
The throned monarch better than
his crown.

William Shakespeare (1564–1616), *The merchant of Venice*, 1596–7, IV. i

27. Mercy seasons justice.

William Shakespeare (1564–1616), ibid.

28. Nothing emboldens sin so much as
mercy.

William Shakespeare (1564–1616), *Timon of Athens*, 1607–8, III. v

99. MINISTER

1. Public bodies and Ministers must
be compelled to observe the law;
and it is essential that bureaucracy
should be kept in its place.

Danckwerts L.J. (1888–1978), *Bradbury* v. *Enfield London Borough Council*, [1967] 1 W.L.R. 1311 at 1325

100. MONEY

1. If you imposed the decimal
coinage in this country you would
have a revolution within a week.

Herbert Henry Asquith (1852–1928), *Imperial Conference 1911*, Cd 5745, pp. 165–70; quoted in N.E.A. Moore, *The decimalisation of Britain's currency*

2. Money speaks sense in a language
all nations understand.

Aphra Behn (1640–89), *The rover*, III. i

3. Money ... [is] a pledge.

John Bellers (1654–1725), quoted in A. Ruth Fry, *Writings*, 1935, p. 39

4. The love of money is the root of all evil.

   Bible, Authorized Version, 1 Timothy, 6: 10

5. It has been said that the love of money is the root of all evil. The want of money is so quite as truly.

   Samuel Butler (1835–1902), *Erewhon* 1872, ch. 10

6. Money is the fruit of evil as often as the root of it.

   Henry Fielding (1707–54), quoted in Esar and Bentley, *The treasury of humorous quotations*

7. Bad money drives out good money. ['Gresham's law']

   Sir Thomas Gresham (1519–79). The phrase occurs in a Royal Proclamation of 1560, when Gresham was a leading government adviser.

8. Put not your trust in money, but put your money in trust.

   Oliver Wendell Holmes (1809–94), *The autocrat of the breakfast table*, 1858, II

9. One cannot help regretting that where money is concerned it is so much the rule to overlook moral obligations.

   Malins V.C. (1805–82), *Ellis* v. *Houston* (1878), 10 Ch.D 236 at 240

10. The counterfeit money is never lost.

    Greek proverb, trans. George Karamelios

11. No man will take counsel, but every man will take money: therefore money is better than counsel.

    Jonathan Swift (1667–1745), *Thoughts on various subjects*, 1706

101. MORALITY

1. It's only if it has a moral basis that the law can command respect.

   Lord Denning, *Sunday Times*, 1 August 1982

2. If the laws are good, morals are good; if the laws are bad, morals are bad; if laws, good or bad, are not observed at all, the worst condition of a society, then there is no morality at all.

   Denis Diderot (1713–84), *Supplement to Bougainville's 'Voyage'*, IV

3. The bottom seems to have dropped out of morality.

   Lord Hailsham, *Observer*, 'Sayings of the week', 15 December 1985

4. Of what efficacy are empty laws, without morals to enforce them?

   Horace (65–8 BC), *Odes*, trans. C. Smart, bk III, ode XXIV

5. A state with defective laws will have defective morals.

   Seneca (4 BC–AD 65), *Ad Lucilium epistulae morales*, epis. XCIV, 39

6. Moral feeling is a force — a force by which men's actions are restrained within certain prescribed bounds; and no legislative

mechanism can increase its results one iota.

Herbert Spencer (1820–1903), *Social statics*, 1870, pt III, ch. XXI, sec. 7

7. Of all abuses of law, the greatest and most pernicious, because to it all the rest may generally be referred, is the setting up of the laws as a system of morality, and making them the guide of our conscience, which a law never can be.

Richard Whately (1787–1863), *Thoughts and apothegms*, 1856, pt VI

102. MOTIVE

1. In any case of injustice it makes a great difference whether the wrong is done on impulse, or whether it is committed deliberately and with premeditation; for offences committed on impulse are less culpable than those committed by design and with malice.

Cicero (106–43 BC), *De officiis*, bk I, ch. VIII

2. It is not essential, as the deceived husband said, to prove a motive where the facts are plain.

A.P. Herbert (1890–1971), *More uncommon law*, 1982, 'Rex v. Bopple, avoid litigation'

3. I am satisfied in nature,
   Whose motive, in this case, should
                          stir me most
   To my revenge.

William Shakespeare (1564–1616), *Hamlet*, 1599–1600), V. ii

4. Whenever a man does a thoroughly stupid thing, it is always from the noblest motives.

Oscar Wilde (1854–1900), *The picture of Dorian Gray*, 1891, ch. VI

103. MOTOR VEHICLES

1. We must not allow ourselves to be warped by any prejudice against motor cars, and so to strain the law against them.

Lord Alverstone C.J. (1842–1915), *Bastable* v. *Little*, [1907] 1 K.B. 59 at 62

2. In some people's views, to kill someone with a motor-car happens to be a 'respectable' criminal offence.

Lord Hutchinson, House of Lords, 9 July 1984

3. It has often been said that more legal ingenuity has been devoted to circumventing the avowed purpose of the breathalyser legislation ... than any other legislation, save possibly the Finance Acts.

Lord Roskill, *Morris* v. *Beardmore*, [1980] 3 W.L.R. 283 at 297

104. MURDER

1. Thou shalt not kill.

Bible, Authorized Version, Exodus, 20: 13

2. Homicide, *n.* The slaying of one human being by another. There are four kinds of homicide: felonious,

excusable, justifiable and praise-worthy, but it makes no great difference to the person slain whether he fell by one kind or another — the classification is for the advantage of the lawyers.

Ambrose Bierce (1842–1914?), *The devil's dictionary*, 1911

3. The only difficulty is committing a murder without committing oneself as a murderer.

G.K. Chesterton (1874–1936), *The scandal of Father Brown*, 1935, 'The quick one'

4. Society is at the mercy of a murderer without a motive.

G.K.Chesterton (1874–1936), quoted in R. Mark, *In the office of constable*, 1978, p. 176

5. Thou shalt not kill; but needst not strive
Officiously to keep alive.

Arthur Hugh Clough (1819–61), *The latest decalogue*, 1862

6. It is absolutely barbarous to murder a sick person, who is usually quite unable to bear it.

Thomas De Quincey (1785–1859), *On murder, considered as one of the fine arts*, 1827

7. Murder may pass unpunished for a time,
But tardy justice will o'ertake the crime.

John Dryden (1631–1700), *The cock and the fox*, 1700

8. Murder in the murderer is no such ruinous thought as poets and romancers will have it.

Ralph Waldo Emerson (1803–82), *Essays, second series*, 1844, 'Experience'

9. Murder is as fashionable a crime as a man can be guilty of.

John Gay (1685–1732), *The beggar's opera*, 1728, I. iv

10. There are only about 20 murders a year in London and not all are serious — some are just husbands killing their wives.

Commander G.H. Hatherill of Scotland Yard, *Observer*, 'Sayings of the week', 21 February 1954

11. By the old laws of England, the husband was called the *lord* of the wife; he was literally regarded as her sovereign, inasmuch that the murder of a man by his wife was called treason (*petty* as distinguished from *high* treason).

John Stuart Mill (1806–73), *The subjection of women*, 1869, ch. II

12. For murder, though it have no tongue, will speak
With most miraculous organ.

William Shakespeare (1564–1616), *Hamlet*, 1599–1600, II. ii

13. Thou shalt have a license to kill.

William Shakespeare (1564–1616), *Henry IV pt II*, 1597–8, IV. iii

14. Now does he feel
His secret murders sticking on his hands.

William Shakespeare (1564–1616), *Macbeth*, 1605, V. ii

15. Truth will come to light; murder cannot be hid long.

William Shakespeare (1564–1616), *The merchant of Venice*, 1596–7, II. ii

16. Murder's as near to lust as flame to smoke.

William Shakespeare (1564–1616), *Pericles*, 1608–9, I. i

17. Bloody homicide.

William Shakespeare (1564–1616), *Richard III*, 1592–3, V. ii

18. Mercy but murders, pardoning those that kill.

William Shakespeare (1564–1616), *Romeo and Juliet*, 1595–6, III. i

19. The spirit of murder works in the very means of life.

Alfred, Lord Tennyson (1809–92), *Maud*, 1855, pt I, sec. I, st. X

105. NATIONALISATION

1. If you want to show that crime doesn't pay, put it in the hands of the government.

Anonymous, quoted in M.Z. Hepker, *A modern approach to tax law*, 1975, p. 7

2. There could be no greater triumph of hope over experience than to advocate more nationalisation. And I do not see how any free society can make it a crime for consenting adults to exchange money for teaching or medical care, however distasteful some of the social consequences may be.

Bryan Magee, 'Why I quit the Labour Party', *Sunday Times*, 24 January 1982

106. NEIGHBOURS

1. Neighbour, *n.* One whom we are commanded to love as ourselves, and who does all he knows how to make us disobedient.

Ambrose Bierce (1842–1914?). *The devil's dictionary*, 1911

2. A good lawyer is a bad neighbour.

Benjamin Franklin (1706–90), *Poor Richard's almanac*, 1737

3. A quarrelsome man has no good neighbours.

Benjamin Franklin (1706–90), ibid., 1746

4. An unpeacable man hath no neighbour.

Thomas Fuller (1654–1734), *Gnomologia*, 1732, no. 662

5. You must ask your neighbours, if you shall live in peace.

Thomas Fuller (1654–1734), ibid., no. 5,961

6. Love your neighbour, yet pull not down your hedge.

George Herbert (1593–1633), *Jacula prudentum*, 1651

7. No man can live longer in peace than his neighbour pleases.

James Kelly, *Scottish proverbs*, 1721, N, no. 15

8. From the poetry of Lord Byron they drew a system of ethics, compounded of misanthropy and voluptuousness, a system in which the two great commandments were, to hate your neighbour, and to love your neighbour's wife.

   Lord Macaulay (1800–59), *Moore's life of Lord Byron*, June 1831

9. Love your neighbours, but don't pull down the fence.

   Chinese proverb

10. I must live amongst my neighbours.

    William Shakespeare (1564–1616), *Henry IV pt II*, 1597–8, II. iv

107. OATH

1. Oath, *n.* In law, a solemn appeal to the Deity, made binding upon the conscience by a penalty for perjury.

   Ambrose Bierce (1842–1914?), *The devil's dictionary*, 1911

2. It is ill to make an unlawful oath, but worse to keep it.

   James Kelly, Scottish proverbs, 1721, I, no. 360

3. The oath of a lover is no stronger than the word of a tapster.

   William Shakespeare (1564–1616), *As you like it*, 1596–1600, III. iv

4. Weigh oath with oath and you will nothing weigh:
   Your vows to her and me, put in two scales,
   Will even weigh; and both as light as tales.

   William Shakespeare (1564–1616), *A midsummer night's dream*, 1596, III. ii

5. You are not oathable.

   William Shakespeare (1564–1616), *Timon of Athens*, 1607–8, IV. iii

108. OFFICIAL SECRETS ACT

1. While the Official Secrets Act is used as it is in this country [UK], bungling and incompetence of all kinds can flourish undetected and the taxpayer will pay dearly for this.

   Leslie Chapman, *Your disobedient servant*, 1978, ch. 18, 'The Official Secrets Act'

2. The Official Secrets Act is not to protect secrets but to protect officials.

   Jonathan Lynn and **Antony Jay**, *Yes minister*, 1981, ch. 7

3. I was born in the year which saw the enactment of the Official Secrets Act. I hope to live long enough to see the death of my contemporary.

   Lord Scarman, *Observer*, 'Sayings of the week', 2 December 1984

109. PARDONS

1. Amnesty is an act by which rulers must often pardon the injustices

they have committed.

Anonymous: graffiti, Sorbonne, 1968, quoted in R. Reisner and L. Wechsler, *Encyclopaedia of graffiti*

2. A general law offering pardon and reward to the criminal who informed against his accomplices, would be an invitation to the commission of all sorts of crimes.

Jeremy Bentham (1748–1832), *Rationale of reward,* 1825, bk I, ch. XIV

3. Pardon, *v.* To remit a penalty and restore to a life of crime. To add to the lure of crime the temptation of ingratitude.

Ambrose Bierce (1842–1914?), *The devil's dictionary,* 1911

4. When by a pardon'd murderer
   blood is spilt
   The judge that pardon'd, hath the
   greatest guilt.

Sir Thomas Denham (1615–68). *Of justice,* 1667

5. Hopes of pardon mend not, but encourage criminals.

Thomas Fuller (1654–1734), *Gnomologia,* 1732, no. 2,548

6. Pardoning the bad is injuring the good.

Thomas Fuller (1654–1734), ibid., no. 3,842

7. It is as cruel to pardon all as to pardon none.

Seneca (4 BC–AD 65), *De clementia,* bk I, ch. II

8. By the merit of vile gold, dross,
   dust,

Purchase corrupted pardon of a
man,
Who in that sale sells pardon from
himself.

William Shakespeare (1564–1616), *King John,* 1596–7, III. i

9. Mercy is not itself, that oft looks
   so;
   Pardon is still the nurse of second
   woe.

William Shakespeare (1564–1616), *Measure for measure,* 1604–5, II. i

10. This is his pardon; purchas'd by
    such sin,
    For which the pardoner himself is
    in.

William Shakespeare (1564–1616), ibid., IV. ii

11. Do what you will, to you it doth
    belong
    Yourself to pardon for self-doing
    crime.

William Shakespeare (1564–1616), *Sonnets,* LVIII

110. PARLIAMENT

1. That the pretended power of suspending of laws, or the execution of laws, by regal authority, without the consent of Parliament is illegal.

Anonymous, English Bill of Rights, 1 December 1689, 1 & 2 William & Mary, sess. 2 c.2.

2. The House of Lords is like Heaven. Everyone wants to get there sometime but not just yet.

Anonymous, quoted by Lord Denning, *The family story,* p. 184

3. *Queen Elizabeth*: Now, Mr. Speaker, what hath passed in the Lower House?
Mr Popham: If it please your Majesty, seven weeks.

Francis Bacon (1561–1626), *Apothegms*, 1624

4. A Parliament is nothing less than a big meeting of more or less idle people.

Walter Bagehot (1826–77), *English constitution*, 1867, ch. V

5. Parliamentary government is being asked to solve the problem which so far it has failed to solve: that is how to reconcile parliamentary popularity with sound economic planning.

Aneurin Bevan (1897–1960), quoted by Denis Healey, *The Times*, 17 April 1975

6. The theory of the English parliamentary system is fascinating for amateurs who know neither its historical evolution nor its prosaic practical operation.

Wilfred E. Binkley, *President and Congress*, 3rd edn, 1962, ch. XVII

7. England is the mother of Parliaments.

John Bright (1811–89), Speech, Birmingham, 18 January 1865

8. We have a maxim in the House of Commons and written on the walls of our House, that the old ways are the safest and surest ways.

Sir Edward Coke, (1552–1634), Speech, 8 May 1628

9. People say that moving the law forward should be left to Parliament, and not the judges. Of course, when you look at some of the judges they may be right.

Lord Denning, *Sunday Times*, 1 August 1982

10. The House of Lords is a model of how to care for the elderly.

Frank Field, *Observer*, 'Sayings of the week', 24 May 1981

11. When I am sitting [on the Woolsack in the House of Lords] I amuse myself by saying 'Bollocks!' *sotto voce* to the bishops.

Lord Hailsham, *Sunday Times*, 25 August 1985

12. I often think it is a pity that God did not have a committee stage before he drafted the Ten Commandments.

Sir Alan Herbert (1890–1971), quoted in *Pass the port again*, 1981, p. 172

13. The only majority that matters in Britain is the majority in the House of Commons.

Michael Heseltine, *Observer*, 'Sayings of the week', 6 November 1983

14. No new right in the law, fully-fledged with all the appropriate safeguards, can spring from the head of a judge deciding a particular case: only Parliament can create such a right.

Megarry V.C., *Malone v. Metropolitan Police Commissioner*, [1979] 2 W.L.R. 700 at 725–6

15. Immortal power is not a human

right, and therefore cannot be a right of Parliament. The Parliament of 1688 might as well have passed an act to have authorized themselves to live forever, as to make their authority live for ever.

Thomas Paine (1737–1809), *Rights of man*, 1791

16. Parliament itself would not exist in its present form had people not defied the law.

Arthur Scargill, *Observer*, 'Sayings of the week', 6 April 1980

17. All are involved in a Parliament.

John Selden (1584–1654), *Table-talk*, 1689, 'Parliament'

18. Women are supposed to have no political power; but clever women put stupid husbands into parliament and into ministerial offices quite easily.

George Bernard Shaw (1856–1950), Letter to Clement Scott, January 1902

19. As though conduct could be made right or wrong by the votes of some men sitting in a room in Westminster.

Herbert Spencer (1820–1903), *Social statics*, 1870, pt IV, ch. XXX, sec. 7

20. Nowhere in the world has radical social change ever been accomplished by Parliament.

Peter Tatchell, *Observer*, 'Sayings of the week', 16 January 1983

21. The English derivation of *parliament*, or *parlement* from the French *parler*, has no better

authority than a mere whim or notion ... We might as well derive *parler* from *parliament*, and both from a *parcel* of gossips, because they are loquacious.

Noah Webster (1758–1843), *A collection of essays*, no. XXIII, 1789, pp. 259–60

22. The House of Commons is terribly outdated, an old man's club with too much spare time boozing.

Shirley Williams, *Observer*, 'Sayings of the year', 3 January 1982

111. PARTNERSHIPS

1. The partner of my partner is not my partner. (*Socii mei socius, meus socius not est.*)

Legal maxim

2. One of the most fruitful sources of ruin to men of the world is the recklessness or want of principle of partners, and it is one of the perils to which every man exposes himself who enters into partnership with another.

Malins V.C. (1805–82), *Mackay v. Douglas* (1872), 14 Eq. 106 at 118

112. PATENTS

1. A patent does not give you the right to make something or do anything except to appear in court as the plaintiff in an action for infringement.

Earl of Halsbury, House of Lords, 20 February 1985

113. PERJURY

1. False and perjur'd.

   William Shakespeare (1564–1616), *Cymbeline*, 1609–10, III. iv

2. Nay to be perjur'd, which is worst of all.

   William Shakespeare (1564–1616), *Love's labour's lost*, 1594–5, III. i

3. Thus pour the stars down plagues for perjury.

   William Shakespeare (1564–1616), ibid., V. ii

4. Now, to our perjury to add more terror,
   We are again forsworn, — in will and error.

   William Shakespeare (1564–1616), ibid.

5. Why this is flat perjury.

   William Shakespeare (1564–1616), *Much ado about nothing*, 1598–9, IV. ii

6. What scourge for perjury
   Can this dark monarchy afford?

   William Shakespeare (1564–1616), *Richard III*, 1592–3, I. iv

114. PICKPOCKETS

1. 'Are you afraid of having your pockets picked?' 'Alas!' replied Mr. Beveridge, 'it would take two men to do that.' 'Hugh!' snorted the Emperor, 'are you so d–d strong, are you?' 'I mean,' answered his *vis-à-vis* ... 'that it would take one man to put something in and another to take it out.'

   Storer Clouston (1870–1944), *The lunatic at large*, pt I, ch. II

2. Shall I not take more ease in mine inn, but I shall have my pocket picked?

   William Shakespeare (1564–1616), *Henry IV, pt I*, 1597–8, III. iii

3. Pickpockets, each hand lusting for all that is not its own.

   Alfred, Lord Tennyson (1809–92), *Maud*, 1855, pt I, sec. I, st. VI

115. PIRACY

1. Piracy, *n.* Commerce without its folly-swaddles, just as God made it.

   Ambrose Bierce (1842–1914?), *The devil's dictionary*, 1911

2. Charity and piracy are things of the past. They were always closely akin, for pirates were very charitable, and ever in their train were troops of sturdy beggars.

   Elbert Hubbard (1856–1915), *Notebook*, p. 16

3. There be ... water-thieves and land thieves; I mean pirates.

   William Shakespeare (1564–1616), *The merchant of Venice*, 1596–7, I. iii

4. Notable pirate! thou salt-water thief!

   William Shakespeare (1564–1616), *Twelfth night*, 1599–1600, V. i

116. PLAINTIFF

1. Court Fool, *n.* The plaintiff.

   Ambrose Bierce (1842–1914?),
   The devil's dictionary, 1911

2. I should be sorry to think that, if a wrong has been done, the plaintiff is to go without a remedy simply because no one can find a peg to hang it on ... where there is a right there should be a remedy.

   Denning L.J., *Abbott* v. *Sullivan*, [1952] 1 K.B. 189 at 200

3. In a vast majority of cases, the verdict is for the plaintiff ... because he who has it in his power to decide whether he will go to law or not, and resolves to expose himself to the expense and trouble of a lawsuit, has probably a good foundation for his claim.

   Sydney Smith (1771–1845),
   Counsel for prisoners

117. POACHING

1. That *Caput lupinum* that *hostis humani generis*, as an honourable friend of mine once called him in his place, that *fera naturae* — a poacher.

   Henry Peter Brougham (1778–1868), House of Commons, 7 February 1828

2. A keeper is only a poacher turned outside in, and a poacher is a keeper turned inside out.

   Charles Kingsley (1819–75), *The water babies*, 1863, ch. 1

3. The law may multiply penalties by reams. Squires may fret and justices commit, and gamekeepers and poachers continue their nocturnal wars. There must be game on Lord Mayor's day, do what you will. You may multiply the crimes by which it is procured; but nothing can arrest its inevitable progress from the wood of the esquire to the spit of the citizen.

   Sydney Smith (1771–1845), *Game laws*

118. POLICE

1. Every American citizen is by birth a sworn officer of the state. Every man is a policeman.

   Henry Ward Beecher (1813–87), *Proverbs from Plymouth pulpit*, 1887

2. Police, *n.* An armed force for protection and participation.

   Ambrose Bierce (1842–1914?), *The devil's dictionary*, 1911

3. The police are, on the whole, such a fine body of men that they do not abuse the powers which they have.

   Lord Denning, *Freedom under the law*, 1949, p. 24

4. A police officer who does not learn the Judges' Rules syllable by syllable is a fool; but the police officer who carries out the Judges' Rules day by day, syllable by syllable, is an even greater fool.

   Lord Elystan-Morgan, House of Lords, 9 July 1984

5. When constabulary duty's to be done,

The policeman's lot is not a happy one.

Sir W.S. Gilbert (1836–1911), *Pirates of Penzance*, 1880, II

6. For the middle class, the police protect property, give directions, and help old ladies. For the urban poor, the police are those who arrest you.

Michael Harrington, *The other America*, 1962, ch. 1

7. I would like to see a return to the good old fashioned policeman: 16 stone and six feet four inches tall.

James Horsfall, *Observer*, 'Sayings of the week', 26 June 1983

8. Forget about the cosy image of Dixon of Dock Green.

Jim Jardine, *Observer*, 'Sayings of the week', 19 July 1981

9. The police ... are the anvil on which society beats out the problems of political and social justice, of extremism, violence and nonconformity generally.

Sir Robert Mark, 'Pigs in the middle', *Observer*, 29 November 1981

10. Very few people even consider the police as human beings with some of the virtues, failures and talents common to all.

Sir Robert Mark, Foreword to *Notes taken at the time*, 1983

11. The police are the only 24-hour social service in the country.

Commander Alex Marnoch, *Observer*, 'Sayings of the week', 20 February 1983

12. The difference between a police state and a state where the police are efficient, but democratically controlled, is a mighty thin one.

Lord Scarman, *Observer*, 'Sayings of the week', 10 June 1984

13. The parish make the constable, and when the constable is made he governs the parish.

John Selden (1584–1654), *Table-talk*, 1689, 'People'

14. The police force needs not exceptionally high standards of education, but very great integrity and strength of character, combined with the wisdom which comes to some — though not all — men when they have had a wide and varied experience of human nature.

Sir Percy Sillitoe, *Cloak without dagger*, 1955, ch. 9

15. Policemen are soldiers who act alone: soldiers are policemen who act in unison.

Herbert Spencer (1820–1903), *Social statics*, 1870, pt III, ch. XXI, sec. 8

16. Police work is seventy per cent common sense. That's what makes a policeman, common sense and an ability to make a quick decision.

Joseph Wambaugh, *The new centurions*, 1971, ch. 5

17. The police are like jam in a sandwich.

Peter Wright, *Observer*, 'Sayings of the year', 30 December 1984

119. POLITICS

1. All we men had grown used to our wives and mothers, and grand-mothers, and great-aunts all pouring a chorus of contempt upon our hobbies of sport, drink and party politics. And now comes Miss Pankhurst, with tears in her eyes, owning that all the women were wrong and all the men were right.

   G.K. Chesterton (1874–1936), *What's wrong with the world*, 1910, pt III, ch. 7

2. There is absolutely no justification in present-day English society for the law to be broken for political or self-interested ends.

   Sir Michael Havers, *Observer*, 'Sayings of the week', 15 April 1984

3. Every political measure will, forever, have an intimate connection with the laws of the land; and he, who knows nothing of these, will always be perplexed, and often foiled by adversaries having the advantage of that knowledge over him.

   Thomas Jefferson (1743–1826), Letter to T.M. Randolph Jr, 6 July 1787

4. Politics is a practical profession. If a criminal has what you want, you do business with him.

   Charles Laughton, quoted in H. Haun, *The movie quote book*

5. Get thee glass eyes;
   And, like a scurvy politician, seem
   To see the things thou dost not.

   William Shakespeare (1564–1616), *King Lear*, 1605–6, IV. vi

6. *Napoleon*: I can't stand women meddling in politics.
   Madame de Staël: Sire, in a country where women have been sent to the guillotine you can't blame them for asking why this happens to them.

   Mme de Staël, (1766–1817), quoted in E. Larsen, *Wit as a weapon*

7. We're not in politics, but we have to be; it's the only way we can survive. Politics is today's method of power.

   Vincent Teresa. *My life in the Mafia*, 1974, ch. 7

8. A political prediction publicly uttered will often have had, or supposed to have had, a great share in bringing about its own fulfillment. He who gives out, for instance, that the people will certainly be dissatisfied with such and such a law, is, in this doing his utmost to *make* them dissatisfied.

   Richard Whately (1787–1863), *Thoughts and apothegms*, 1856, pt VI

120. POLYGAMY
See also 15. Bigamy

1. Polygamy, *n.* A house of atonement, or expiatory chapel, fitted with several stools of repentance, as distinguished from monogamy, which has but one.

   Ambrose Bierce (1842–1914?), *The devil's dictionary*, 1911

2. Polygamy may well be held in
   dread,

Not only as a sin, but as a *bore*:
Most wise men with *one* moderate
                              woman wed,
Will scarcely find philosophy for
                              more.

Lord Byron (1788–1824), *Don Juan*, canto VI, 1823, st. XII

3. Had God intended polygamy for the species, it is probable that he would have begun with it, especially as, by giving to Adam more wives than one, the multiplication of the human race would have proceeded with a quicker progress.

William Paley (1743–1805), *The principles of moral and political philosophy*, 1784, bk III, pt III, ch. VI

121. PORNOGRAPHY

1. Pornography is the undiluted essence of anti-female propaganda.

Susan Brownmiller, *Against our will*, 1975, ch. 12

2. It'll be a sad day for sexual liberation when the pornography addict has to settle for the real thing.

Brendan Francis, quoted in E.F. Murphy, *The Macmillan treasury of relevant quotations*

3. It is a quirk of human nature that jurymen faced with a choice between a pornographer and a do-gooder will usually choose the former.

Sir Robert Mark, *In the office of constable*, 1978, ch. 13

122. POVERTY

1. Forma Pauperis (Latin). In the character of a poor person — a method by which a litigant without money for lawyers is considerately permitted to lose his case.

Ambrose Bierce (1842–1914?), *The devil's dictionary*, 1911

2. Poverty begets sedition and villainy.

Robert Burton (1577–1640), *Anatomy of melancholy*, 'Democritus to the reader'

3. Poverty, of course, does not mean destitution.

Evershed M.R. (1899–1966), *Re Coulthurst's Will Trusts*, [1951] 1 All E.R. 774 at 776

4. How vainly shall we endeavour to repress crime by our barbarous punishment of the poorer class of criminals so long as children are reared in the brutalizing influences of poverty, so long as the bite of want drives men to crime.

Henry George (1839–97), *Social problems*, 1883, ch. IX

5. Numerous penal laws grind every rank of people, and chiefly those least able to resist oppression, the poor.

Oliver Goldsmith (1728–74), *The citizen of the world*, 1762, letter LXXX

6. If poverty is the mother of crime, stupidity is its father.

La Bruyère (1645–96), *Characters*, 1688, 'Of man'

123. PRECEDENT

1. What of that? Shall not we give judgement because it is not adjudged in the books before? We will give judgement according to reason, and if there be no reason in the books, I will not regard them. [Said in argument that there were no cases in the books on the point in issue.]

   Anderson C.J. (1530–1605), *Anon.* (1588), Gould. 96

2. In all usages and precedents, the times be considered wherein they first began; which if they were weak or ignorant, it derogateth from the authority of the usage, and leaveth it for suspect.

   Francis Bacon (1561–1626), *The advancement of learning*, bk II, 12

3. Precedent, *n.* In law, a previous decision, rule or practice which, in the absence of a definite statute, has whatever force and authority a judge may choose to give it, thereby greatly simplifying his task of doing as he pleases. As there are precedents for everything, he has only to ignore those that make against his interest and accentuate those in the line of his desire. Invention of the precedent elevates the trial-at-law from the low estate of a fortuitous ordeal to the noble attitude of a dirigible arbitrament.

   Ambrose Bierce (1842–1914?), *The devil's dictionary*, 1911

4. I believe that *obiter dicta*, like the proverbial chickens of destiny, come home to roost sooner or later in a very uncomfortable way to the Judges who have uttered them, and are a great source of embarrassment in future cases.

   Bowen L.J. (1835–94), *Cooke* v. *New River Company* (1888), 38 Ch.D 56 at 71

5. All bad precedents began as justifiable measures.

   Julius Caesar (100–44 BC), attributed

6. What is the argument on the other side? Only this, that no case has been found in which it has been done before. That argument does not appeal to me in the least. If we never do anything which has not been done before, we shall never get anywhere. The law will stand still whilst the rest of the world goes on; and that will be bad for both.

   Denning L.J., *Packer* v. *Packer*, [1954] P. 15 at 22

7. We are not to be deterred by the absence of authority in the books. Our forefathers always held that the law was locked in the breasts of the judges, ready to be unlocked whenever the need arose.

   Lord Denning M.R., *Re P. (G.E.) (An Infant)*, [1965] 1 Ch. 568 at 583

8. A precedent embalms a principle. The principle may be right or may be wrong — that is a question for discussion; but at the first glance it is right to conclude that it is a principle that has been acted upon and recognised by those who preceded us.

   Benjamin Disraeli (1804–81), House of Commons, 22 February 1848

9. Why should you stand so much on precedents? The times hereafter will be good or bad: If good, precedents will do no harm; if bad, power will make a way where it finds none.

   Sir Fulke Greville (1554–1628), quoted in Francis Bacon, *Apothegms*

10. Legal precedents are like statistics. If you manipulate them, you can prove anything.

    Arthur Hailey, *Airport*, 1968, pt 3, ch. 11

11. When a court finds two precedents in conflict, it must follow the later one.

    Learned Hand (1872–1961), *The bill of rights*, 1958, I

12. One precedent creates another. They soon accumulate, and constitute law.

    Junius, *Letters*, 1772, 'Dedication to the English nation'

13. There is nothing too absurd but what authority can be found for it.

    Manisty J. (1808–90), *Henderson v. Preston* (1888), 4 T.L.R. 632 at 633

14. I am not unduly troubled by the absence of English authority: there has to be a first time for everything, and if the principles of English law, and not least analogies from existing rules, together with the requirements of justice and common sense, pointed firmly to such a right existing, then I think the court should not be deterred from recognising the right.

    Megarry V.C., *Malone* v. *Metropolitan Police Commissioner*, [1979] 2 W.L.R. 700 at 725

15. The error of those who reason by precedents drawn from antiquity, respecting the rights of man, is that they do not go far enough into antiquity. They do not go the whole way … if we proceed on, we shall at last come out right; we shall come to the time when man came from the hand of his maker.

    Thomas Paine (1737–1809), *Rights of man*, 1791

16. No crime has lacked a precedent.

    Seneca (4 BC–AD 65), *Hippolytus*

17. I may example my digression by some mighty precedent.

    William Shakespeare (1564–1616), *Love's labour's lost*, 1594–5, I. ii

18. It must not be; there is no power in Venice
    Can alter a decree established:
    'Twill be recorded for a precedent,
    And many an error, by the same example,
    Will rush into state: it cannot be.

    William Shakespeare (1564–1616), *The merchant of Venice*, 1596–7, IV. i

19. Not all precedents are good precedents, and the fact that it has been done before indicates that it is high time we stopped doing it now.

    Lord Simon, House of Lords, 21 January 1985

20. A precedent embalms a principle.

    Lord Stowell (1745–1836), attributed

21. It is a maxim among these lawyers, that whatever hath been done before, may legally be done again ... There, under the name of *precedents*, they produce as authorities to justify the most iniquitous opinions; and the judges never fail of decreeing accordingly.

    Jonathan Swift (1667–1745), *Gulliver's Travels*, 1726, pt IV, ch. V

22. Precedents are dangerous things.

    George Washington (1732–99), Letter to Henry Lee, 31 October 1786

23. For advising a poet to leave off writing, and turn lawyer, because he is dull, and impudent, and says or writes nothing now, but by precedent.

    William Wycherley (1640–1716), *The plain dealer*, III. i

124. PRISON

1. Prison, *n.* A place of punishments and rewards. The poet assures us that — 'Stone walls do not a prison make', but a combination of the stone wall, the political parasite and the moral instructor is no garden of sweets.
   (see 124.13).

   Ambrose Bierce (1842–1914?), *The devil's dictionary*, 1911

2. Prisons are built with stones of law, brothels with bricks of religion.

   William Blake (1757–1827), *The marriage of heaven and hell* (1790–3), 'Proverbs of hell'

3. People do not come out of gaol as they went in. A boy may enter the prison-gate merely as a robber of an orchard; he may come out of it 'fit for' — I will not say 'treasons' — but certainly 'stratagems and spoils'.

   Henry Peter Brougham (1778–1868), House of Commons, 7 February 1828

4. A removal to Alcatraz is ... considered in the underworld as ... the reward of distinguished field service that cannot be overlooked.

   Alistair Cooke, *Talk about America*, 1968, 'Alcatraz'

5. One learns patience in a prison.

   Feodor Dostoevski (1821–81), *The house of the dead*, 1861, ch. II

6. It only makes a man worse to go to prison and be corrupted.

   E.M. Forster (1879–1970), *A passage to India*, 1924, pt I, ch. 7

7. Girls pick up all sorts of things in prison. We can hardly expect her to be honest.

   John Galsworthy (1867–1933), *Windows*, 1922, I

8. Our present prisons ... find or make men guilty ... enclose wretches for the commission of one crime, and return them, if

returned alive, fitted for the perpetration of thousands.

Oliver Goldsmith (1728–74), *The vicar of Wakefield*, 1766, ch. XXVII

9. Jail can't teach a person to do good and Siberia can't teach a person to do good.

   Maxim Gorki (1868–1936), *The lower depths*, III

10. As long as other men are in prison, I, too, am in bonds.

    Elbert Hubbard (1856–1915), *Notebook*, p. 113

11. Two months in jail'll remove freckles.

    Frank McKinney Hubbard (1868–1930), *New sayings by Abe Martin*, 1917

12. Prison: … An institution where even crooks go wrong.

    Frank McKinney Hubbard (1868–1930), *The Roycroft dictionary*, 1923

13. Stone walls do not a prison make,
       Nor iron bars a cage;
    Minds innocent and quiet take
       That for an hermitage.

    Richard Lovelace (1618–58), *To Althea, from prison*, IV

14. Any person who claims to have deep feelings for other human beings should think a long, long time before he votes to have other men kept behind bars — caged. I am not saying that there shouldn't

be prisons, but there shouldn't be bars.

Malcolm X (1925–65), *Autobiography*, 1965, ch. 10

15. Prison of course is the school of crime *par excellence*. Until one has gone through that school one is only an amateur.

    Henry Miller (1891–1980), *The air conditioned nightmare*, 1945, 'The soul of anaesthesia'

16. If you can't do time, don't do crime.

    John Morgan, after being sentenced to 7 years' imprisonment, *Daily Telegraph*, 18 May 1985

17. Prison reform will not work until we start sending a better class of person there.

    Laurence J. Peter, *Peter's quotations*, 1977

18. Let prisons swallow 'em.

    William Shakespeare (1564–1616), *Timon of Athens*, 1607–8, IV.iii

19. The most anxious man in a prison is the governor.

    George Bernard Shaw (1856–1950), *Maxims for revolutionists*, 1903

20. The facilities for getting into jail seem to be ample. We want more organisations for keeping people out.

    Charles Dudley Warner (1829–1900), *Backlog studies*, 1873, 'Eighth study', p. 209

21. I know not whether Laws be right,
    Or whether Laws are wrong;
    All that we know who lie in gaol
    Is that the wall is strong;
    And that each day is like a year,
    A year whose days are long.

    Oscar Wilde (1854–1900), *The ballad of Reading Gaol*, 1898, V, i

22. Every prison that men build
    Is built with bricks of shame,
    And bound with bars lest Christ
                         should see
    How men their brothers maim

    Oscar Wilde (1854–1900), ibid., V, iii

23. The vilest deeds like poison weeds,
    Bloom well in prison-air;
    It is only what is good in Man
    That wastes and withers there.

    Oscar Wilde (1854–1900), ibid., V, v

125. PROHIBITION

1. There is a crying for wine in the streets; all joy is darkened, the mirth of the land is gone.

   Bible, Authorized Version, Isaiah, 24:11

2. Stolen waters are sweet.

   Bible, Authorized Version, Proverbs, 9:17

3. I am inclined to think that stating the Prohibitionist arguments is one of the best ways of attacking Prohibition.

   G.K. Chesterton (1874–1936), *Come to think of it*, 1931, ch. XXXV, 'On prohibition'

4. The best thing about prohibition may have been its end.

   Alistair Cooke, *Alistair Cook's America*, 1973, ch. 10

5. Forbidden fruit a flavour has
   That lawful orchards mock;
   How luscious lies the pea within
   The pod that Duty locks!

   Emily Dickinson (1830–86), *Poems*, pt I, no. LXXXVII

6. We find many things to which the prohibition of them constitutes the only temptation.

   William Hazlitt (1778–1830), *Characteristics*, 1823, CXL

7. What is lawful has no attraction, but what is unlawful is fascinating.

   Ovid (43 BC–AD 17), *Amores*, bk II, XIX, 1. 3

8. If you covet something which is not yet prohibited, there is always a fear that prohibition may come.

   Tacitus (*c.*55–*c.*117), *Annals*, bk III, sec. 54

126. PROOF

1. Proof, *n.* Evidence having a shade more of plausibility than of unlikelihood. The testimony of two credible witnesses as opposed to that of only one.

   Ambrose Bierce (1842–1914?), *The devil's dictionary*, 1911

2. Let proof speak.

   William Shakespeare (1564–1616), *Cymbeline*, 1609–10, III. i

147

3. And this may help to thicken other
proofs
That do demonstrate thinly.

   William Shakespeare (1564–
   1616), *Othello*, 1604–5, III. iii

4. That which I shall report will bear
no credit,
Were not the proof so nigh.

   William Shakespeare (1564–
   1616), *The winter's tale*, 1610–11,
   V. i

5. Most true, if ever truth were preg-
nant by circumstance: that which
you hear you'll swear you see,
there is such unity in the proofs.

   William Shakespeare (1564–
   1616), ibid., V. ii

6. Questions of proof are not satis-
factorily left to ignorant or
untrained minds, announcing
decisions of major consequence in
a few unexplained monosyllables.

   Glanville Williams, *Sunday
   Times*, 18 April 1982

127. PROPERTY
See also 84. Land

1. The right of property enables an
industrious man to reap where he
has sown.

   Anonymous

2. Is it not lawful for me to do what I
will with mine own?

   Bible, Authorized Version,
   Matthew, 20:15

3. Property has its duties as well as its
rights.

   Benjamin Disraeli (1804–81),
   Sybil, 1845, bk II, ch. XI

4. 'Th' accurate delimitation o' th'
concept property would afford a
theme especially apposite fer
amplificative philosophical dis-
quisition; however, you've chosen
your path in life an' must take th'
consequences,' said Justice Marsh
Swallow, in sentencin' Stew Nugen
this mornin'.

   Frank McKinney Hubbard (1868–
   1930), *New sayings by Abe Martin*, 1917

5. Property rights are of course
human rights, i.e., rights which are
possessed by human beings. The
introduction of the wholly false
distinction between property rights
and human rights in many policy
discussions is surely one of the all
time great semantic flimflams.

   Michael C. Jensen and **William
   H. Meckling**, 'Theory of the firm',
   Journal of Financial Economics,
   3, 1976, p. 307

6. *Where there is no property, there is
no injustice* is a proposition as certain as any demonstration in
Euclid: for the idea of property,
being a right to any thing, and the
idea to which the name injustice is
given, being the invasion or violation of that right.

   John Locke (1632–1704), *Essay
   concerning human understanding*,
   1690, bk IV, ch. III, sec. 18

7. No one, I am sure, by the light of
nature ever understood an English
mortgage.

   Lord Macnaghten (1830–1913),
   Samuel v. *Jarrah Timber & Wood
   Paving Corpn. Ltd.*, [1904] A.C.
   323 at 326

8. [Property] A patent entitling one man to dispose of another man's labour.

    Thomas Robert Malthus (1766–1834), attributed

9. The right of property has not made poverty, but it has powerfully contributed to make wealth.

    J.R. McCulloch (1789–1864), *Principles of political economy*, new edn, pt I, ch. II, p. 87

10. The theory of the Communists may be summed up in a single sentence: Abolition of private property.

    Karl Marx (1818–83) and **Friedrich Engels** (1820–95), *The Communist manifesto*, 1848, II

11. The laws of property have never yet conformed to the principles on which the justification of private property rests. They have made property of things which never ought to be property, and absolute property where only a qualified property ought to exist.

    John Stuart Mill (1806–73), *Principles of political economy*, ed. Ashley, bk II, ch. I, 3

12. The institution of property, when limited to its essential elements, consists in the recognition, in each person, of a right to the exclusive disposal of what he or she have produced by their own exertions, or received either by gifts or fair agreement, without force or fraud, from those who produced it.

    John Stuart Mill (1806–73), ibid., ch. II, 1

13. Property is theft.

    Pierre-Joseph Proudhon (1809–65), *What is property*, ch. I

14. Laws are always useful to those who have property, and harmful to those who have nothing.

    Jean Jacques Rousseau (1712–78), *The social contract*, 1762, bk I, ch. IX, note

15. Without that sense of security which property gives, the land would still be uncultivated.

    François Quesnay (1694–1774), *Maximes*, IV

16. Property assures what toil acquires.

    Richard Savage (?–1743), *Of public spirit*, 1736

17. Law in a free country, is, or ought to be the determination of the majority of those who have property in land.

    Jonathan Swift (1667–1745), *Thoughts on various subjects*, 1711

18. Property is the most ambiguous of categories. It covers a multitude of rights which have nothing in common except that they are exercised by persons and enforced by the state.

    R.H. Tawney (1880–1962), *The acquisitive society*, 1921, ch. V

19. That low, bestial instinct which men call the right of property.

    Leo Tolstoy (1828–1910), *First stories*, 'Story of a horse'

20. If property had simply pleasures, we could stand it, but its duties make it unbearable. In the interest of the rich we must get rid of it.

    Oscar Wilde (1854–1900), *The soul of man under socialism*, 1912, p. 9

21. Property is an instrument of humanity. Humanity is not an instrument of property.

    Woodrow Wilson (1856–1924), Speech, 18 September 1912

128. PUBLIC OPINION

1. The reason why the law is carried into effect in England is, because the feeling of the people is in favour of it, and every man is willing to become and is in reality a peace officer, in order to further the ends of justice.

   John Bright (1811–89), House of Commons, 13 December 1847

2. In effect, to follow, not to force the public inclination: to give a direction, a form, a technical dress, and a specific sanction, to the general sense of the community, is the true end of legislature.

   Edmund Burke (1729–97), Letter to the Sheriffs of Bristol, 3 April 1777

3. The history of the world is the record of the weakness, frailty and death of public opinion.

   Samuel Butler (1835–1902), *Notebooks*, ed. Festing Jones, ch. VII

4. I read this morning an awful, though anonymous, manifesto in the great organ of public opinion, which always makes me tremble.

   Benjamin Disraeli (1804–81), House of Commons, 13 February 1851

5. Public opinion's always in advance of the Law.

   John Galsworthy (1867–1933), *Windows*, 1922, I

6. Laws they are not ... which public approbation hath not made so.

   Richard Hooker (*c.*1554–1600), *Of the laws of ecclesiastical polity*, 1594, bk I, ch. X, 8

7. Public opinion is the great natural restraining force. We are ruled by Public Opinion, not by Statute law. If Statute-law expresses the Zeitgeist it is well, but often law hampers and restrains Public Opinion.

   Elbert Hubbard (1856–1915), *Notebook*, p. 33

8. Public opinion will not tolerate in America a heartless judiciary. At last the people judge the judge.

   Elbert Hubbard (1856–1915), ibid., p. 120

9. Laws that do not embody public opinion can never be enforced.

   Frank McKinney Hubbard (1868–1930), *Epigrams*, 1923

10. We know no spectacle so ridiculous as the British public in one of its periodical fits of morality.

    Lord Macaulay (1800–59), *Moore's life of Lord Byron*, June 1831

11. What we call public opinion is a modern form of ethical custom and is organized in all manner of voluntary associations.

Roscoe Pound (1870–1964), *Social control through law*, 1968, I

12. Opinion is of more power than law.

Sydney Smith (1771–1845), *Game laws*

13. In a free and republican government, you cannot restrain the voice of the multitude. Every man will speak as he thinks.

George Washington (1732–99), Letter to Lafayette, 1 September 1778

14. There is nothing more disgusting in British political life than the sight of a Conservative who thinks he has public opinion behind him.

Auberon Waugh, *Spectator*, 15 March 1986

129. PUBLIC POLICY

1. Public policy — it is a very unruly horse, and when once you get astride it you never know where it will carry you.

Burrough J. (1750–1839), *Richardson* v. *Mellish* (1824), 2 Bing. 229 at 252

2. The law relating to public policy cannot remain immutable. It must change with the passage of time. The wind of change blows on it.

Danckwerts L.J. (1888–1978), *Nagle* v. *Feilden*, [1966] 1 All E.R. 689 at 696

3. With a good man in the saddle, the unruly horse [public policy] can be kept in control. It can jump over obstacles. It can leap the fences put up by fictions and come down on the side of justice.

Lord Denning M.R., *Enderby Town Football Club Ltd.* v. *Football Association Ltd.*, [1971] 1 Ch. 591 at 606–7

4. It seems to me that this public policy is a high horse to mount and is difficult to ride when you have mounted it.

A.L. Smith L.J. (1836–1901), attributed

130. PUNISHMENT

1. The object of the punishment is the reformation of the sufferer, and that of revenge the gratification of the agent.

Aristotle (384–322 BC), *Rhetoric*, trans. Welldon, bk I, ch. X

2. All punishment is mischief: all punishment in itself is evil.

Jeremy Bentham (1748–1832), *Principles of morals and legislation*, 1789, ch. XV, II

3. My punishment is greater than I can bear.

Bible, Authorized Version, Genesis, 4:13

4. Gallows, *n.* A stage for the performance of miracle plays, in which the leading actor is translated to heaven. In this country [USA] the gallows is chiefly

remarkable for the number of people who escape it.

Ambrose Bierce (1842–1914?), *The devil's dictionary*, 1911

5. Guillotine, *n.* A machine which makes a Frenchman shrug his shoulders with good reason.

Ambrose Bierce (1842–1914?), ibid.

6. Pillory, *n.* A mechanical device for inflicting personal distinction.

Ambrose Bierce (1842–1914?), ibid.

7. Rope, *n.* An obsolescent appliance for reminding assassins that they too are mortal. It is put around the neck and remains in place one's whole life long.

Ambrose Bierce (1842–1914?), ibid.

8. But for the grace of God there goes John Bradford.

John Bradford (1510?–55), [on seeing some criminals going to execution], quoted in the *Dictionary of national biography*

9. 'Hanging is too good for him', said Mr Cruelty.

John Bunyan (1628–88), *Pilgrim's progress*, 1678, pt I

10. I take it for granted, gentlemen, that we sympathize in a proper horror of all punishment further than as serves for an example.

Edmund Burke (1729–97), Letter to the Sheriffs of Bristol, 3 April 1777

11. Experience shows that the frequent repetition of capital punishment has never yet made men better.

Catherine the Great (1729–96), quoted by J. Bright, House of Commons, 3 May 1864

12. The punishment shall fit the offence.

Cicero (106–43 BC), *De legibus*, bk III, ch. XX

13. Care should be taken that the punishment should not be out of proportion to the offence.

Cicero (106–43 BC), *De officiis*, bk I, ch. XXV

14. The first interest of laws
    Was to correct th' effect, and
                       check the cause;
    And all the ends of punishment,
    Were only future mischiefs to pre-
                                    vent.
    But justice is inverted when
    Those engines of the law,
    Instead of pinching vicious men,
    Keep honest ones in awe;
    Thy business is, as all men know,
    To punish villains not to make men
                                      so.

Daniel Defoe (1660–1731), *A hymn to the pillory*, 1703

15. The newly appointed judge soon discovers that the most difficult and detestable of his tasks is that of deciding the matter of sentencing.

Lord Edmund Davis, House of Lords, 24 January 1985

16. Crime and punishment grow out of one stem. Punishment is a fruit that unsuspected ripens within the

flower of the pleasure which concealed it.

Ralph Waldo Emerson (1803–82), *Essays, first series*, 1841, 'Compensation'

17. Is not all punishment inflicted beyond the merit of the offence, so much punishment of innocence!

Benjamin Franklin (1706–90), Letter to Benjamin Vaughan, 14 March 1785

18. Law cannot persuade, where it cannot punish.

Thomas Fuller (1654–1734), *Gnomologia*, 1732, no. 3, 148

19. Man punishes the action, but God the intention.

Thomas Fuller (1654–1734), ibid., no. 3, 332

20. To punish and not prevent, is to labour at the pump, and leave open the leak.

Thomas Fuller (1654–1734), ibid., no. 5,216

21. We will hang you, never fear, Most politely, most politely!

Sir W.S. Gilbert (1836–1911), *Princess Ida*, 1884, I

22. My object all sublime
I shall achieve in time —
To let the punishment fit the
crime —
The punishment fit the crime.

Sir W.S. Gilbert (1836–1911), *The Mikado*, 1885, II

23. Well it were if rewards and mercy alone could regulate the common-wealth, but since punishments are sometimes necessary, let them at least be rendered terrible, by being executed but seldom, and let justice lift her sword rather to terrify than revenge.

Oliver Goldsmith (1728–74), *Citizen of the world*, 1762, letter LXXXI

24. Men are not hanged for stealing horses but that horses may not be stolen.

Lord Halifax (1633–95), *Political thoughts and reflexions*

25. The fear of punishment may be necessary to the suppression of vice; but it also suspends the finer motives to virtue.

William Hazlitt (1778–1830), *Characteristics*, 1823, CXXXI

26. Punishment is lame, but it comes.

George Herbert (1593–1633), *Jacula prudentum*, 1651

27. Seldom hath punishment, though lame of foot, failed to overtake a villain.

Horace (65–8 BC), *Odes*, trans. C. Smart, bk III, ode II

28. Punishment presses as a companion upon guilt.

Horace (65–8 BC), ibid.

29. Every man who gets whipped for a sin claims that other men have done more, and been whipped less.

E.W. Howe (1853–1937), *Country town sayings*, 1911

30. We are punished by our sins not for them.

   Elbert Hubbard (1856–1915), *Notebook*, p. 12

31. Punishment ... The justice that the guilty deal out to those that are caught.

   Frank McKinney Hubbard (1868–1930), *The Roycroft dictionary*, 1923

32. Never take the taws, when a word will do the turn.

   James Kelly, *Scottish proverbs*, 1721, N, no. 72

33. Shew me the man, and I'll show you the law.

   James Kelly, ibid., S, no. 37

34. The only effect of public punishment is to show the rabble how bravely it can be borne.

   Walter Savage Landor (1775–1864), *Imaginary conversations*, 1824–9, 'Diogenes and Plato'

35. If ... any thing be imprinted on the mind of all men as a law, all men must have a certain and unavoidable knowledge, that certain, and unavoidable punishment will attend the breach of it.

   John Locke (1632–1704), *Essay concerning human understanding*, 1690, bk I, ch. III, 13

36. There should be one weight and one measure. Decimation is always an objectionable mode of punishment.

   Lord Macaulay (1800–59), *Moore's life of Lord Byron*, June 1831

37. How many condemnations have I seen more criminal than the crimes themselves?

   Michel de Montaigne (1533–92), *Essays*, bk III, 1595, 'Of experience'

38. The unreasonable severity of the laws obstructs their execution.

   Charles de Secondat, Baron de Montesquieu (1689–1755), *The spirit of the laws*, 1748, bk VI, 13

39. Criminals collected together corrupt each other; they are worse than ever, when at the termination of their punishment they re-enter society.

   Napoleon I (1769–1821), *Table talk and opinions*, 1868, p. 100

40. The proper end of human punishment is not the satisfaction of justice, but the prevention of crimes.

   William Paley (1743–1805), *The principles of moral and political philosophy*, 1784, bk VI, ch. IX

41. Nothing so upholds the laws as the punishment of persons whose rank is as great as their crime.

   Cardinal Richelieu (1585–1642), quoted in L.J. Peter, *Peter's quotations*

42. The time that precedes punishment is the severest part of it.

   Seneca (4 BC–AD 65), *De beneficiis*, bk II, ch. V

43. No one resorts to punishment until

he has exhausted all the means of correction.

Seneca (4 BC–AD 65), *De clementia*, bk I, ch. XIV

44. For the person who administers punishment nothing is so unfitting as anger, since punishment is much better at producing reform if inflicted with judgement.

Seneca (4 BC–AD 65), *De ira*, bk I, ch. XV

45. Punishment postponed can still be exacted, but once exacted it cannot be recalled.

Seneca (4 BC–AD 65), ibid., bk II, ch. XXII

46. Judicious punishment!

William Shakespeare (1564–1616), *King Lear*, 1605–6, III. iv

47. That were a punishment too good for them.

William Shakespeare (1564–1616), *Much ado about nothing*, 1598–9, III. iii

48. A punishment more in policy than in malice; even so as one would beat his offenceless dog to affright an imperious lion.

William Shakespeare (1564–1616), *Othello*, 1604–5, II. iii

49. Punishment is only a pretence of cancelling one crime with another.

George Bernard Shaw (1856–1950), *Major Barbara*, 1905, Preface

50. There is an end to the law, if every man is to measure out his punish-

ment for his own wrong.

Sydney Smith (1771–1845), *Game laws*

51. There must be some injustice in every great example of punishment, but what is hard for the few is compensated by the benefit to the whole.

Tacitus (*c.*55–*c.*117), *Annals*, bk XIV, sec. 44

52. Certainty is more effectual than severity of punishment.

Henry D. Thoreau (1817–62), *The comparative moral policy of severe and mild punishments*, 1835

53. 'Your great grandfather was hanged'
'That is a l– –'
'Silence! Hanged sir. But it was not his fault. He could not help it.'
'I am glad you do him justice.'

Mark Twain (1835–1910), *Lionizing murderers*

54. I'm all for bringing back the birch, but only between consenting adults.

Gore Vidal, quoted in Hearn Stephenson, *Contradictory quotations*

55. You felons on trial in courts.
You convicts in prison-cells, you sentenced assassins chain'd and handcuff'd with iron,
Who am I too that I am not on trial or in prison?
Me ruthless and devilish as any, that my wrists are not chain'd with iron, or my ankles with iron?

Walt Whitman (1819–91), *You felons on trial in courts*

56. I have no doubt that reformation is a much more painful process than punishment, is indeed punishment in its most aggravated and moral form.

Oscar Wilde (1854–1900), *The critic as artist*, pt II

57. Strike not from Law's firm hand
that awful rod,
But leave it thence to drop for lack
of use:
Oh, speed the blessed hour,
Almighty God!

William Wordsworth (1770–1850), *Sonnets upon the punishment of death*, XIII, 'Conclusion'

131. QUARRELS

1. The quarrels of relations are harder to reconcile than any other.

John Arbuthnot (1667–1735), *Law is a bottomless pit*, 1712, pt II, ch. V

2. If they could excite hatred enough in one of the parties towards the other, they seemed to be of the opinion that they had gone half the way towards reconciling the quarrel.

Edmund Burke (1729–97), *Letter to the Sheriffs of Bristol*, 3 April 1777

3. If you cannot avoid a quarrel with a blackguard, let your lawyer manage it, rather than yourself. No man sweeps his own chimney, but employs a chimney sweeper, who has no objection to dirty work, because it is his trade.

C.C. Colton (1780–1832), *Lacon*, 1820, vol. I, CCCXIV

4. There must be two at least to a quarrel.

Thomas Fuller (1654–1734), *Gnomologia*, 1732, no. 4,942

5. Go not for every grief to the physician, nor every quarrel to the lawyer, nor for every thirst to the pot.

George Herbert (1593–1633), *Jacula prudentum*, 1651

6. Quarrels are built on a misunderstanding.

Elbert Hubbard (1856–1915), *Notebook*, p. 82

7. Quarrels would not last long if the fault were only on one side.

François Duc de La Rochefoucauld (1613–80), *Maxims*, 1678

8. Patch a quarrel.

William Shakespeare (1564–1616), *Anthony and Cleopatra* 1606–7, II. ii

9. We quarrel in print, by the book, as you have books for good manners.

William Shakespeare (1564–1616), *As you like it*, 1596–1600, V. iv

10. Come, let us four to dinner: I dare
say
This quarrel will drink blood
another day.

William Shakespeare (1564–1616), *Henry VI pt I*, 1589–90, II. iv

11. No quarrel, but a slight contention.

    William Shakespeare (1564–1616), *Henry VI pt III*, 1590–1, I. ii

12. In the managing of quarrels you may say he is wise; for either he avoids them with great discretion, or undertakes them with a most Christian-like fear.

    William Shakespeare (1564–1616), *Much ado about nothing*, 1598–9, II. iii

132. RACE RELATIONS

1. God ... hath made of one blood all nations of men for to dwell on the face of the earth.

    Bible, Authorized Version, Acts, 17:26

2. Deep-rooted racial prejudice probably takes about five years of concentrated psychotherapy to dispel.

    Chief Inspector Ian McKenzie, *Observer*, 'Sayings of the week', 16 January 1983

133. RAPE

1. Rape. It is not proper, by a gross and puerile joke, to deny the existence of this crime, and to diminish the horror of it.

    Jeremy Bentham (1748–1832), *Principles of morals and legislation*, 1789, ch. XIV

2. [Rape] is nothing more or less than a conscious process of intimidation by which *all men* keep *all women* in a state of fear.

    Susan Brownmiller, *Against our will*, 1975, ch. 1

3. All men are rapists and that's all they are. They rape us with their eyes, their laws and their codes.

    Marilyn French, attributed

4. The House of Lords has decided it's a man's belief that matters in a rape case; there are very few women among the judges of the House of Lords.

    John Mortimer, *Rumpole of the Bailey*, 1978, 'Rumpole and the Honourable Member'

5. It would be much better if young women should stop being raped much earlier in the proceedings than some of them do.

    Mr Justice Stabler, *Observer*, 'Sayings of the week', 8 January 1961

6. The [rape] victim's suffering might be reduced if our courtroom procedure did not resemble something between a Pontifical High Mass in the Tridentine Rite and a comic opera. In a British courtroom, an ordinary act like eating a sausage can be made, under cross-examination, to sound like some bizarre perversion.

    Auberon Waugh, *Sunday Telegraph*, 23 September 1984

134. RECEIVING

1. No receiver, no thief.

    Thomas Fuller (1654–1734), *Gnomologia*, 1732, no. 3,620

157

2. The receiver
   Is as bad as the thiever.

   Thomas Fuller (1654–1734), ibid., no. 6,162

3. Evill gotten goods never proveth well.

   John Heywood (1506–65), *Proverbs*, 1546, pt I, ch. XI

4. Where there be no receivers, there be no thieves.

   John Heywood (1506–65), ibid., ch. XII

5. A receipter is worse than a thief.

   James Kelly, *Scottish proverbs*, 1721, A, no. 86

135. RELIGION

1. A mixture of the ingredients of a clergyman and a justice of the peace, though each might be good in itself, frequently made a nauseous compound.

   Henry Peter Brougham (1778–1868), House of Commons, 29 February 1828

2. As between different religions the law stands neutral, but it assumes that any religion is at least likely to be better than none.

   Cross J., *Neville Estates Ltd.* v. *Madden*, [1961] 3 All E.R. 769 at 781

3. Religion concerns the spirit in man whereby he is able to recognise what is truth and what is justice; whereas law is only the application, however imperfectly, of truth and justice in our everyday affairs.

   Lord Denning, *The changing law*, 1953, p. 122

4. The laws of the realm do admit nothing against the law of God.

   Hobart C.J. (?–1625), *Colt & Glover* v. *Bishop of Coventry and Lichfield* (1612), Hob. 140 at 149

5. No one gives a fig about the Ten Commandments any more.

   Lord Chief Justice Lane, *Observer*, 'Sayings of the week', 22 May 1983

6. The Christian religion has all the marks of the utmost utility and justice: but none more manifest than the severe injunction it lays indifferently upon all to yield absolute obedience to the civil magistrate, and to maintain and defend the laws.

   Michel de Montaigne (1533–92), *Essays*, bk I, 'Of custom'

7. Penal laws should be avoided in respect of religion.

   Charles de Secondat, Baron de Montesquieu (1689–1755), *The spirit of the laws*, 1748, bk XXV, 12

8. The bishop is in the nature of an ecclesiastical sheriff.

   North C.J. (1637–85), *Walwyn* v. *Awberry* (1677), 1 Mod. 258 at 260

9. Persecution is not an original feature in *any* religion; but it is always the strongly-marked feature of all law-religions, or religions

established by law.

Thomas Paine (1737–1809), *Rights of man*, 1791

10. The effects of penal laws, in matters of religion, are never confined to those limits in which the legislature intended they should be placed.

Sydney Smith (1771–1845), *The Peter Plymley letters*, 1807, V

11. The Gospel and the Law of late
    Have been at sad dissension
Before the Judge and Magistrate:
    Old Satan's last invention.
Of course the Law upholds the
                                Law,
    The Gospel over-ruling:
And those who have St Paul in
                                awe
    Must seek more modern
                        schooling.

James Thomson (1834–82), *Law* v. *Gospel*, I

136. REVENGE

1. Revenge is a kind of wild justice; which the more man's nature runs to, the more ought law to weed it out.

Francis Bacon (1561–1626), *Essays*, 1625, IV, 'Of revenge'

2. A dead body revenges not injuries.

William Blake (1757–1827), *The marriage of Heaven and Hell*, 1790–3, 'Proverbs of hell'

3. Justice, our law and our law courts are for the taming and regulating of revenge.

Samuel Butler (1835–1902),

Notebooks, ed. Festing Jones, ch. XXI

4. Revenge never repairs an injury.

Thomas Fuller (1654–1734), *Gnomologia*, 1732

5. In taking revenge a man is but even with his enemy; but in passing it over, he is superior.

Thomas Fuller (1654–1734), ibid., no. 2,821

6. It costeth us more to revenge injuries, than to bear them.

Thomas Fuller (1654–1734), ibid., no. 2,835

7.   Revenge, at first though sweet,
Bitter ere long back on itself
                            recoils.

John Milton (1608–74), *Paradise Lost*, bk IX, 1. 171

8. In revenge and in love woman is more barbarous than man.

Friedrich Nietzsche (1844–1900), *Beyond good and evil*, ch. 4

9. In any wild country, where the power of the law is little felt or heeded, and where everyone has to rely upon himself for protection, men soon get to feel that it is in the highest degree unwise to submit to any wrong without making an immediate and resolute effort to avenge it upon the wrongdoers.

Theodore Roosevelt (1858–1918), 1886, quoted in *Time*, 28 October 1985

10. Both my revenge and hate

Loosing upon thee in the name of
justice,
Without all terms of pity.

William Shakespeare (1564–
1616), *All's well that ends well*,
1602–4, II. iii

11. Men are readier to pay back an
injury rather than a benefit,
because gratitude is a burden
whereas revenge is a pleasure.

Tacitus (*c.*55–*c.*117), *Annals*, bk
IV, ch. 3

12. Guilt escaping, passion might then
plead
In angry spirits for her old free
range,
And the 'wild justice of revenge'
prevail.

William Wordsworth (1770–
1850), *Sonnets upon the punishment of death*, VIII

137. RIGHTS

1. Right, *n.* Legitimate authority to
be, to do or to have; as the right to
be a king, the right to do one's
neighbour, the right to have
measles and the like.

Ambrose Bierce (1842–1914?),
The devil's dictionary, 1911

2. What people have always sought is
equality of rights before the law.
For rights that were not open to all
equally would not be rights.

Cicero (106–43 BC), *De officiis*,
bk II, ch. XII

3. The right of a man to work is just

as important to him, if not more
important, than his rights of
property.

Denning L.J., *Abbott* v. *Sullivan*,
[1952] 1 K.B. 189 at 204

4. A right to silence is a very misleading expression. A man has not
a right to silence. What he has is a
privilege against self-incrimination.

Lord Denning, House of Lords, 9
July 1984

5. When one is concerned with the
sophisticated criminal, or the
habitual criminal, one does not
have to tell him what his rights are,
because he knows.

Lord Hooson, House of Lords, 9
July 1984

6. There is no exception to God's law
on human rights.

Kenneth Kaunda, *Sydney
Morning Herald*, 'Sayings of the
week', 14 September 1985

7. Rights matter most when they are
claimed by unpopular minorities.

Justice Michael Kirby, *Sydney
Morning Herald*, 'Sayings of the
week', 30 November 1985

8. What rights are his that dare not
strike for them?

Alfred, Lord Tennyson (1809–
92), *The last tournament*, 1871, 1.
525

9. It is not desirable to cultivate a
respect for the law, so much as for
the right. The only obligation

which I have a right to assume is to do at any time what I think is right.

Henry D. Thoreau (1817–62), *Resistance to civil government*, 1849

10. Men are not always *right* in their use of their rights.

Richard Whately (1787–1863), *Thoughts and apothegms*, 1856, pt VI

138. RIOTS

1. Riot, *n.* A popular entertainment given to the military by innocent bystanders.

Ambrose Bierce (1842–1914?), *The devil's dictionary*, 1911

2. Riots are the politics of the excluded.

John Bohstedt, *The Times*, 4 November 1985

3. O my poor kingdom, sick with civil blows!
When that my care could not withhold thy riots,
What wilt thou do when riot is thy care?

William Shakespeare (1564–1616), *Henry IV* pt II, 1597–8, IV. iv

4. He is a sworn rioter.

William Shakespeare (1564–1616), *Timon of Athens*, 1607–8, III. ii

5. It is a misfortune in [the Southern] states, that the freemen of a *whole county* assemble at elections. This is one principal cause, why the elections are attended with tumults, riots, quarrels, bloody noses, and in a few instances with death. The laws of a republic should guard against all large collections of people for good or bad purposes: they are always dangerous.

Noah Webster (1758–1843), *A collection of essays*, no. XXVII, 1790, 'Miscellaneous remarks'

139. SECURITY

1. A bad padlock invites a pickpocket.

Thomas Fuller (1654–1734), *Gnomologia*, 1732, no. 2

2. No lock will hold,
Against the power of gold.

Thomas Fuller (1654–1734), ibid., no. 6,236

3. When you walk laden with gold you must look out for robbers.

St Jerome (*c.*342–420), *Letters*, XXII

4. We have locks to safeguard necessaries,
And pretty traps to catch petty thieves.

William Shakespeare (1564–1616), *Henry V*, 1598–9, I.ii

140. SEX

1. There were many things which a girl under 16 needed to practise, but sex was not one of them.

Lord Brandon, *Gillick* v. *West Norfolk and the Wisbech Area*

*Health Authority and the DHSS,
The Times,* 18 October 1985

2. Contraceptives do not, in themselves, directly assist in the crime
of unlawful sexual intercourse.

Mr Justice Woolf, *Observer*, 'Sayings of the week', 31 July 1983

141. SMUGGLING

1. These days anyone can become a
smuggler quite unwittingly. The
quirks of the official mind make
sure that sooner or later, some-
where or other virtually everything
the traveller packs into his suitcase
or the importer wants to import is
either prohibited entry or charged
exorbitant rates of duty.

Timothy Green, *The smugglers,*
1969, 'Finale'

2. The smuggler ... [is] a person
who, though no doubt highly
blameable for violating the laws of
his country is frequently incapable
of violating those of natural justice,
and would have been, in every
respect, an excellent citizen had
not the laws of his country made
that a crime which nature never
meant to be so.

Adam Smith (1723–90), *The
wealth of nations,* 1776, bk V, ch.
II

3. The smuggler can compete with
the spirit merchant on account of
the great duty imposed by the
revenue; but where there is no
duty to be saved the mere thief ...
can never be long the rival of him
who honestly and fairly produces

the articles in which he deals.

Sydney Smith (1771–1845),
Game laws

142. SPORT

1. The libel laws ... have always
made it virtually impossible to
write a really good racing book
about anything but the horses.

Jeffrey Bernard, *Spectator*, 29
March 1986

2. Cheating has always been a part of
cricket and, as long as there are
laws to try and get round, always
will be.

Dickie Bird, *Not out*, 1978, ch. 3

3. There is not a worse constituted
tribunal on the face of the earth,
not before the Turkish cadi, than
that at which summary convictions
on the game-laws take place; I
mean a bench or a brace of sporting justices.

Henry Peter Brougham (1778–
1868), House of Commons, 7
February 1828

4. He brought an eye for all he saw;
   He mixt in all our simple sports;
   They pleased him, fresh from
                    brawling courts
And dusty purlieus of the law.

Alfred, Lord Tennyson (1809–
92), *In memoriam*, 1850,
LXXXIX, 1. 9

143. SUICIDE

1. [Suicide is] ... a man rushing into

the presence of his maker unasked.

Lord Denning, *The family story*, 1981, p. 100

2. Suicide ... Self-murder; the horrid crime of destroying one's self.

Samuel Johnson (1709–84), *A dictionary of the English language*, 1755

3. I wish these people would show more efficiency about these overdoses. How much trouble they would save. [Referring to a defendant who had attempted suicide.]

Mr Justice Bertrand Richards, *Observer*, 'Sayings of the week', 24 July 1983

144. TAX

1. I have to refer to the attached form. I regret so grave I am unable to complete the form as I do not know what is meant by filling this form. However, I am not interested in this income service. Could you please cancel my name in your books, as this system has upset my mind and I do not know who registered me as one of your customers. [Reply sent by a newly independent Zimbabwean to the Commissioner of Income Tax in Salisbury.]

Anonymous

2. A woman's income chargeable to income tax shall ... (for any year) during which she is a married woman living with her husband be deemed for income tax purposes to be his income and not to be her income.

Anonymous, *UK Income and Corporation Taxes Act*, 1970, sec. 37

3. *Lord Aylstone*: Is it possible to be registered for VAT [Value Added Tax] if one is carrying out something that is completely illegal ... Would the Customs and Excise register, for example, a burglar, a prostitute, or a brothel?
Noble lords: Yes!

Lord Aylestone, House of Lords, 14 January 1985

4. Render therefore unto Caesar the things which are Caesar's.

Bible, Authorized Version, St Matthew, 22: 21

5. And it came to pass in those days, that there went out a decree from Caesar Augustus that all the world should be taxed.

Bible, Authorized Version, St Luke, 2:1

6. Oh what a tangled web we weave when we practice to relieve.

Sir Hermann Black, *Sydney Morning Herald*, 'Sayings of the week', 6 July 1985

7. An economy breathes through its tax loopholes.

Barry Bracewell-Milnes, 'Tax avoidance can be good news for the tax collector', *Daily Telegraph*, 16 July 1979

8. It is through the magistracy, more than through any other agency — except, indeed, that of the tax-

gatherer — that the people are brought directly into contact with the government of the country.

Henry Peter Brougham (1778–1868), House of Commons, 7 February 1828

9. To tax and to please, no more than to love and be wise, is not given to men.

Edmund Burke (1729–97), *Speech on American taxation,* 19 April 1774

10. Would twenty shillings have ruined Mr Hampden's fortune? No! but the payment of half twenty shillings, on the principle that it was demanded would have made him a slave.

Edmund Burke (1729–97), ibid.

11. Taxing is an easy business. Any projector can contrive new compositions; and bungler can add to the old.

Edmund Burke (1729–97), House of Commons, 11 February 1780

12. That a great reluctance to pay taxes existed in all the colonies, there can be no doubt. It was one of the marked characteristics of the American People long after their separation from England.

G.S. Callender (1865–1915), *Selections from the economic history of the United States 1765–1860,* 1909, p. 123

13. There is no such thing as a good tax.

Winston Churchill (1874–1965), *Observer,* 'Sayings of the week', 6 June 1937

14. No man in this country is under the smallest obligation, moral or other, so to arrange his legal relations to his business or to his property as to enable the Inland Revenue to put the largest possible shovel into his stores.

Lord Clyde (1863–1944), *Ayrshire Pullman Motor Services and D.M. Ritchie* v. *The Commissioners of Inland Revenue* (1929), 14 Tax Cas. 754 at 763

15. The Inland Revenue is not slow — and quite rightly — to take every advantage which is open to it under the taxing statutes for the purpose of depleting the taxpayer's pocket.

Lord Clyde (1863–1944), ibid., at 764

16. The art of taxation consists in so plucking the goose as to obtain the largest amount of feathers with the smallest possible amount of hissing.

Jean Baptiste Colbert (1619–83), attributed

17. The avoidance of tax may be lawful, but it is not yet a virtue.

Lord Denning M.R., *Re Weston's Settlements,* [1969] 1 Ch. 223 at 245

18. 'It was as true,' said Mr. Barkis, 'as taxes is. And nothing's truer than them.'

Charles Dickens (1812–70), *David Copperfield,* 1850, ch. 21

19. There are few greater stimuli to human ingenuity than the prospect of avoiding fiscal liability. Experi-

ence shows that under this stimulus human ingenuity outreaches Parliamentary prescience.

Diplock L.J. (1907–85), *Commissioners of Customs & Excise* v. *Top Ten Promotions Ltd.*, [1969] 3 All E.R. 39 at 69

20. An Englishman's home is his tax haven.

    Economist, 17 November 1979, p. 78

21. In this world nothing can be said to be certain, except death and taxes.

    Benjamin Franklin (1706–90), Letter to Jean Baptiste Le Roy, 13 November 1789

22. There can be no taxation without misrepresentation.

    J.B. Handelsman, quoted by Y. Barzel, 'An alternative approach to the analysis of taxation', *Journal of Political Economy*, 1976, p. 1177

23. Death, avers Peter Pan, is an awfully big adventure, but the Inland Revenue has not yet claimed that it is [not] an associated operation. [Associated operation defined by Finance Act 1936 s. 18 (2).]

    Harman J. (1894–1970), *Bambridge* v. *I.R.C.*, [1954] 1 W.L.R. 1265 at 1268

24. Now it is notorious — and is, indeed, a long standing injustice — that the scale of the taxpayer's allowances under schedule E are on an altogether more niggardly and restricted scale than under Schedule D. Indeed, it has been

said that the pleasure of life depends nowadays upon the schedule under which a man lives.

Lord Justice Harman (1894–1970), quoted in Gwyneth McGreggor, *Employees' deductions under the income tax*

25. It is the small owner who offers the only really profitable and reliable material for taxation. ... He is made for taxation. ... He swarms; he is far more tied to his place and his calling than the big owner; he has less skill, and ingenuity as regards escape; and he still has a large supply of 'ignorant patience of taxation.'

    Auberon Herbert (1836–1906), quoted in F. Coffield, *A popular history of taxation*

26. One-half the world don't know how th' other half dodges taxes.

    Frank McKinney Hubbard (1868–1930), *New sayings by Abe Martin*, 1917

27. The wisdom of man never yet contrived a system of taxation that would operate with perfect equality.

    Andrew Jackson (1767–1845), speech, 1832

28. Excise. ... A hateful tax levied upon commodities, and adjudged not by the common judges of property, but wretches hired by those to whom excise is paid.

    Samuel Johnson (1709–84), *Dictionary of the English language*, 1755

29. Income tax, if I may be pardoned

for saying so, is a tax on income.

Lord Macnaghten (1830–1913), *L.C.C.* v. *A.G.*, [1901] A.C. 26 at 35

30. Taxation is a most flexible and effective but also a dangerous instrument of social reform. One has to know precisely what one is doing lest the results diverge greatly from one's intentions.

Gunnar Myrdal, *The political element in the development of economic theory*, 1953, p. 188

31. Taxation without representation is tyranny.

James Otis (1725–83), attributed

32. That which angers men most is to be taxed above their neighbours.

Sir William Petty (1623–87), *A treatise of taxes and contributions*, 1662

33. Taxes, after all, are the dues that we pay for the privileges of membership in an organised society.

Franklin D. Roosevelt (1882–1945), speech, 21 October 1936

34. There is no equity about a tax.

Rowlatt J. (1862–1945), *Cape Brandy Syndicate* v. *I.R.C.*, [1921] 1 K.B. 64 at 71

35. You'll be whipp'd for taxation one of these days.

William Shakespeare (1564–1616), *As you like it*, 1596–1600, I. ii

36. All is fair in love, war and tax evasion.

Tom Sharpe, *The throwback*, 1978, ch. 19

37. The nation should have a tax system which looks like someone designed it on purpose.

William E. Simon, quoted in US Treasury, *Blueprints for basic tax reform*, 1977

38. Like old ships' hulls the tax codes of the western nations are barnacled with exemptions, reliefs and concessions.

The Times, 14 December 1985

39. WARD'S LAW: Pay nothing in tax today that you can argue about tomorrow.

Christopher Ward, *How to complain*, 1976, p. 221

40. In such experience as I have had with taxation — and it has been considerable — there is only one tax that is popular, and that is the tax that is on the other fellow.

Sir Thomas White (1866–1955), debate in the Canadian Parliament, 1917

41. It would be strange if taxation by interest groups should not result in taxation according to interest.

Knut Wicksell (1851–1926), quoted in R.A. Musgrave, *Theory of public finance*, 1959, p. 59

145. THEFT

1. Thou shalt not steal.

Bible, Authorized Version, Exodus, 20:15

2. Plunder, *v.* To take the property of another without observing the decent and customary reticences of theft. To effect a change of ownership with the candid concomitance of a brass band.

   Ambrose Bierce (1842–1914?), *The devil's dictionary*, 1911

3. When a man is robbed of a trifle on the highway, it is not the two-pence lost that constitutes the capital outrage.

   Edmund Burke (1729–97), *Speech on conciliation with America*, 22 March 1775

4. Kill a man's family, and he may brook it,
   But keep your hands out of his breeches' pocket.

   Lord Byron (1788–1824), *Don Juan*, canto X, st. LXXIX

5. Stolen sweets are best.

   Colley Cibber (1671–1757), *The rival fools*, 1709, I

6. Thou shalt not steal; an empty feat,
   When it's so lucrative to cheat.

   Arthur Hugh Clough (1819–61), *The latest decalogue*, 1862

7. All stealing is comparative. If you come to absolutes, pray who does not steal?

   Ralph Waldo Emerson (1803–82), *Essays, second series*, 1844, 'Experience'

8. Beggars may sing before a thief.

Thomas Fuller (1654–1734), *Gnomologia*, 1732, no. 964

9. He that finds a thing, steals it, if he endeavours not to restore it.

   Thomas Fuller (1654–1734), ibid., no. 2,104

10. It is easy to rob an orchard, when none keep it.

    Thomas Fuller (1654–1734), ibid., no. 2,925

11. The friar preached against theft, when he had a goose up his sleeve.

    Thomas Fuller (1654–1734), ibid., no. 4,548

12. He that steals an egg, will steal an ox.

    George Herbert (1593–1633), *Jacula prudentum*, 1651

13. When the steede is stolne shut the stable durre.

    John Heywood (1506–65), *Proverbs*, 1546, pt I, ch. X

14. To robbe Peter and pay Poule.

    John Heywood (1506–65), ibid., ch. XI

15. Chaunge bee no robbry.

    John Heywood (1506–65), ibid., pt II, ch. IV

16. The traveller with nothing sings as he passes a thief.

    Juvenal (fl. AD 1st–2nd cent.), *Satires*, II

17. Fair exchange is no rob'ry.

    James Kelly, *Scottish proverbs*, 1721, F, no. 27

18. Whatever is guarded is desired more. Security itself attracts thieves.

    Ovid (43 BC–AD 17), *Amores*, bk III, iv, 1. 25

19. There's warrant in that theft
    Which steals itself, when there's no
    mercy left.

    William Shakespeare (1564–1616), *Macbeth*, 1605–6, II. i

20. The robb'd that smiles steals something from the thief;
    He robs himself that spends a
    bootless grief.

    William Shakespeare (1564–1616), *Othello*, I. iii

21. He that is robb'd, not wanting
    what is stolen,
    Let him no know't, and he's not
    robb'd at all.

    William Shakespeare (1564–1616), ibid., III. iii

22. There is boundless theft
    In limited professions.

    William Shakespeare (1564–1616), *Timon of Athens*, 1607–8, IV. iii

23. O, theft most base,
    That we have stol'n, what we do
    fear to keep!

    William Shakespeare (1564–1616), *Troilus and Cressida*, 1597–1602, II. ii

24. *Mendoza*: I am a brigand: I live by robbing the rich.
    Tanner: I am a gentleman: I live by robbing the poor.

    George Bernard Shaw (1856–1950), *Man and superman*, III

146. THIEVES

1. Better scare a thief than snare him.

    Aesop (fl. *c.*550 BC), 'The farmer and the lion', *Fables*

2. Old thieves never die, they just steal away.

    Anonymous

3. All bad men are not thieves, although all thieves are bad men.

    Aristotle (384–322 BC), *Rhetoric*, trans. Welldon, bk II, ch. XXIV

4. Men do not despise a thief, if he steal to satisfy his soul when he is hungry.

    Bible, Authorized Version, Proverbs, 6: 30

5. A certain man went down from Jerusalem to Jericho, and fell among thieves.

    Bible, Authorized Version, St Luke, 10: 30

6. Robber, *n.* A candid man of affairs.

    Ambrose Bierce (1842–1914?), *The devil's dictionary*, 1911

7. In a very plain sense the proverb says, call one a thief, and he will steal.

    Thomas Carlyle (1795–1881), *Sartor resartus*, 1836, bk II, ch. I

8. Justice must be a very good thing because I see here that it even has to be practised among thieves.

    Miguel De Cervantes (1574–1615), *Don Quixote*, 1614, pt II, ch. LX

9. They say that even thieves have a code of laws to observe and obey.

   Cicero (106–43 BC), *De officiis*, bk II, ch. XI

10. As to the profession of robber [in the eighteenth century] exercised on the roads of England, it was a liberal profession, which required more accomplishments than either the bar or the pulpit; from the beginning it presumed a most bountiful endowment of heroic qualifications — strength, health, agility, and exquisite horsemanship, intrepidity of the first order, presence of mind, courtesy, and a general ambidexterity of powers for facing all accidents, and for turning to a good account all unlooked-for contingencies.

    Thomas De Quincey (1785–1859), *Autobiography*, ch. XVI

11. The thief steals from himself.

    Ralph Waldo Emerson (1803–82), *Essays, first series*, 1841, 'Compensation'

12. An hundred thieves cannot strip one naked man, especially if the skin's off.

    Benjamin Franklin (1706–90), *Poor Richard's almanac*, 1755

13. A fair booty makes many a thief.

    Thomas Fuller (1654–1734), *Gnomologia*, 1732, no. 86

14. A thief knows a thief, as a wolf knows a wolf.

    Thomas Fuller (1654–1734), ibid., no. 430

15. A thief passes for a gentleman, when stealing has made him rich.

    Thomas Fuller (1654–1734), ibid., no. 431

16. All are not thieves that dogs bark at.

    Thomas Fuller (1654–1734), ibid., no. 502

17. Opportunity makes the thief.

    Thomas Fuller (1654–1734), ibid., no. 3,810

18. The great thieves punish the little ones.

    Thomas Fuller (1654–1734), ibid., no. 4,565

19. The thief is sorry he is to be hanged, but not that he is a thief.

    Thomas Fuller (1654–1734), ibid., no. 4,788

20. When the enterprising burglar's not a-burgling.

    Sir W.S. Gilbert (1836–1911), *Pirates of Penzance*, 1880, II

21. Thieves are the finest people in the world!

    Maxim Gorki (1868–1936), *The lower depths*, I

22. When thieves fall out, true men come to their good.

    John Heywood (1506–65), *Proverbs*, 1546, pt II, ch. IX

23. A thief believes everybody steals.

    E.W. Howe (1853–1937), *Country town sayings*, 1911

24. He that shews his purse, bribes the thief.

    James Kelly, *Scottish proverbs,* 1721, H, no. 28

25. To rob even a corpse.

    Proverb, quoted by Aristotle, *The rhetoric,* bk II, ch. VI

26. We hang little thieves and take our hats off to great ones.

    German proverb

27. Beauty provoketh thieves sooner than gold.

    William Shakespeare (1564–1616), *As you like it,* 1596–1600, I. iii

28. What simple thief brags of his own attaint?

    William Shakespeare (1564–1616), *The comedy of errors,* 1592–3, III. ii

29. A plague upon't, when thieves cannot be true to one another!

    William Shakespeare (1564–1616), *Henry IV pt I,* 1597–8, II. ii

30. Suspicion always haunts the guilty mind;
    The thief doth fear each bush an officer.

    William Shakespeare (1564–1616), *Henry VI pt III,* 1590–1, V. vi

31. What know the laws
    That thieves do pass on thieves.

    William Shakespeare (1564–1616), *Measure for measure,* 1604–5, I. v

32. Every true man's apparel fits your thief.

    William Shakespeare (1564–1616), ibid., IV. ii

33. His thefts were too open; his filching was like an unsuccessful singer; he kept not time.

    William Shakespeare (1564–1616), *The merry wives of Windsor,* 1597–1601, I. iii

34. Rich preys make true men thieves.

    William Shakespeare (1564–1616), *Venus and Adonis,* 1592

35. Why don't thieves dress with aprons — so convenient for storing stolen goods?

    Sydney Smith (1771–1845), quoted in W. Jerrold, *Bon-Mots of Sydney Smith and R. Brinsley Sheridan,* p. 58

147. TORTS

1. You cannot do wrong without suffering wrong.

   Ralph Waldo Emerson (1803–82), *Essays, first series,* 1841, 'Compensation'

2. There is no wrong without a remedy. (*Ubi jus ibi remedium.*)

   Legal maxim

3. No wrong is done to a person who consents to it. (*Volenti non fit injuria.*)

   Legal maxim

4. What would be a nuisance in Belgrave Square would not necessarily

be so in Bermondsey.

Thesiger, L.J. (1838–80), *Sturges v. Bridgman* (1879), 1 Ch.D. 852 at 865

148. TRADE UNIONS

1. Trade unionists and the courts should be kept far apart.

   Winston Churchill (1874–1965), attributed

2. Management and union may be likened to that serpent of the fables who on one body had two heads that fighting with poisoned fangs, killed themselves.

   Peter Drucker, *The new society*, 1951, ch. 14

3. I cannot help thinking that the English Bar is probably the oldest and tightest trade union in the world.

   Sir Patrick Hastings (1880–1952), *Observer*, 'Sayings of the week', 21 May 1921

4. Most workers want nothing more of the law than that it should leave them alone.

   Lord Wedderburn, quoted in *The Times*, 19 March 1986

149. TREASON

1. *English* treasons never can succeed,
   For they're so open-hearted, you may know
   Their own most secret thought, and others too.

   Daniel Defoe (1660–1731), *The true-born Englishman*, 1701, pt II

2. Treason doth never prosper:
   what's the reason?
   For if it prosper, none dare call it treason.

   Sir John Harington (1561–1612), *Epigrams*, 'Of treason'

3. Treason is not inherited.

   William Shakespeare (1564–1616), *As you like it*, 1596–1600, I. iii

4. Treason and murder ever kept together,
   As two yoke-devils sworn to either's purpose.

   William Shakespeare (1564–1616), *Henry V*, 1598–9, II. ii

5. Treason's secret knife.

   William Shakespeare (1564–1616), *Henry VI pt II*, 1590–1, III. i

150. TRESPASS

1.   noTiS
   Trespaser's will be persekuted to the full extent of 2 mongrel dogs which ain't never been overly soshibil with strangers and 1 dubble barrel shot gun which ain't loaded with no sofy pillers. Dam if I ain't tired of this hel raisin on my proputy.

   Anonymous: sign posted on a public road in South Georgia, quoted in H.L. Mencken, *Americana*, 1925, 'Georgia'

151. TRIAL

1. Trial, *n.* A formal inquiry designed

171

to prove and put upon record the blameless characters of judges, advocates and jurors.

Ambrose Bierce (1842–1914?), *The devil's dictionary*, 1911

2. I'll be judge, I'll be jury,
Said cunning old Fury:
I'll try the whole cause,
And condemn you to death.

Lewis Carroll (1832–98), *Alice's adventures in wonderland*, 1865, ch. III

3. Sentence first — verdict afterwards.

Lewis Carroll (1832–98), ibid., ch. XII

4. Battledore and shuttlecock's a wery good game, vhen you an't the shuttlecock and two lawyers the battledores, in which case it gets too excitin' to be pleasant.

Charles Dickens (1812–70), *The Pickwick papers*, 1837, ch. XX

5. That trial is not fair, where affection is the judge.

Thomas Fuller (1654–1734), *Gnomologia*, 1732, no. 4,373

6. Let mine trial be mine own confession.

William Shakespeare (1564–1616), *Measure for measure*, 1604–5, V. i

7. Before I be convict by course of law.
To threaten me with death is most unlawful.

William Shakespeare (1564–1616), *Richard III*, 1592–3, I. i

8. Are you going to hang him *anyhow* — and try him afterward?

Mark Twain (1835–1910), *A trial*, 1872

9. The wisest lawyer never discovers the merits of his cause 'till the trial.

William Wycherley (1640–1716), *The country wife*, I. i

152. TRUSTS

1. ... uses were but imaginations.

Anderson C.J. (1530–1605), *Chudleigh's case* (1595), 1 Rep. 113b at 140a

2. A trust is an office necessary in the concerns between man and man, and ... if faithfully discharged, attended with no small degree of trouble and anxiety.

Lord Hardwicke L.C. (1690–1764), *Knight* v. *Earl of Plymouth* (1747), Dick. 120 at 126

3. I am 'in a fiduciary position' — which is always a ———— uncomfortable position.

F.W. Maitland (1850–1906), *The letters of Frederic William Maitland*, ed. C.H.S. Fifoot, 1965, p. 122, letter no. 137

153. TRUTH

1. The lip of truth shall be established forever;
But a lying tongue is but for a moment.

Bible, Authorized Version, Proverbs, 12: 19

2. Buy the truth, and sell it not.

   Bible, Authorized Version, ibid., 23: 23

3. Speak ye every man the truth to his neighbour; execute the judgement of truth and peace in your gates.

   Bible, Authorized Version, Zechariah, 8: 16

4. Ye shall know the truth, and the truth shall make you free.

   Bible, Authorized Version, St John, 8: 32

5. Truth fears no trial.

   Thomas Fuller (1654–1734), *Gnomologia*, 1732, no. 5,297

6. Truth makes the devil blush.

   Thomas Fuller (1654–1734), ibid., no. 5,306

7. Truth needs the wisdom of the serpent as well as the simplicity of the dove.

   Sir Arthur Helps (1813–75), *Friends in council*, 1847, ch. 1

8. Is not the truth the truth?

   William Shakespeare (1564–1616), *Henry IV pt I*, 1597–8, I. iv

9. The lawyer's truth is not Truth, but consistency, or a consistent expediency, and is not concerned chiefly to reveal the justice that may consist with wrong-doing.

   Henry D. Thoreau (1817–62), *Resistance to civil government*, 1849

10. Truth is stranger than fiction, but

not near as plentiful.

   Frank McKinney Hubbard (1868–1930), *New sayings by Abe Martin*, 1917

154. TYRANNY

1. No tyranny ought to be endured which makes free speech dangerous.

   Henry Ward Beecher (1813–87), *Proverbs from Plymouth pulpit*, 1887

2. Bad laws are the worst sort of tyranny.

   Edmund Burke (1729–97), speech at Bristol, previous to the election, 1780

3. Wherever law ends, tyranny begins.

   John Locke (1632–1704), *Of civil government*, 1690, ch. XVIII

4. Tyranny is the desire of universal rule outside its sphere.

   Blaise Pascal (1623–62), *Pensées*, 1670, pt I

155. VICE

1. It is the nature of vice or crime that it takes away moral stamina.

   Henry Ward Beecher (1813–87), *Proverbs from Plymouth pulpit*, 1887

2. As crimes are evils against organised forms of society, so vices

are evils against the unorganised forms of society.

Henry Ward Beecher (1813–87), ibid.

3. If virtue had everything her own way, she would be insufferable as dominant factions generally are. It is the function of vice to keep virtue within reasonable bounds.

Samuel Butler (1835–1902), *Notebooks*, ed. Festing Jones, ch. II

4. Vice is its own reward.

Quentin Crisp, *The naked civil servant*, 1968, ch. 2

5. Vice know she's ugly, so puts on her mask.

Benjamin Franklin (1706–90), *Poor Richard's almanac*, 1746

6. A vicious man's son has a good title to vice.

Thomas Fuller (1654–1734), *Gnomologia*, 1732, no. 451

7. As virtue is its own reward, so vice is its own punishment.

Thomas Fuller (1654–1734), ibid., no. 743

8. It is easier to run from virtue to vice, than from vice to virtue.

Thomas Fuller (1654–1734), ibid., no. 2,931

9. Till vice gets an habit, there is a remedy for it.

Thomas Fuller (1654–1734), ibid., no. 5,046

10. Vice is its own punishment, and sometimes its own cure.

Thomas Fuller (1654–1734), ibid., no. 5,354

11. There is some virtue in almost every vice.

William Hazlitt (1773–1830), *Characteristics*, 1823, CCLXXIV

12. Where vice is, vengeance follows.

James Kelly, *Scottish proverbs*, 1721, W, no. 127

13. What often stops us from concentrating on a single vice is that we have several of them.

François Duc de La Rochefoucauld (1613–80), *Maxims*, 1678

14. It is clear that those vices which destroy domestic happiness ought to be as much as possible repressed. It is equally clear that they cannot be repressed by penal legislation. It is therefore right and desirable that public opinion should be directed against them.

Lord Macaulay (1800–59), *Moore's life of Lord Byron*, June 1831

15. Vices and frailties correct each other, like acids and alkalies. If each vicious man had but one vice, I do not know how the world would go on.

Richard Whately (1787–1863), *Thoughts and apothegms*, 1856, pt VI

156. VIOLENCE

1. I really think that this assault was

carried to a very inconsiderate length, and that if an author is to go and give a beating to a publisher who has offended him, two or three blows with a horse-whip ought to be quite enough to satisfy his irritated feelings.

Lord Abinger C.B. (1767–1844), *Fraser* v. *Berkeley* (1836), 7 Car. & P. 621 at 626

2. Nations are not primarily ruled by laws; less by violence.

Edmund Burke (1729–97), *Thoughts on the causes of the present discontents*, 1770

157. WAR

1. Laws are dumb in war.

Cicero (106–43 BC), *Pro Milone*, ch. IV

2. The Roman sword would never have conquered the world if the grand fabric of Roman Law had not been elaborated to save the man behind the sword from having to think for himself.

F.M. Cornford (1874–1943), *Microcosmographia academica*, 1908, V

3. Where drums beat, law is silent.

James Kelly, *Scottish provebs*, 1721, W, no. 151

4. War makes thieves, and peace hangs them.

James Kelly, ibid., no. 154

158. WEALTH

1. Lay not up for yourselves treasures upon earth, where moth and rust doth corrupt, and where thieves break in and steal.

Bible, Authorized Version, St Matthew, 6:19

2. The persons who compose the Independent classes are Dependent upon two things: first, upon the *industry* of their fellow creatures; second, upon *injustice* which enables them to command it.

John Gray (1799–1883), *Lectures on human happiness*, 1825

3. What need a rich man be a thief?

James Kelly, *Scottish proverbs*, 1721, W, no. 133

4. It is better that a man should tyrannise over his bank balance than over his fellow-citizens.

John Maynard Keynes (1883–1946), *The general theory of employment, interest and money*, bk VI, ch. 24

5. The distribution of wealth depends on the laws and customs of society.

John Stuart Mill (1806–73), *Principles of political economy*, ed. Ashley, bk II, ch. I, 1

6. Wealth, in a commercial age, is largely made up of promises.

Roscoe Pound (1870–1964), *An introduction to the philosophy of law*, 1922, ch. 6

159. WILLS

1. The power of making a will, is an instrument placed in the hands of individuals for the prevention of private calamity.

   Jeremy Bentham (1748–1832), *Principles of the civil code*, pt II, ch. V

2. Legacy, *n.* A gift from one who is legging it out of this vale of tears.

   Ambrose Bierce (1842–1914?), *The devil's dictionary*, 1911

3. When you have told anyone you have left him a legacy the only decent thing to do is to die at once.

   Samuel Butler (1835–1902), attributed

4. If a man can't forge his own will, whose will can he forge?

   Sir W.S. Gilbert (1836–1911), *Ruddigore*, 1887, II

5. Disinherit: 1. The prankish action of the ghosts in cutting the pockets out of trousers. 2. To leave great sums of money to lawyers.

   Frank McKinney Hubbard (1868–1930), *The Roycroft dictionary*, 1923

6. No customer brings so much grist to the mill.
   As the wealthy old woman who makes her own will.

   Lord Charles Neaves (1800–76), attributed

7. Let's talk of graves, of worms, and epitaphs;

Make dust our paper, and with rainy eyes
Write sorrow on the bosom of the earth.
Let's choose executors, and talk of wills.

   William Shakespeare (1564–1616), *Richard II*, 1595–6, III. ii

8. Men should not sin in their graves.

   Strange M.R. (1696–1754), *Thomas* v. *Britnell* (1751), 2 Ves. Sen. 313 at 314

160. WITNESSES

1. A Kerry witness ... one who will swear to anything.

   Anonymous, quoted by Ferdinand Mount, *Spectator*, 7 June 1986

2. The body is the chief witness in every murder.

   G.K. Chesterton (1874–1936), *The scandal of Father Brown*, 1935, 'The point of a pin'

3. Lawyers hold that there are two kinds of particularly bad witness: a reluctant witness, and a too willing witness.

   Charles Dickens (1812–70), *The Pickwick papers*, 1837, ch. XXXIV

4. Often people do not know that they may be important witnesses simply because ... they may not understand the significance of something they have seen, or,

indeed, of something they have noticed not seeing in a particular case.

Lord Elton, House of Lords, 2 July 1984

5. One eye-witness is better than ten hearsays.

   Thomas Fuller (1654–1734), *Gnomologia*, 1732, no. 3,750

6. There is a witness every where.

   Thomas Fuller (1654–1734), ibid., no. 4,886

7. And with a smile set a witness even on a brother.

   Hesiod (*fl. c.*8th cent. BC), *Works and days*, trans. A.W. Mair

8. If you will make't an action, call witness to't.

   William Shakespeare (1564–1616), *Cymbeline*, 1609–10, II. iii

9. You cannot witness for me, being slain.

   William Shakespeare (1564–1616), *Henry VI pt I*, 1589–90, IV. v

10. God is my witness.

    William Shakespeare (1564–1616), *Henry VI pt II*, 1590–1, I. iii

11. But now I find I had suborn'd the witness.

    William Shakespeare (1564–1616), *Othello*, 1604–5, III. iv

Index of Authors and Sources

In this index the entries refer to individual quotations rather than pages. Each entry contains two numbers, the first of which indicates the number of the topic and the second the actual quotation. For example, under Abinger, the first reference is 50.1. This refers to the first quotation appearing under the 50th topic, which is 'Defamation'. The numbers and titles of the topics appear at the top of the pages.

Where an author is quoted frequently it did not seem very helpful to provide each reference. Therefore, to save space, where the number of quotations from a single author exceeds 25 the name is simply marked with an asterisk.

INDEX OF AUTHORS AND SOURCES

Index of Key Words

This index is arranged alphabetically, both for the key words and for the entries following each key word. Each entry gives part of the quotation to indicate the context and the key word itself is then abbreviated. Like the index of authors and sources, the reference consists of two numbers, the first of which indicates the topic and the second the quotation itself. For example, an entry under 'Forest' reads 'laws ... like a vast f. 85.19'. This refers to the 19th quotation appearing under the 85th topic, which is 'Law'.

Abstract: A. liberty 93.5
Abundance: A. of law breaks no law 85.121
Academe: Our court shall be a little A. 41.27
Accessory: I am your a. 1.2
Accomplice: Topic 1
Accountants: Topic 2
Accus'd: being a. a crafty murderer 65.17
Accusation: Guilt has very quick ears to an a. 65.4
justifies himself before a. 65.5
Accusations: clear conscience laughs at false a. 33.5
Accuse: Topic 3
no man is bound to a. himself 65.12
What is the evidence that doth a. me? 58.14
Accused: absence of the a. 50.14
to detain one a. of unusualness 10.1
Accuser: no a. so dreaded ... as the conscience 33.16
Accuses: guilty conscience self a. 33.14
Acquit: juries ... occasionally a. a defendant 80.19
Acquittal: triumphant verdicts of a. 80.44
Acquitted: than that he should be tried and a. 43.10
Acre: for an a. of barren ground 84.10
Action: limitation of a. 97.13
Activists: judges ... judicial a. 79.75
Administration: a. of human justice 83.12
a. of justice is the firmest pillar 83.75
makes the a. of justice stink 27.31
Adultery: Topic 4
Adversaries: Do as a. do in law 88.76
Advocacy: Topic 5
Advocate: good have no need of an a. 72.12
Affection: where a. is the judge 151.5
Agency: Topic 6
Agent: a. of injustice 24.1
Agree: A., for the law is costly 40.2

Agreements: a. between spouses 97.2
Men keep their a. 36.3
Agricultural: a. community again to two classes 26.6
Agriculture: nation depended on a. 27.20
Alcatraz: A removal to A. 124.4
Alcohol: tears and misery ... caused by a. 77.3
Alibi: Topic 7
Alimony: Topic 8
Alive: needst not strive officiously to keep a. 104.5
All-binding: manacles of the a. law 85.181
Altar: sacrifices made at the a. 97.27
American: A. attitude to the law 85.39
Every A.'s guarantee of freedom 16.2
Amnesty: A. is an act by which rulers 109.1
Anger: a. does not become a judge 79.78
hire out words and a. 88.59
nothing so unfitting as a. 130.44
Antic: old father a. the law 85.174
Apes: scholar at court is an ass among a. 41.10
Apology: Never make a defence or a. 51.1
Appeals: Topic 9
Aprons: Why don't thieves dress with a. 146.30
Arbitrary: a. system indeed must always be 39.7
an a. decision 78.3
Arguments: lies well steel'd with weighty a. 94.21
Aristocracy: a monarchy, an a. and a democracy 35.9
Armed: only a man a. to the teeth 86.3
Arms: benefit of law of a. 51.10
Laws ... hold their tongues amongst a. 85.45
Army: like Virgil's a. 88.1
Arrest: Topic 10
We can a. and prevent monopoly 27.34
Arson: Topic 11

Fine: What is a f. lie 94.23
Fines: Topic 61
Fingers: Lawyers' f. 60.6
Fire: careless in the use of f. 11.1
Fire-side: those who form ... his f. 59.2
Fish: f. hangs in the net 26.12
    some f. some frogs 41.13
Fishery: ladies of the British f. 95.1
Five: For so long as you have f. pounds
    60.1
Flood: corruption, like a general f. 39.13
Folly: prolific mother of f. 48.4
Folly-swaddles: Commerce without its f.
    115.1
Fool: a f., with judges 79.21
    one man ... for making a f. of another
      43.8
    think truth were a f. 94.15
Fooleries: little f. of our draftsmen 92.4
Fools: amongst f. a judge 79.21
    built on the heads of f. 88.43
Foot: Chancellor ... still had only the
    length of his f. 56.11
    varies like the Chancellor's f. 56.9
    we call a f., a Chancellor's f. 56.16
Footsteps: the art of tracing f. 53.6
Forbidden: F. fruit a flavour has 125.5
Force: judge is to suppress f. 79.4
Foreign: f. laws of God and man 85.111
Forest: laws ... like a vast f. 85.19
Forge: If a man can't f. his own will 159.4
Forms: lawyer has his f. 88.10
Forswear: Accuse some innocent and f.
    myself 3.6
Fountain: inexhaustible f. of dishonesty
    48.2
Fox: f. should not be of the jury 80.22
Frailties: Vices and f. correct each other
    155.15
Frailty: forget what human f. is 83.73
France: as the laws are written in F. 30.2
    in F. it is the presiding judge 79.55
Fraud: Topic 62
    Judge is to suppress force and f. 79.4
Free: Man is born f. 93.21
    Trade is in nature f. 27.17
Freedom: Constitution ... source of their f.
    35.12
    Every American's guarantee of f. 16.2
    jury ... lamp that shows that f. lives
      80.14
    laws impinge on individual f. 93.19
    too much f. 93.9
Free speech: F. does not mean f. 93.29
Friar: f. preached against theft 145.11
Friend: f. in court 41.9
Friends: eat and drink as f. 88.76
Frogs: some fish some f. 41.13

Frowning: Unto the f. judge 58.14
Fruit: good tree cannot bring forth evil f.
    67.1
    Money ... f. of evil 100.6
Fudge: Though all my law is f. 79.41

Gallows: save a thief from the g. 98.10
Gambling: Topic 63
Gaming: G. ... child of avarice 63.2
Gates: g. of mercy shall be all shut up
    98.16
Gentleman: I am a g. I live by robbing the
    poor 145.24
    thief passes for a g. 145.15
Ghosts: these g. of the past 83.8
Glaring: faced with g. injustice 79.24
Glass: earth is made of g. 42.16
Gloster: G. is as innocent 72.16
Goblins: That mouldeth g. swift as frenzy's
    thoughts 33.28
God: But for the grace of G. there goes
    John Bradford 130.8
    foreign laws of G. and man 85.111
    G. is my witness 160.10
    juries are like Almighty G. 80.34
    The true laws of G. 85.51
    unwritten laws of G. 85.198
Goddess: why the g. is blindfolded 83.42
Gold: against the power of g. 139.2
    G. delights to penetrate 18.5
    When you walk laden with g. 139.2
Good: g. and upright magistrate 79.51
    G. is a g. doctor 96.2
    G. laws cause better laws 92.35
    The law is g. 85.33
Good faith: Foundation of justice is g.
    83.20
    g. is the basis of all mercantile
      transactions 27.11
Goodlier: He were much g. 68.10
Goose: steals the g. from off the common
    26.2
Government: Topic 64
    four pillars of g. 83.9
    g. is ... governed by the constitution
      35.10
    g. which imprisons unjustly 24.2
Governments: this that makes their g. slow
    52.6
Governs: best which g. not at all 64.19
Grace: But for the g. of God there goes
    John Bradford 130.8
Grand juries: G. ... only censors of this
    Nation 80.20
Graves: Men should not sin in their g.
    159.8
Greater: g. the man, the g. the crime 42.22
Gresham's law: G. 100.7

INDEX OF KEY WORDS

194

House of Commons: H. is terribly
outdated 110.22

House of Lords: H. is like H. 110.2

Houses: Laws, like h. 85.46
lawyer's h. are built 88.43

Human: forget what h. frailty is 83.73
law has respect for h. infirmity 85.22

Humane: H. law 85.90
more h. and enlightened penal system
42.36

Humanity: H. is the second virtue of the
Courts 83.62
judge dealing with h. 79.52
Property is an instrument of h. 127.21

Humorous: desire to be h. in court 41.4

Humour: judges with a sense of h. 79.68

Hundred: h. thieves cannot strip one naked
man 146.12
takes a h. years to make a law 92.2

Hunger: Where there is h., law is not
regarded 85.85

Hungry: h. judges soon the sentence sign
43.14
satisfy his soul when he is h. 146.4
than a h. judge 79.96

Husband: Bigamy having one h. too many
15.1
evidence of a wife for or against her h.
58.9
h. who commits adultery 4.2
happy marriage ... blind wife and a
deaf h. 97.24
only one h. at a time 97.1
readiness to shoot the h. 4.1

Huzzas: gain the h. of thousands 79.63

Idiot: law is an ass — a i. 97.12

If: much virtue in i. 94.16

Ignorance: I. and crime are not cause and
effect 42.58
I. of the law excuses no man 51.9
i. of the law is no excuse 51.5
i. of the law 95.14
twelve people of average i. 80.40

Ignorant: i., blundering, blind thing, the
law 85.112
person i. of legal matters 41.29

Ill-managed: law-suit is like an i. dispute
95.8

Illegal: masses will resort to i. methods 3.3

Illegitimacy: Topic 69

Illiterate: Juries ... i. plebians 80.39

Imaginations: uses were but i. 152.1

Impartial: cold neutrality of an i. judge
79.15

Impey: Chief Justice I. 18.6

Impossible: When you have eliminated the
i. 53.5

Imprisons: government which i. unjustly
24.2

Impulse: whether the wrong is done on i.
102.1

Incorruption: assurance of i. 39.4

Indentures: makes i. as he goes 88.32

Indicted: No one who has been i. 72.4

Indictment: drawing up an i. against a
whole people 76.1

Inexcusable: knowledge rendereth a crime
i. 42.21

Informers: Topic 70

Infringe: not partial to i. our laws 91.3

Inheritance: land ... is the original i. 84.8

Inherited: Crimes, like lands, are not i.
42.51
Treason is not i. 149.3

Iniquity: Gaming ... brother of i. 63.2
Sparing justice feeds i. 83.70

Injury: Crime may be said to be i. 42.3
He that defends an i. 51.4
I. is to be measured by malice 47.1

Injustice: Topic 71
better than cheap i. 83.16
blazoning our i. everywhere 50.18
fear of suffering i. 83.46
female fugitive from i. 54.6
Justice, is worse than i. 41.8
One man's justice is another's i. 83.26

Inland Revenue: I. to put the largest
possible shovel 144.14

Inn: take more ease in mine i. 114.2

Innocence: Topic 72
shield of i. 85.40
silence often of pure i. 95.35
timid i. 42.40

Innocent: Accuse some i. 3.6
better ... than to condemn an i. one
65.27
every man is i. in his own eyes 83.23
excuses the guilty, condemns the i.
65.11
given to the military by i. bystanders
138.1

Insanity: Topic 73

Inscrutable: i. workings of Providence
79.86

Insolvencies: able to trace bankruptcies
and i. 14.1

Insolvency: Topic 74

Instinct: low, bestial i. 127.19

Institutions: rocks on which all civil i.
83.45

Insurance: Topic 75

Integrity: presumption of i. 21.3

Intelligent: conversation of i. barristers
88.69

Intend: If a man is not too mad to i. 73.8

not a crime to i. to commit a crime 42.24

Intentions: i. of legislative actions 92.8

Interest: long-legged i. 48.1

International: presence of great i. struggles 83.3

International Law: Topic 76

Interprets: lawyer i. truth 88.37

Intolerance: law may be only the i. 85.192

Intoxication: Topic 77

Intuition: more or less trained i. 81.3

Iron: Nor i. bars a cage 124.13

Jack Ketch: unsympathetic as J. 88.45

Jails: visiting j. 44.17

Jam: police are like j. in the sandwich 118.17

Jargon: peculiar cant and j. 30.13

Jealous: Law ... is a j. mistress 85.201

Jeffreys: classed with Lord J. 79.22

Jewel: Honesty is a fine j. 68.4

John: But for the grace of God there goes J. Bradford 130.8

    made possible ... Magna Carta under J. 96.2

Judge: character of j. in my own cause 78.2

    cover the iniquity of one corrupt j. 39.3

    Equity ... matter of the length of the j.'s ears 56.12

    He whose father is a j. 43.4

    I'll be j., I'll be jury 151.2

    j. under the influence of government 64.14

    No man can be j. in his own cause 78.5

    overspeaking j. is no well-tuned cymbal 83.10

    People j. the j. 128.8

    Unto the frowning j. 58.14

Judgement: Topic 78

    proceed to j. 79.83

    shallow spirit of j. 85.175

Judges: Topic 79

    hungry j. soon the sentence sign 43.14

    J. answer to the question of law 41.22

    Jurymen ... but ephemeral j. 82.1

    law was locked in the breasts of the j. 123.7

    Parliament, the Press and the J. 35.3

    robes of all the good j. 39.3

    The j. all ranged 41.16

    what the j. had for breakfast 85.6

    When j. steal themselves 39.16

    when the right judge j. wrongly 79.90

Judicial: J. power ... may be a check 64.13

    judges ... j. activists 79.75

    worst of all j. failings 41.4

Judicious: J. punishment 130.46

Jungle: this is the Law of the j. 85.125

Juries: Topic 80

    j. will not convict 43.3

Jurisprudence: Topic 81

    In civil j. 25.2

Jurors: Topic 82

    j. to the matter of fact 41.22

Jury: I'll be judge, I'll be j. 151.2

    May work and worm into a j.'s hearts 79.18

    We're the j. 47.2

Jury-men: wretches hang that j. may dine 43.14

Just: Law has never made men a whit more j. 85.206

    O j. but severe law 85.181

Justice: Topic 83

    every purpose but that of delaying j. 56.2

    Government's ungirt when j. dies 64.10

    half evidence will not do quarter j. 58.10

    Injustice all round is j. 71.12

    injustice in clamouring for j. 71.7

    J. ... among thieves 146.8

    j. in her net of law 85.159

    J. is the end of government 64.11

    J., is worse than injustice 41.8

    J. seen to be done 83.40

    j. should rouse itself 42.29

    j., while she winks at crimes 72.3

    j. without trial 43.15

    Liberty plucks j. by the nose 93.22

    Mercy seasons j. 98.27

    My aim is j. 20.2

    No fee, no j. 60.1

    Poetic j. 83.59

    Revenge is a kind of wild j. 136.1

    tardy j. will o'ertake the crime 104.7

    The more certain j. is 20.7

    this living temple of j. 28.6

    Thou robbed man of j. 58.13

    Thwackum was for doing j. 98.4

    Unwhipp'd of j. 42.48

    When Mr J. was a counsellor 88.4

    where mystery begins j. ends 30.4

Justices: bench or a brace of sporting j. 142.3

    J. come and go 83.71

Keeper: k. is only a poacher 117.2

Kentish: A K. jury 80.23

Kerry: A K. witness 160.1

Key: have taken away the k. of knowledge 88.6

Kill: K. a man's family 145.4

    k. someone with a motor-car 103.2

    let's k. all the lawyers 88.74

    license to k. 104.13

Protection: Innocence is no p. 72.8
Providence: inscrutable workings of p. 79.86
Public: Only effect of p. punishment 130.34
Public Opinion: Topic 128
Public Policy: Topic 129
Publisher: author is to go and give a beating to a p. 156.1
Punish: Great thieves p. little ones 146.17
   To p. villains not to make men so 130.14
Punished: madman is only p. by his madness 73.1
Punishment: Topic 130
   barbarous p. of the poorer class 122.4
   let the p. fit the crime 130.22
   offence ... less horror than the p. 43.6
   p. called trigamy 15.3
   p. of minor offences 39.6
   Penitent ... awaiting p. 65.1
   The certainty of p. is of more consequence 53.9
   vice is its own p. 155.7
   who can judge of crimes by p. 42.9
Punishments: Pecuniary p. 61.1
Purlieus: dusty p. of the law 142.4
   walk within the p. of the law 91.2
Purse: petitioner ... that spares his p. 95.16
   shews his p., bribes the thief 146.24
Pusey: Uncle Jeff P. 73.3

Qualifications: qualifies all his q. 88.28
Qualifies: q. all his qualifications 88.28
Quarrels: Topic 131
Quarrelsome: q. man has no good neighbours 106.3
Quarter: half evidence will not do q. justice 58.10
Queen: Ruler of the Q.'s Navee 90.1
Queen's bench: in the q. both law and conscience 41.23
Quiddits: where be his q. now 88.73
Quillets: sharp q. of the law 85.175
   where be his quiddits now, his q. 88.73

Race Relations: Topic 132
Ransom: The r. the happy pay to the devil 8.1
Rape: Topic 133
Raskills: take care o' r. 85.75
Rational: body of law is more r. 30.9
Rattling: r. on every side 48.9
Reap: Give a man security that he may r. 84.6
Reason: Crime is never founded upon r. 42.33

R. is the life of the law 85.61
   That takes the r. prisoner 73.7
Receiving: Topic 134
Red-robed: to visualize the terrible r. figure 79.17
Redemption: Nothing akin to foul r. 98.24
Redressed: If it be confessed, it is not r. 31.13
Referee: judge acts as a kind of r. 79.55
Reform: lawyers do not take law r. seriously 88.39
Reformation: r. is a much more painful process 130.56
   r. of the sufferer 130.1
Reformers: Law r. have to be as adventurous 85.77
Regulating: R. the prices of goods 27.6
Relations: quarrels of r. 131.1
Relieve: practice to r. 144.7
Religion: Topic 135
   Equity ... same that the spirit is in r. 56.15
   Liberty, next to r. 93.1
   where mystery begins, r. ends 30.4
Remedy: no wrong without a r. 147.2
Render: R. therefore unto Caesar 144.4
Repeal: body of men who meet to r. laws 32.1
   r. a few silly laws 92.20
   r. of bad or obnoxious laws 85.97
Repeating: why counsel are always r. themselves 79.72
Repent: Married in haste, we may r. at leisure 97.11
Repented: I was a lawyer, I have r. 88.81
Repents: He that r. of his own act 31.2
Representation: Taxation without r. is tyranny 144.31
Republic: cannot cause serious trouble in a r. 39.12
Republics: it is for r. to have laws 3.3
Resisted: He hath r. law 85.172
Responsibility: Where there is no r. 71.1
Responsible: law which requires parents to be more r. 59.1
Revenge: Topic 136
   Justice ... system of r. 83.43
   stir me most to my r. 102.3
Reverence: exaggerated r. for their system 88.66
Revolution: imposed the decimal coinage ... r. within a week 100.1
Revolving door: criminal-justice system ... had a r. 44.14
Reward: r., the conscience flies out 33.25
   Vice is its own r. 155.4
Rewards: Crimes, like virtues, are their own r. 42.19

INDEX OF KEY WORDS

liar ... I'll show you a t. 94.11
No receiver, no t. 134.1
Opportunity makes the t. 146.17
penalties to the t. 42.16
salt-water t. 115.4
save a t. from the gallows 98.10
Set a t. to catch a t. 53.7
that smiles steals something from the t. 145.20
traveller with nothing sings as he passes a t. 145.16
What need a rich man be a t. 158.3
Thiever: receiver is as bad as the t. 134.2
Thieves: Topic 146
All t. who could my fees afford 60.3
fell among t. 146.5
t. of mercy 98.15
War makes t. 157.4
where t. break in and steal 158.1
Thing: started, like a guilty t. 65.15
Thousand: t. pounds' worth of law 40.3
Thriller: English t. writers 44.8
Thunder: quiet conscience sleeps in t. 33.8
Thunderbolt: innocents 'scape not the t. 72.15
Thwackum: T. was for doing justice 98.4
Time: If you can't do t. 124.16
t. that precedes punishment 130.42
To-day: That which is law t. 85.50
Tongue: lying t. is but for a moment 153.1
murder, though it have no t. 104.12
T. was the lawyer 41.5
Tongue-tied: vanish t. in their guiltiness 65.19
Tongues: conscience hath a thousand t. 33.26
Had I a hundred t. 42.59
Laws ... hold their t. amongst arms 85.43
Tools: Words are the lawyer's t. 88.22
Torts: Topic 147
Torture: no worse t. than the t. of the laws 79.5
Touchstone: t. of common sense 80.3
Tower: burn down the T. too 11.3
Track: such as reveals in the woods the t. 42.16
Tracks: know the t. of a thief 53.1
Trade: T. is in nature free 27.17
Trade Unions: Topic 148
Train: T. up a child 23.2
Transgression: no law, there is no t. 85.202
Traps: t. for money 85.107
Traveller: t. with nothing sings as he passes a thief 145.16
Treason: Topic 149
cannot commit t. 38.3
t. is not own'd when 'tis described 42.15
Treasure: he that has stolen the t. 3.2

Treasures: Lay not up for yourselves t. upon earth 158.1
Treaty of Rome: T. like an incoming tide 92.12
Tree: Corruption is a t. 39.2
good t. cannot bring forth evil fruit 67.1
Trespass: Topic 150
laws of t. are enacted 84.2
Trial: Topic 151
justice without t. 43.15
Truth fears no t. 153.5
who refuses to come to a t. 31.1
Trifle: When a man is robbed of a t. 145.3
Trifles: does not concern itself with t. 85.128
Trigamy: punishment called t. 15.3
Triumph: t. of hope over experience 97.20
Trout: when you find a t. in the milk 58.16
Truant: I have been a t. in the law 85.176
True: as t. ... as taxes is 144.18
Trust: put your money in t. 100.8
what fool Honesty is! and T. 68.14
Trusters': cut your t. throats 14.7
Trusts: Topic 152
Truth: Topic 153
accusers ... never knew what t. meant 3.5
Any fool can tell the t. 94.7
any kind of human t. 41.31
cause of t. and justice 88.21
establishment of t. 43.11
I want the t. 58.17
Is not the t. the t. 153.8
Justice is t. in action 83.24
lawyer interprets t. 88.37
lie always needs a t. 94.3
prevent a person telling the whole t. 58.5
Tell a lie and find a t. 94.2
think t. were a fool 94.15
to find out the t. 79.20
Twelve: Amongst t. judges may not one be found 79.18
bringing t. men into a box 80.7
Twenty: Would t. shillings have ruined Mr Hampden 144.10
Types: all the t. of crime 42.59
Tyrannical: power without justice is t. 83.57
Tyrannise: t. over his bank balance 158.4
Tyranny: Topic 154
legislation imposed on t. 66.4
Taxation without representation is t. 144.31
Tyrant: Though t. kings, of t. laws restrain 64.12
Tyrants: the law of t. 85.194

Unalterable: talk of an u. law 92.40
Uncivil law: the U. shall make it mine 25.4
Understood: people obliged to obey laws
they never u. 30.10
Under-wear: insurance policy is like old u.
75.2
Underwriter: u. knows nothing 75.1
Unfee'd: breath of an u. lawyer 60.5
Ungirt: Government's u., when justice dies
64.10
Union: Management and u. 148.2
United States: U. ... has an unwritten
constitution 35.6
Unjust: An u. society 86.1
Every u. decision 56.6
Unlawful: commission of u. acts by others
42.56
ill to make an u. oath 107.2
Unnecessary: U. laws 85.107
Unobserved: Laws or ordinances u. 55.7
Unpalatable: U. statute law 85.166
Unpeaceable: u. man hath no neighbour
106.4
Unpunished: offence committed by many
goes u. 42.34
Unsuit: I demand an u. 95.21
Unwritten: u. laws of God 85.198
United States ... has an u. constitution
35.6
Upright: good and u. magistrate 79.51
O wise and u. judge 79.84
Used: it will be u. against you 10.2
Useless: No one is entirely u. 44.1
Uses: u. were but imaginations 152.1

Vacation: lawyers in the v. 88.71
Vacuum: Equity abhors a beneficial v.
56.8
Vacuum-cleaner: criminal justice system
... likened to a v. 43.13
VAT: possible to be registered for V.
144.3
Vengeance: private v. comes in 43.3
Where vice is, v. follows 155.12
Verbal: A v. contract 36.1
Verdict: returning a perverse v. 80.25
Sentence first — v. afterwards 151.3
Verdicts: triumphant v. of acquittal 80.44
Verses: said to criticise my v. 88.58
Vice: Topic 155
Vilest: The v. deeds like poison weeds
124.23
Villain: smile, and smile and be a v. 49.2
Villains: To punish v. not to make men so
130.14
V. are usually the worst casuists 4.1
When rich v. have need of poor ones
42.49

Villainy: Poverty begets sedition and v.
122.2
Villany: Nothing is sacred now but v.
42.39
Violate: Those who v. the law 85.207
Violence: Topic 156
Virgil: like V.'s army 88.1
Virtue: Crime like v. has its degrees 42.40
Crimes, like v. 42.19
if v. had everything her own way 155.3
Justice is not a cloistered v. 83.7
Successful crime goes by the name of v.
42.43
Virtues: crimes ... cherished by our v.
42.45
Justice sums up all v. 59.60
Virtuous: cannot make men v. 41.25
Visage: confront the v. of the offence
98.14
Vitiates: Insanity v. all acts 73.4
Voluminous: laws are ... apt to be v. 92.50

Wages: w. of sin is alimony 8.2
Waking: crime depends on somebody not
w. 42.8
Walls: Stone w. do not a prison make
124.13
War: Topic 157
Watch-dog: director is really a w. 29.1
Water-flowing: mercy dried their w. tears
98.18
Water-thieves: w. ... I mean pirates 115.3
Wax: 'tis the bee's w. 88.74
Weak: for the w. too strong 85.159
Wealth: Topic 158
Wedding: W. is destiny, and hanging
likewise 97.15
Weeds: The vilest deeds like poison w.
124.23
Weigh: W. but the crime 42.52
Weighty: lies well steel'd with w.
arguments 94.21
Well-breakfasted: w. juryman 82.3
Whereas: The W. of almost every preamble
92.43
Whipped: who gets w. for a sin 130.29
Whistle: Let the law go w. 85.190
Whit: Law has never made men a w. more
just 85.206
White: w. is black 88.78
Widow: while the w. weeps 83.69
Wife: evidence of a w. for or against her
husband 58.9
happy marriage ... blind w. and a deaf
husband 97.24
if every w. ought to be a slave 92.29
Wig: w. full of learning 41.5
Wild: Revenge is a kind of w. justice 136.1

Will: w. of the nation 85.115

William: oppressions of W. the Norman 96.2

Wills: Topic 159

Windward: Just to the w. of the law 91.1

Windy: w. side of the law 85.189

Winks: justice, while she w. at crimes 72.3

Wise: O w. and upright judge 79.84

Wisest: continual expedients of the w. laws 55.6

  The w. man sometimes acts weakly 21.1

Witch: Accountants are the w. doctors 2.1

Witness: bewildering an honest w. 45.4

  In real life the w.'s fortitude 45.2

  Liar ... An expert w. 94.12

  no w. so terrible ... as the conscience 33.16

  w. of a good conscience 33.22

Witnesses: Topic 160

  method of examining w. apart 92.42

  oral examination of w. 45.4

Wives: Who married three w. at a time 15.6

Woe: Pardon is still the nurse of second w. 98.22

Wolf: holds a w. by the ears 95.12

Woman: litigation ... started by a w. 95.27

man has embraced w. 92.52

Women: acceptance of w.'s equality 92.37

  given w. so much power 85.117

  of her w. lawyer to me 88.72

  very few w. among the judges 133.4

  Were w. permitted to plead 95.1

Wooden: justice ... has a w. leg 83.25

  some judges are ... w. headed 79.72

Woolsack: made the Lord Chancellor sit on a w. 27.20

Words: hire out w. and anger 88.59

  to sell w. 88.65

  W. are the lawyer's tools 88.22

World: Lawyers run the w. 88.18

Worm: w. of conscience 33.24

Wrangling: our w. lawyers 95.11

Wrath: law ... malevolent engine of w. 85.113

Wrecked: all civil institutions have been w. 83.45

Wretches: w. hang that jury-men may dine 43.14

Writers: English thriller w. 44.8

Wrong: cannot do w. without suffering w. 147.1

  no w. without a remedy 147.2

Wrongly: when the right judge judges w. 79.90